What Are You Doing Here?

My Autobiography

BARONESS FLOELLA BENJAMIN DBE

PAN BOOKS

First published 2022 by Macmillan

This paperback edition first published 2023 by Pan Books
an imprint of Pan Macmillan
The Smithson, 6 Briset Street, London EC1M 5NR
EU representative: Macmillan Publishers Ireland Ltd, 1st Floor,
The Liffey Trust Centre, 117–126 Sheriff Street Upper,
Dublin 1, D01 YC43
Associated companies throughout the world
www.panmacmillan.com

ISBN 978-1-5290-7106-1

1 3 5 7 9 8 6 4 2

A CIP catalogue record for this book is available from the British Library.

Typeset in Sabon by Jouve (UK), Milton Keynes
Printed and bound by CPI Group (UK) Ltd, Croydon, CR0 4YY

What Are You Doing Here?

Floella Benjamin was born on the Caribbean island of Trinidad in 1949, and came to England in 1960 as part of the *Windrush* generation. She has enjoyed a successful career as a children's presenter, best known for the iconic BBC TV programmes *Play School* and *Play Away*, and has also worked as an actress, writer, producer, working peer and an active advocate for the welfare and education of children. Her broadcasting work has been recognized with a Special Lifetime Achievement BAFTA and an OBE. She was appointed a Baroness in the House of Lords in 2010 and a Dame in the 2020 New Year Honours list, and is the Chair of the Windrush Commemoration Committee. *What Are You Doing Here?* is her first adult autobiography, after previously writing her classic memoir *Coming to England* and the acclaimed *Sea of Tears*.

In 2022, it was one of Her Majesty the Queen's last wishes to appoint Floella to the prestigious Order of Merit, which is held by only twenty-four people. Floella is the first Caribbean person to receive the order, but she is sure she won't be the last.

*To my unbelievably strong and determined family –
Marmie, Dardie, Sandra, Lester, Ellington,
Roy Jr and Cynthia.*

*My supportive guardian angels who have loved
and protected me.*

*My golden children Aston and Alvina who have
made me proud.*

*And my beloved and devoted husband Keith who
is the wind beneath my wings.*

Chapter One

What am I doing here? That thought didn't cross my mind. Even though I'd never set foot in a proper theatre before, not even to sit in the audience, let alone walked out onto a vast black stage in London's West End. The spotlights blazed down on me. As I stared out into the darkness of the auditorium, knowing an invisible audience was waiting to see what I was made of, joy and determination took charge of me.

The year was 1969. I was twenty years old and I had that inexplicable feeling my life was about to change for ever. I couldn't predict where this path would lead. I couldn't have imagined then that over fifty years later, men and women of a certain age would rush up to me with adoration in their eyes:

'I love you, Floella. I've loved you ever since I first saw you on *Play School.*'

I couldn't have dreamed that I'd one day be discussing government policy with my *Play School* babies – now government ministers, party leaders, prime ministers – in the Houses of Parliament.

At that moment all I knew was this: I was in the right place. I was born to do this. Now I just had to prove it.

'Floella Benjamin,' announced the stage manager.

From the pitch-black auditorium came a voice. A man's

1

voice. I couldn't see its owner but he sounded a little bored. After all, to him I was just one more of a small crowd of young hopefuls who had gathered at the Shaftesbury Theatre stage door that day. This was the era of open auditions. Anyone who'd spotted the newspaper ad that had brought me here could just walk off the street and have a go. The director of this touring musical had been auditioning all week.

'So, love, what are you going to sing for us?'

That was easy. I'd chosen a favourite Cole Porter number. I'd performed it with my father's band at countless weddings and working men's clubs since my early teens.

'"I've Got You Under My Skin",' I announced confidently, turning to the pianist at the edge of the stage. I thought of my father Dardie . . . 'In the key of F.'

The intro struck up, loud and familiar. From the time I was born, I've thrown my entire being into everything I do. I believe that if something's worth doing, you should do it to the very best of your ability. So, I threw myself into this song, ready to enjoy every note.

'"*Use your mentality! Wake up to reality!*"' I sang, the broadest of smiles on my lips.

My voice soared, my eyes sparkled and I was transported to my favourite place . . . Far, far away from reality. A magical place, temporarily out of time. How I loved to sing. It felt almost like soaring into space. I didn't want this song to end. But when it did, the voice from the stalls was enthusiastic.

'Wonderful! Wonderful!'

They liked me, I thought. *They really liked me.* This was going better than I could have hoped.

'Can you move, love? Can you dance?'

Could I move? Could I dance? I'd been dancing since I could walk.

This time the pianist struck up with a pop song. Maybe it

was a hit by the Supremes? I can't remember now, but I'd mod-
elled myself on that world-famous Motown girl group when I'd
chosen my outfit, so I looked the part. After smuggling my
costume out of the house that morning so that my mother
Marmie couldn't stop me, I'd changed at lunchtime in my office
toilet, before covering up my glamour with a maxi coat and
slipping out to the theatre while everyone else was eating their
sandwiches. I felt extremely sophisticated in my leopard-print
mini dress and knee-high leather boots. My make-up was striking too – plenty of eyeshadow, rouge and lipstick. I wore a
shiny black pageboy wig over my own Afro-styled hair.

I thought of Marmie, and her deep faith in me. Perhaps she
wouldn't approve of what I was doing right now, but nothing
could shake the sense of self-worth she'd carefully instilled in
me. *Believe in yourself, Floella*, I told myself. I looked like a
star, and I was ready to dance like one. What I lacked in
curves – my figure was Twiggy-thin in those days – I'd make
up for in energy and flair. I began to gyrate wildly as the music
took over my body. Could I move? Nobody could doubt my
enthusiasm.

But although I'd pinned a flower to my fashionable wig, I
hadn't actually pinned my wig on.

One quick spin and whoosh! I went one way. My wig went
the other.

A roar of invisible laughter came from the stalls.

As I tried to grab the wig, I realized that my short dress had
ridden up to become even shorter and my underwear was on
full display. I knew I couldn't let my embarrassment show. *Keep
smiling*, I told myself. *Keep dancing.*

I must have impressed, despite everything, because the next
thing I knew I was being asked to stay back to read.

I was auditioning for a groundbreaking new musical called
Hair, about a group of young anti-establishment hippies in

New York City rebelling not just against the Vietnam War, but against their conservative parents. The plot revolves around the main character's decision whether or not to burn his draft card. The epitome of the Swinging Sixties counterculture, *Hair* had taken Broadway and then London by storm, and was breaking boundaries in every way. The infamous nude scene had been all over the papers.

Neither of my parents would have agreed to my audition for the touring production of the show, if they'd known what I was up to, though I hoped Dardie at least would understand my desire to join the wonderful world of showbiz. Marmie was another matter altogether. I had a proper job in a bank, didn't I? I had security. Marmie wasn't going to be too keen on me giving up all that. Dardie's meagre earnings as a musician had thoroughly disillusioned her about following a dream career as an entertainer.

The stage manager, a young woman called Daisy, gave me a script and showed me my lines. Luckily, I recognized the opening of the Gettysburg Address – familiar to me because Dardie would often recite by heart every word of Martin Luther King's 1963 'I have a dream' speech. When King spoke of Abraham Lincoln's Emancipation Proclamation, and the light of hope it gave to millions of enslaved African Americans, his opening words echoed the beginning of Abraham Lincoln's speech:

'Four score and seven years ago . . .'

I was really enjoying myself now, and looking forward to returning to the spotlight for the next stage of the audition. I knew my American accent would be perfect. Dardie had taken us to the cinema since we were tiny, and many of my party pieces were imitations of American stars. Meanwhile, other girls were coming off stage in tears.

'Next!' the voice kept saying. 'Next!'

How much longer would I have to wait? I looked at my

watch and began to panic. My lunch break had vanished, and I was definitely going to be late back to the office. I explained my situation to the stage manager, and luckily she was able to get me moved up the list to perform the final task.

Once again, I brought all the emotion I could muster to the speech. I stood and spoke as proudly as any president. For those moments I *was* Abraham Lincoln. I had no idea how irreverent the lines were in the context of this musical, but that didn't matter.

'Wonderful, Floella,' said the voice again when I'd finished. 'Just hang around a bit longer now while we make up our minds.'

Hang around? No chance! I thought of the battles ahead – not just with Marmie, but with my employer too. What if this didn't work out? I had a good job with Barclays Bank and I couldn't risk losing that. And there was one particular manager, very aggressive in his manner. I can see him now. He had a podgy face and glasses, and used to walk with his neck always jutting out ahead of him so you felt his head was about to slide off his body. I felt as if he'd leap on any opportunity to put me down. I couldn't let him get me on this.

I don't know what possessed me. I hate injustice, and it didn't seem fair that I was putting my job at risk by having to wait even longer. I decided it was time to speak out.

'Listen!' I said, fearlessly. 'I don't know who you are out there, but I've got a proper job in a bank, you know. I've already been here for ages, and this is my lunch hour. I've got to get back to the office.'

In my head, I was doing a quick calculation. My salary at the bank was twenty pounds a week. I usually made another five pounds from singing in the band with Dardie and my brothers. But it wasn't just the money I was worrying about now. Everyone knew the reputation of this show. I'd better be quite clear about my terms to have any chance of convincing Marmie this was the job for me.

'If you do want me in your show, you'd better make up your mind. Oh, and by the way, I want thirty pounds a week and I'm not taking my clothes off! Do you want me or don't you?'

I didn't wait for an answer. I just left.

When I got back to the office, the phone rang, and to my joy and amazement I discovered I'd got the job.

PART 1

CHILDHOOD LASTS A LIFETIME

Chapter Two

What a nerve I had! Where did I get such confidence? With no training, no experience, how did I know what to do when I got up on that stage? Why wasn't I overawed like so many of the other girls there?

At that moment, everything I'd learned in life came back to me. Performing to an audience was something I was perfectly accustomed to doing. But there was something else that told me I had the ability to set my own rules and boundaries that day. At the time it felt like instinct. But I realize now that my deep self-belief was rooted in my childhood years in Trinidad and London. I have my parents to thank. I'll always be grateful for the way they brought me up. They coated me in love, always, and, between them, they gave me strength from the moment I was born. They made me who I was at the age of twenty and they made me who I am today. You see, I believe childhood lasts a lifetime. Mine certainly has.

Marmie and Dardie moulded me in very different ways.

My dad was a hero to us all, and also our great entertainer. He opened our eyes to the wonders of the world, filling our days with excitement and joy. We adored him. One of the most important things I learned from Dardie was how to perform. When he played the saxophone and we danced and sang, we felt like the luckiest, happiest children on earth. He led the way, and showed me how it was done. So even when I was very small, our next-door neighbour in Trinidad would often point to me and say:

'You see this girl, Flo? She's going to be on the stage one day.'

How did he know? Because he always saw me up on the 'gallery'. We lived in a lovely white wooden house on stilts, and that's what we called the veranda. Amongst us children, I was the entertainer of the family, putting on a show for the others, or amusing visitors.

'Sing a song!' my mother would encourage if anyone came to the house.

'Do a dance!' Dardie would tell me. 'Recite a poem for our guest.'

I was born in Marabella, a town not far from Pointe-à-Pierre in Trinidad, the southernmost island in the Caribbean. It's closer to Venezuela than to any other country. Marmie, who'd believed the old wives' tale that breastfeeding prevents pregnancy, used to say I came quickly into the world, and I've been in a hurry to do things ever since. When I made my first appearance on 23 September 1949, just eleven months after my older sister Sandra, Trinidad was still firmly part of the British Empire, and the site of Britain's largest oil refinery. Nearly everyone in Pointe-à-Pierre worked there, including my father.

By day, Dardie was an oil field policeman. Every morning he'd set off in his crisply ironed khaki uniform to patrol the enormous refinery near the forest, and every evening he'd be just as smart as we ran to meet him coming home. To us, he seemed a giant of a man, scooping his smallest children up in his arms as if they were feathers. We fought for the privilege of polishing his brass buttons, longing to be the one chosen to make them gleam. I loved using the special tool that you had to slot around each one so that the Brasso wouldn't dirty the fabric.

By night, and at weekends, he was a musician. He had taught himself to play the saxophone thanks to my mother, who persuaded her brother to give her husband an instrument he owned but couldn't actually play. Dardie's first love was jazz, although there wasn't much call for it in Trinidad then. Calypso and steel pan were the music of choice. Dardie's eyes and ears were set further afield. He named three of his six children after American jazz musicians, including me. My namesake was the great singer Ella Fitzgerald – but he added 'Flo' to the beginning, short for Flower. After me, on Boxing Day in 1950, came Lester, named after Lester Young, the hip saxophonist from New Orleans who started his career in 'Count' Basie's orchestra and invented 'cool'. Then the gaps between babies became a little longer. There was Ellington, born in November 1952, named in honour of pianist and bandleader Duke Ellington, the composer of genius who wrote so many of the jazz standards Dardie loved to play. He learned them from the hard and breakable black records and sheet music he used to order specially from America. America! How glamorous! My youngest brother arrived in October 1954, and was named after our dad, Roy, so we always called him Junior. And after Junior came Cynthia, the baby of the family, born in May 1956. So, before my parents were thirty years old – and Marmie and Dardie were both born in the same year, 1926 – they had six lively children. In those early days, we four big ones were a noisy gang, always running around, fighting and having fun while Marmie looked after the little ones, Junior and Cynthia.

But long before the others were born, I was showing my character, as Dardie always liked to remind me.

'Flo has always been fast with herself,' he'd tell people.

11

'Before you knew it – at eight months old – she was walking. None of this creeping for Flo.'

By the age of fifteen months I was dancing, and talking too, and bossing around my big sister Sandra, who was so much smaller and quieter than I was that we looked like twins, especially since Marmie always dressed us alike. The way she turned us out was legendary. On special occasions we were eye-catching in matching dresses she'd made herself, with neat little white socks and our hair in plaits and ribbons.

By Christmas 1950, Marmie was heavily pregnant with our little brother, Lester. On Boxing Day she knew her time had come. Mrs Jackson, the midwife, was summoned from across the road and Marmie told Dardie to look after me and Sandra, to keep us out of the way while she was in labour. Since he had a gig with his band that day, playing at a *fête* – that's what we called a big party in Trinidad – he just took us along with him.

So, there he was, playing away to all the mums and dads and kids, Latin and swing to start off with. And, as he told the story, there was I, dancing along too. But when the calypso music struck up, I was not too happy. These people weren't dancing properly. So, I got up on stage myself.

'No, no, no! You're getting this all wrong!' I said. And without a second thought, I showed them how their dancing should really be done.

'Wind up your waist!' Marmie used to say. And that's exactly what I did, completely unafraid to tell all the guests at that *fête* the right way to move your body to the calypso beat.

According to Dardie, everyone stared in amazement at this fifteen-month-old child gyrating her tiny hips and ordering them around. They'd never seen anything like it.

And whenever Dardie told that story, Marmie would add:

'And she hasn't changed a bit. She's still telling people what to do.'

It's true that I've never been afraid to speak out. If I see something that's not right to me, I'll ask questions. I had that confidence because I also had that pride which both my parents, in their different ways, made sure was at the core of every one of their children. So, although we came out very differently, all six of us with different ambitions and interests, we all believed in ourselves wholeheartedly. You might say we were programmed to have self-confidence. It's a family inheritance.

It also comes from the fact that Marmie constantly bathed us in love. She adored having a family, and lived for her children. She defended us from injustice as a lioness defends her cubs from danger. She knew what it meant to have happiness snatched away, for her mother died in 1930 when she was only four, and eight years later she also lost her beloved father. She was abandoned to the care of a wicked couple who treated her like their servant, so after an early childhood filled with love, she had to grow up quickly. At the age of twelve, she was forced to leave school to work for them. They had a grand house with polished floors, a piano and beautiful furniture, and she spent her days keeping the property immaculate. But this didn't make her bitter or resentful. In fact, it gave her aspirations.

She often used to run away because of the bad treatment she had to endure but was always forced to return, until eventually, at the age of sixteen, she could take it no more. She secured a job as a daily help to an ex-pat family linked to the oilfields where Dardie worked, and Marmie met my father there on one of her days off. They were almost exactly the same age: Dardie was born in July 1926, while Marmie's birthday was just three months later. She was very beautiful, and lots of men made a play for her, but Dardie won her heart by talking to her about culture, music and history, and they married in 1948, the same year my sister was born.

Marmie was someone who could only see the positive things

in life. She had no self-pity and she taught us never to dwell on the negative. If you see yourself as a victim, only you will be the loser.

'That house gave me something to aim for,' Marmie told us.

The room she loved best in our little white house in Trinidad was the living room, which was only used on special occasions. She kept it beautifully. It was my job and Sandra's to keep it spotless, polishing the furniture every day and making sure it was always clean and shining. With a vase on the table of gorgeously coloured tropical flowers from the garden, starched curtains and white lace doilies, it smelled and looked delicious. I can hear the sound of Marmie's rocking chair now, gently tipping back and forth while she fed the newest baby. As she rocked, she directed our work, or sang. She was always singing, although she had a terrible voice. And you could judge her mood by her choice of song.

Marmie made our home-world safe and secure. But she was a hard taskmistress. Sandra and I were expected to do our share of the housework – even ironing with a coal-filled iron and scrubbing the floors – while she looked after the babies, and filled the house with song and the smell of her miraculous cooking. Day after day, she effortlessly conjured the most amazing meals from her kitchen, so that each one tasted like the best we'd ever eaten: chicken, dumplings, pigtail or fish which Sandra and I went to buy from the fishermen's wharf down the lane. On Saturdays it was sweet-scented cakes and coconut drops, which we helped her make. Whatever Marmie cooked had that special touch.

'You've got to eat because it makes you big and strong!' she used to insist.

We didn't need encouragement. We thought she was a magician.

She was also a firm disciplinarian. She had to be, especially with me and Ellington, because we were so naughty and very noisy. At home, we behaved ourselves in the living room but ran riot in the children's bedroom, the most joyful part of the house. Here we had endless pillow fights, chased each other around and competed to jump the highest on the beds. I was always in trouble for something – usually fighting with Ellington. In fact, my mother even kept a small suitcase packed for me, ready to dispatch with me if I really misbehaved.

'Oh, don't send her away, Marmie!' Sandra would beg, for I was her chief protector in life, just as Ellington was for Lester. 'Don't send her away!'

I knew she never would. It was a fantastical threat. I knew nothing would separate her from her children. It was unimaginable.

Chapter Three

While Marmie made us strong and confident by coating us in love, Dardie introduced us to the big wide world beyond our home and shores. He would give us regular quizzes on geography and history; we could name all the countries of the world, and reel off their capitals and population sizes at the drop of a hat. But he also made sure we knew our family heritage, and its significance.

Dardie's mother had also died when he was just a little boy, and he was brought up by his powerful father, Leonard Benjamin. Both men found Antigua, the island of their birth, too small for their adventurous spirits. At nineteen, Dardie travelled over 400 miles to the larger island of Trinidad to make a new life for himself, while my grandfather moved 3,000 miles away to America not many years later. So I never met him, but from the way Dardie spoke about him, I felt I knew him.

Leonard was born in 1888, and he was a tailor by profession, making uniforms for soldiers, prison officers and policemen. His father was a wealthy merchant who made a fortune running a fleet of schooners and trading cargo from island to island. *His* father had been born into slavery in Barbuda. Not everyone enslaved in the Caribbean was put to work in the sugar cane fields: the plantations and the lucrative sugar trade needed skilled tradespeople too, such as blacksmiths and carpenters, boatbuilders, stonemasons and tailors. My great-great-grandfather was emancipated on the stroke of midnight on 1 August 1834, following the 1833 Slavery Abolition Act. This made buying or owning slaves illegal in most of the British Empire, although in the colonies only enslaved children under six were instantly freed; everyone else was renamed an 'apprentice', which changed very little. Even after this form of servitude ended, it wasn't easy for Black people to make a living. The sugar trade was in decline, and plantation owners preferred to bring in indentured workers from India, China and Europe, paying them with plots of land, rather than let the formerly enslaved people from Africa have land of their own. But Leonard's grandfather's skills helped future generations of his family thrive.

An activist as well as an influential speaker, Leonard was a co-founder of the Antiguan Trades and Labour Union, which led a battle against the White sugar barons for better working conditions and higher pay. In Antigua's first general election on 26 July 1946, he was one of five union-backed candidates elected with a big share of the votes to the Executive Council of the federal colony of the Leeward Islands. Leonard Benjamin was the second minister to Vere Bird, who eventually became the first premier of the nation when it was made an autonomous associated state of the United Kingdom in 1976. On independence in 1981, Bird became Antigua and Barbuda's first prime minister. So, from 1946 till 1951, serving as Bird's deputy, my grandfather was effectively the country's deputy prime minister. But he and Bird fell out badly, prompting Leonard's move to New York in the late 1950s.

Politics was also in Dardie's DNA and it's in mine too. He was brought up to be a union man through and through. Leonard was known as one of the most gifted orators of his

17

generation. No wonder Dardie was such a good storyteller. He was a great one for books too, but the best stories were the ones he told us from his head. From Dardie's lips we lapped up all kinds of tales, although we were never quite sure which were true and which were fantasy. In our imaginations, all the worlds he conjured up came together and made us dream, ensuring that our heritage was in our psyche in more ways than one.

How we loved the folk tales he told us about Anansi, the trickster spider-man. These were stories of cunning and quick-wittedness saving the day, of turning the tables on your enemies with ingenuity and clever talking. They were brought to the Caribbean from West Africa with the men, women and children enslaved during the Atlantic slave trade, and their shape-shifting hero was celebrated as a symbol of survival and resistance. Had Dardie learned the fables from his own father? Did he consciously see them as a way to teach his children about their history and heritage? In years to come, when I grew up and became a presenter on *Play School* and *Play Away*, and later *Tree House*, *Playabout*, *Hullaballoo* and *Jamboree*, I'd introduce Anansi to new generations of children. But that's another story.

'To know your future, you have to know your past, your history,' he would quote, sounding just like a philosopher himself. 'Only then can you move forward freely, unburdened by the shackles of your past.'

I have always taken this to heart. Dardie told us heart-rending stories of old Antigua. While darkness gathered around us, and the air filled with the rhythmic chirp of cicadas, we sat on the gallery close to Dardie to hear the tale of brave and rebellious Prince Klaas, enslaved from the Gold Coast. His real name was Kwaku, and he was captured at the age of ten and shipped to the Caribbean. In charge of the biggest, wealthiest plantation in St John's, he spent eight years hatching an elaborate plan – Dardie called it a gunpowder plot – to blow up all the British planters and their wives in a spectacular explosion during a large ball due to be held in 1736. They wanted to make the island of Antigua into the first independent African-ruled nation outside Africa. But the conspiracy was discovered, and he and many others were horrifically tortured and killed.

I remember Dardie describing a mysterious arch of rocks on Antigua's east coast called Devil's Bridge, where distraught Africans threw themselves into the ocean, in the hope their bodies would be returned by the sea to their homeland.

Dardie enchanted us with thrilling stories that expanded our horizons and made us see every possibility in life. This was very deliberate. He knew that without role models, we wouldn't know what we might achieve.

He also told us stories about movies and film stars, and every month he drove us to San Fernando's outdoor cinema. With your ticket, you got a speaker that sat inside the vehicle so that every word and song filled the car. When I was seven years old, he took us to see an unforgettable movie: *Island in the Sun*, starring Jamaican-born Harry Belafonte. His co-star was Dorothy Dandridge, who'd been the first-ever African-American to be nominated for a Best Actress Oscar, for the all-Black musical *Carmen Jones*. We watched their performances through the car windows, projected in Technicolor on a gigantic screen outside, and the experience went into my consciousness and stuck there for ever.

It was huge in every way, this Hollywood film starring Black stars alongside White, telling a story of interracial love and contemporary Caribbean politics. Belafonte was a massive star. Wildly popular, he had recently introduced Trinidadian music to an international audience, selling a record-breaking million copies of his 1956 album *Calypso*. He was also an important confidant and supporter of Martin Luther King Jr and the American civil rights movement, financing the Freedom Rides and voter registration drives, and raising thousands of dollars to release civil rights protesters from jail. Dorothy Dandridge was also a political activist, involved with both the National Association for the Advancement of Colored People (NAACP) and the National Urban League. She broke down barriers throughout her career, while facing racism, racial stereotyping, segregated entertainment venues and a film production code which banned mixed-race love scenes. Until she was cast in a film about a successful slave uprising, she always refused to be cast as a slave or prostitute.

I couldn't have known any of this, nor understood the significance of the film's plot, but I know that seeing this handsome Black man and beautiful Black woman performing on that colourful screen in a Caribbean setting showed me that anything was possible. You've got to see yourself to know you are part of a world that is admired. (Years later, I met Belafonte in Jamaica and told him how much it had meant to me seeing him up there at our drive-in cinema in San Fernando, in a movie actually filmed in the British West Indies. He was thrilled to hear this, and we exchanged stories of how we were both trying to make a difference in the world.)

I was also deeply affected by seeing Lena Horne in the 1943 Vincente Minnelli musical *Cabin in the Sky*, which featured Louis Armstrong and Duke Ellington. Lena Horne was an incredible singer, actor, dancer and civil rights activist – a real pioneer.

'I'm going to grow up to be like her!' I told Dardie. Little did I know then that Horne's race meant she was rarely cast in a leading Hollywood role, and her appearances were often edited out because movie theatres in certain parts of America refused to show any films with Black performers.

Dardie gave us plenty of influential and imposing role models too. On our wall he hung a large framed photograph of Marcus Garvey, dressed in his iconic ceremonial uniform. Standing proudly with a tasselled sword in his hand, he wore a jacket adorned with shiny buttons like my father's, and plenty of gold braid, fringed epaulettes, gold stars on his sleeves and an amazing plumed Napoleon-style hat. Every day his visionary gaze looked out across our living room, as if commanding us to do our best. Garvey was a hero in the Caribbean. His stature and influence were enormous. Born into poverty in Jamaica in 1914, he founded the largest pan-African mass movement ever created, the Universal Negro Improvement Association, or UNIA. When Bob Marley later sang 'Redemption Song', he was quoting a speech by Garvey: 'We are going to emancipate ourselves from mental slavery because whilst others might free the body, none but ourselves can free the mind.'

Garvey's message of racial pride and self-reliance was instilled in us by Dardie, who explained that Garvey wanted the people of the Caribbean to return to Africa. Dardie also told us stories about Haile Selassie, the Emperor of Ethiopia, the King of Kings. An African Emperor! So, we grew up with powerful images of leadership. We understood that Black is beautiful. Dardie gave us aspirations in life. From the moment we were born, he made sure we would aim high. Marmie gave us the confidence to capture what some might see as the impossible.

'You've got to do your best, and then anything is possible!'

This was our parents' strongest message. But though I've always been very competitive, I've never compared myself with anyone. We were brought up as individuals, with our own strengths. We never competed with each other, but we were encouraged to achieve the best we could ourselves. All six of us learned to believe in who we were with our inner souls. And that has carried us all through life. I believe that children need to grow up knowing that they are loved and appreciated and important in the world. That's why I often tell children when I visit schools to shout these words out loud:

'I am worthy! I am worthy! I am worthy!'

We shout the words together, so that the hall rings with affirmation.

Sometimes you need to say something out loud to believe it.

Marmie and Dardie shared a sense of justice, and we children also grew up with a strong moral compass. Marmie's morality was formed above all by her faith. She loved going to church, and on Sundays we always went with her. But not just to one church. By the end of the day, we had visited three! Dressed up beautifully in my Sunday best – a crisply starched and ironed dress with pretty puffed sleeves – I'd spend the morning sitting in awe at the local Pentecostal church. It was all very dramatic there. The preacher seemed as tall as a giant, and his skin was the blackest I'd ever seen. As he stood in the pulpit you had the feeling he was directing his words to your very own heart. The women in that congregation threw themselves into their worship in the most fascinating way. They sang at top volume, fluttered their fans, called out regular 'Hallelujahs' and sometimes were so taken over by 'the spirit' that they rose up from their seats with bodies that shook and trembled.

Although we had a special children's service in the middle of all this, with Bible stories and prayers for our families, after lunch we then went to the Salvation Army Sunday school. The best thing about this was the music. We learned to play different instruments and although I wasn't really much of a musician, I had lots of fun with the cymbals and the triangle. Finally, at six o'clock in the evening, we headed for the Anglican church, our last service of the day.

There was really no chance at all of any of us getting into trouble on a Sunday, and we were exposed to a range of different places of worship – although, sadly I never went inside any of the many Hindu temples, which looked particularly beautiful and intriguing when they were lit up with hundreds of candles for Diwali.

One of the great things about our own island-in-the-sun 1950s childhood was that it was perfectly safe for us to roam free. Marmie could get us out of her hair by sending us out to play and she never had to worry. The worst we'd get up to was climbing trees and shaking the branches to loosen the ripe juicy mangoes or sweet pomme citere, a fruit like a green-and-gold tropical plum that I've never seen in England. This was a time of great freedom. Except at school.

School and home were almost like two different worlds, but I was happy in both. From the age of four, I got dressed each weekday morning in my royal blue tunic and white blouse, and ran off down the lane hand in hand with Sandra to a big two-storey timber building, where children were so quiet and obedient that the classrooms could be separated by no more than a wooden partition.

Teachers were people of status in our community. You had huge respect for them because of the way they presented you with knowledge. They were strict, of course, and there could be no speaking out of turn or messing around in lessons. You arrived on time to be inspected by the headmistress – your nails, clothes and shoes all had to be perfectly clean. (Marmie would check us too, before we left.) If you were late, you got the lash with a thick leather belt. But the teachers were also kind, and extremely dedicated.

It was a very traditional, structured education, and we understood it to be the best in the world. After all, it was British! We learned the three Rs – reading, writing and arithmetic – and much of that learning was by rote, whether times tables or poetry. So, by the time I was six, I could happily recite and act out Tennyson's 'The Beggar Maid' on our gallery stage. It's a poem about a legendary African king who falls in love with a poor girl passing by, a rags-to-riches story:

> So sweet a face, such angel grace,
> In all that land had never been:
> Cophetua sware a royal oath:
> 'This beggar maid shall be my queen!'

But at school we learned nothing about our African heritage or the indigenous Arawak or Carib people who originally inhabited the Caribbean islands. We were cheated out of that. Our curriculum and all our textbooks came from Britain. We learned how to be subjects of the British Empire, and about the countries Britain had conquered. British history. British heroes. British poets. Everything centred on that place far away that we learned to call the Motherland. We were brainwashed to believe that we were part of something great, something magnificent. I sang 'God Save the Queen' and 'Rule Britannia' and 'Land of Hope and Glory' with vigour. I believe all children should sing some sort of anthem every day because, looking back, I see that as something very positive. It wasn't the words that stirred me as a child, I didn't really understand them. It was the emotions of the music and singing that did. They gave me a sense of pride, and made me feel that I belonged.

Chapter Four

And then the arguments began. Sandra and I heard them through the wooden wall that divided the children's bedroom from our parents', low conversations which seemed to go on for hours and hours. We would lie awake and listen and worry. We heard Marmie crying:

'But, Roy, I can't leave my children . . . I'll never leave the children.'

This was reassuring. But it also made us realize that whatever their dispute, we were somehow involved too.

I began to have bad dreams for the first time in my life. I had nightmares about falling. There was nobody to catch me. I didn't even tell Sandra about these. I didn't want them to come true. We didn't talk about what we feared, superstitious that saying something out loud might make it real.

Marmie's songs changed. They became more mournful. There was one in particular, 'Now is the Hour', which she sang over and over again. Dardie began to leave newspapers lying around the house, folded to show advertisements for jobs in England, boat journeys to Britain.

After the Second World War, workers from the British Caribbean were encouraged to come to the Motherland to help rebuild the nation. The United Kingdom was suffering from serious labour shortages, and the newly created National Health Service, as well as British Rail and London Transport, recruited most actively in Jamaica and Barbados. In 1948 immigration law changed: the British Nationality Act gave citizenship to *everyone* living in the UK and its colonies, with automatic right to enter and settle. That was the year the HMT *Empire Windrush*, a troopship coming to England from Australia via the Caribbean, landed at Tilbury, bringing with it 802 British West Indians. Most were men from Jamaica, many former soldiers and airmen who'd spent years defending Britain. But it was a Trinidadian who featured on a now well-known Pathé News report. Aldwyn Roberts, known as 'Lord Kitchener', performed an optimistic song he'd written for the occasion: 'London is the Place for Me'.

Antigua had been too small for my dad. Now Trinidad was becoming too small. The story we were told when we were young was that he wanted to go to London to become a jazz musician and that in Trinidad people only wanted to hear calypso. That was certainly true. But later we learned the full story.

Like his father before him, Dardie's powerful sense of justice and his commitment to human rights had led him into union work at the oil refinery, defending workers' rights at a time when they had very few. And this was beginning to get him into trouble. A colleague had already been jailed for his activism, sent to Carrera Island, off the north-west peninsula. My mother begged Dardie to think of his children.

'Roy, you've got to stop this,' she told him. What would she do if he landed himself in prison too? 'What's going to happen to my six children? Do you want them to end up in an orphanage?'

She didn't want us to have a hero for a father if he couldn't be with us. She was a homemaker, not a breadwinner. She wanted a husband who'd take care of his children.

So yes, he was pulled by the prospects of a better life abroad, and ambition, but he was also looking for a particular kind of safety – and political freedom.

His first thought had been to go to America and join his father. But Grandad Leonard wrote back to tell him to think again. No man could make it in New York with six children in tow, he told him. His White boss Veasey was equally pessimistic about his chances of success in Britain with a large family but, undeterred, Dardie decided that London was the place for him.

The next thing we knew, we were moving.

The plan was that he would go ahead and sort out a place for us all to live, and get a job to pay for our passages over. But to pay for his fare and keep us in his absence, we had to sell almost everything. The gramophone went. His beloved records. The car. He couldn't take them with him. I suppose the picture of Marcus Garvey and much of the beautiful polished furniture went too. We moved out of our lovely house on stilts, where there was room underneath for the washtub and car, and Marmie could grow vegetables at the back – pigeon peas, cassavas, okras, dasheen – and flame-red hibiscus in the little front garden. Gone were the rocking chairs on the gallery. We moved into a much smaller house, in a poorer part of San Fernando, further from the sea, where we were all cramped together.

And suddenly, in September 1958, Dardie was packing a suitcase and his saxophone and he was gone too. Once it had been decided, it all happened very quickly. Just before my ninth birthday, he was gone. Of course, I cried, and cried, and I'd never seen Marmie cry so much, and we children missed him and his marvellous stories, but at least we still had Marmie.

While she waited for the call to join Dardie, life got much

27

harder for her. She had to take on cleaning jobs, and would vanish early in the morning and late in the evening, leaving Sandra and me to take care of the little ones. She sold her jewellery and all our christening silver. I remember finding her in tears one day because she had had to sell her beloved sewing machine.

A few months passed, and then the very worst happened. Once again, the first clue that something was up was Marmie's songs. In her terrible, terrible voice, she began to sing that farewell song again, 'Now is the Hour', which had haunted the house before Dardie left.

But this time she would be sailing, and though she could take four-year-old Junior and two-year-old Cynthia, the rest of us would have to wait a little longer. It would be too hard for the family to establish itself in London with all six of us, so we'd have to join the others later.

She cried and hugged us as she sang, and we would all begin to cry too.

Where would we live? Who would look after us?

'Your Auntie Olive can't look after you,' Marmie told us. Her sister Olive, who died in 2022, well into her nineties, would often say to me during our weekly phone conversations:

'Flo, I tried, but I couldn' look after all'a'yuh. My circumstances were too difficult. I had no space. I had to work. I know you forgive me, though. You must forgive me, or you wouldn't give me all the things you give me and treat me so special.'

'Auntie Olive, of course I understand,' I always replied. 'Of course I don't hold it against you.'

Marmie never held it against her either. She was such a great woman. She knew it wasn't meant to be. Of course, I was secretly relieved when nobody in the family could take care of us. Maybe it meant Marmie wouldn't go.

When we went visiting friends, Marmie would ask if they

could look after us, just for a few months, and then we'd be sent for. A lot of heads were shaken. Everyone seemed to have too many children of their own. And who knew how long it would really be? 'Left-behind' children were more common than we realized. Finally two sets of people agreed, but we would have to be separated.

The moment of parting was almost unbearable. It's hard to write about even now. It was May 1959, and Dardie had been gone for eight months. That was bad enough. But I still couldn't understand how Marmie could break her vow to never leave us behind. We meant everything to each other. My brothers and sisters were also my best friends. What would happen now to our happy family? It felt like the end of the world. A dark veil of unhappiness descended on my life.

Marmie took me and Sandra nearly thirty miles north to Tunapuna. Lester and Ellington were taken in by a family in San Fernando. Perhaps that doesn't sound far, but it felt a world away. We had no hope of seeing them, and had no idea what was happening to our little brothers.

We hardly knew these people in Tunapuna, although we had to call them 'Auntie' and 'Uncle', as a sign of respect. They treated us more like servants than family friends.

'Do the dishes! Clean the floor! Have you swept the yard yet?'

I was used to housework, and accepted my responsibilities at home. Even in my new home, I threw myself into my chores. I had already learned to put my heart into anything I did. But our new 'auntie's' orders were relentless.

'Haven't you finished the ironing? Get me a chicken!'

That meant chasing the fowl round the yard, grabbing it by the wings, wringing its neck and then plucking its feathers. We spent hours picking the husks from rice, grain by grain. It was like being trapped in a fairy tale. She was very superstitious and

29

made us perform an elaborate ritual of sprinkling holy water round the house at five o'clock in the morning to keep away the evil spirits, although it seemed to us that the evil spirits were already inside. We were stopping it getting out. And if we showed any sign of misery:

'Take that look off your face! All ya don't you know how lucky you are? All ya parents gallivanting in England leaving me to look after all ya. Be grateful you're not living in an orphanage.'

When we tried to write and tell our parents, 'Auntie' censored our letters, and gave us a wallop. Sandra and I cried ourselves to sleep most nights. The rest of the time we were kept too busy to think, and after school we found any excuse not to go home. We even snuck into a line of people paying respects to a dead neighbour one afternoon, filing by an open coffin where we saw a dead man lying so peaceful and content that I lost any fear of death. Meanwhile, the family that was supposed to be looking after us spent the money Marmie sent for us on fancy new things for themselves.

It was the worst time of my life. Without each other, I don't know how Sandra and I would have got through it. We held hands whenever we could and sang our favourite songs together to remind us of home. Uprooted from everything, we had to start at a new school. We always arrived exhausted after working since four in the morning. The other children picked on Sandra, because she was new and pretty and small for her age. That was when I began to fight physically, to protect her.

I knew I had to assert myself. If you didn't stand up for yourself, you'd be trampled on. I'd never fought anyone as big as one particular girl who was bullying Sandra, but I had little choice. Fights happened on Fridays, at the end of the day, outside the school gates. Everyone would be watching.

I was nine years old, and skinny. This girl was so much older and taller than me. The other children crowded round us in a big circle, waiting for the action. *Oh my goodness . . .* What was I going to do? She came towards me, ready to lay into me, thinking it would be easy work, I'm sure. My eyes were level with her boobies. So, I just reached out and grabbed them, one in each hand. I squeezed as hard as I possibly could.

She squealed like a pig.

'Let go, let go!' she screamed.

With all my strength, I swung her round, and threw her aside.

And then I dusted off my hands, very deliberately, very confidently. And I looked around at all the other children, staring each one right in the eye.

'Let that be a lesson to all of you,' I said. 'Don't you touch my sister Sandra again. None of you.'

And after that, everybody left us alone.

Later we discovered that Lester and Ellington had suffered even more than me and Sandra during this time. They didn't even have a bed to sleep in, but had to lie underneath somebody else's. They were made to fight for their food like dogs. Winner takes all. The loser went hungry. Every night the woman who was supposed to be looking after them sat in her rocking chair and ordered my brothers to clean her toenails.

The full horror of their situation only became clear to me a few years ago. When Ellington was sixty-five, and managing director of his own construction company, he suddenly revealed something he'd kept hidden in his heart for the best part of his life. The memory and his intense pain were uncovered unexpectedly. It took him by surprise. It was 2018, and I had invited all my family to the Chelsea Flower Show, where I was displaying the special garden which I'd designed and fought hard to

31

fund: the *Windrush* garden, celebrating seventy years since the beginning of the exodus of people from the Caribbean to Britain. All the elements of our life story were there: the gorgeous tropical flowers, the ship itself with little 3-D printed people on board, waving goodbye, and London, represented by a bright red London bus in flowers. I thought my brothers and sisters would love it. But Ellington – big, tough Ellington – was visibly affected when he saw the garden, and his eyes moistened.

'I'm seeing that woman now who was supposed to be looking after me and Lester,' he said angrily. I felt I had forgiven my 'auntie', but my Ellington still hated his so-called guardian with a vengeance. And he told me a story.

One day during that terrible period in our lives, Lester found a magnifying glass. He'd never seen such a thing before.

'What's this for?' he asked.

'Come here and put out your hand,' the woman told him. 'I'll show you.'

Of course, neither Lester nor Ellington knew what was going to happen. It didn't take long for Lester to feel the burning pain of the sun through the glass on his skin. I think the agony for Ellington was not being able to protect Lester from such deliberate cruelty.

If you talk to most Caribbean children who were left behind, they'll tell you similar stories. This kind of thing happened a lot all across the region. People often resented those who went away to England or America, trying to 'better' themselves, and they took it out on their vulnerable offspring. They didn't see you as someone who was suffering, someone who'd lost their connection with their family, someone who needed to be loved or embraced. They were happy to take the money and parcels sent by absent parents, but they offered no comfort.

*

How did we survive those long months apart from our parents and each other?

Love. We had already soaked up so much love, and developed so strong a vision of the world and such confidence in ourselves that we were able to cope with adversity and disruption when it came. Like a well-built house, we had good foundations.

Neuroscientists now know that babies are born with 86 billion brain cells, or neurons, and in the first seven years of life more than one million new neural connections between them are formed every single second. That's how we learn to touch, smell, hear, move, form attachments . . . everything! So, you have to talk to babies, nurture them, show them everything, and it all soaks in. It's like pictures emerging on a blank canvas: everything slowly makes sense, bit by bit.

That's how a child learns what life is all about. So Aristotle's saying '*Give me a child until he is seven and I will show you the man*' has been scientifically proven.

That's why it's so important to give *all* children that love, not just your own. *All* children need love, from the moment they come into the world.

This came home to me forcefully not very long ago, when I was giving a speech at an event in Hull, which was then the City of Culture. Just before I began my talk, a middle-aged woman came in and looked at me, bewildered. She didn't know what to do. She walked around the room, very agitated. It was really quite strange, but I carried on with my speech. After everyone else had left with their selfies and autographs, the woman finally approached me.

'I'm so sorry I acted that way when I saw you, Floella. I'm forty-eight now, but when I was eight years old I was fostered, and my foster parents had two sons. Every day they used to come home and sexually abuse me. The only thing that got me through was seeing your smiling face on television saying, 'Hello! Is everything all right?' And then I knew that somebody in this world loved me. It was you, Floella Benjamin. Whenever I'm going through a crisis, even now, I see your face. And I know you love me.'

I cried that day. I found it easy to pour out my love through that screen because I'd had love poured into me from the moment I was born. My life was easy compared with so many children's. So I can't say this often enough:

All you need is love. All you need is love. All you need is love.

Chapter Five

About fifteen months after she'd left, Marmie finally sent us the good news. We were leaving our world of unhappiness! All four of us were going to join our parents and little brother and sister in London at last. We said goodbye to our tormentors without a second glance. Auntie Olive came to pick me and Sandra up, and took us to her house in Port of Spain, where we were reunited with Lester and Ellington.

How skinny and ill they both looked. It was a terrible shock. Auntie Olive had been just as horrified when she went to visit them for the first time since Marmie left, and then came to see how we were faring. She'd written immediately to her sister to let her know what was happening to us.

Marmie was heartbroken. Her world fell apart, she told us later.

'No more! No more! I can't take it!' she said. Marmie found a nursery school for Junior and Cynthia and persuaded them to keep the little ones as late as possible, so that she could work as many hours as she possibly could to save for our fares. Luckily, she was very charming and people always wanted to help her.

I was actually on my way to the fabled Motherland. It felt as if we were stepping into one of Dardie's exciting adventure stories. Everything I cared about most was in England. That was where I was meant to be. That was where I had been told I belonged. Though we were to travel for two weeks or more over four thousand miles of ocean, in our heads we were simply moving from one part of Britain to another, where the streets were paved with gold.

The ships always left at night, and the wharf at Port of Spain was dark, noisy and crowded. I remember a lot of shouting and shoving, as the night air crackled with emotion – worry and hope and sadness and fear all muddling together. People fretted loudly over their trunks and suitcases, or 'grips', as we called them. Others said prayers for a safe passage. Many were embracing and crying as they said goodbye to loved ones, maybe for the last time. We hugged Auntie Olive tightly, and I quickly found myself in tears too.

The harbour at Port of Spain was too shallow for the big ships to approach, so little motorboats ferried passengers out to the *Marqués de Comillas*. Lowering myself down into the tender as it bobbed on inky black water seemed an impossible step that filled me with terror. The liquid reflections of the quayside lights fractured over and over again. At last Sandra and my brothers coaxed me aboard, and we sped into the unknown, clinging tightly to one another and feeling terribly alone. Even more terrifying was bumping in darkness against the towering bow of the anchored ship, far away from the twinkling lights onshore, and realizing that to get on board I would now have to climb up a shaky rope ladder.

'*Venga! Venga!*'

From above and below, kind Spanish sailors urged me on and offered helping hands, but again I felt wobbly with fear and found it hard to move. I was convinced that at any moment I would slip and plunge into the menacing depths of the swelling seas.

Departure remains a blur. There was so much to take in. Stairs in all directions, numbers, signs, loudspeakers, the thundering bellow of the horn as we began to move. Once a luxury ocean liner travelling between Spain and New York, the *Marqués de Comillas* had been converted into a passenger cargo-ship after the Second World War; now over eight hundred passengers could be accommodated on board. This voyage had already picked up lots of other British citizens in Grenada and Barbados. The tiny cabin we all shared was between decks, right in the belly of the ship, and we took to our bunks gratefully.

My first shock on waking was the dizzying nausea that immediately overwhelmed me. Nobody had warned us about seasickness. Tomato soup and corn puffs were all we could stomach. Sandra took even longer to find her sea legs than I did, but by day five I was able to start exploring and bring her back reports, as Lester, Ellington and I rushed around the ship, investigating every corner of the vessel from the cargo hold to the ballroom. How fascinating it all was! What freedom we had! We were four youngsters aged seven to eleven travelling all on our own! Although Marmie had apparently paid someone to take care of us, nobody ever appeared, and we were left to run wild, until Ellington got into a fight with another boy. They punched and kicked each other, rolling around on deck together locked in combat without a thought of danger.

'Stop! Stop!' Sandra and I were horrified. Even when the captain shouted a furious warning from the bridge, they kept on fighting. Finally, he came down in person, and dragged them from the edge just before they fell overboard.

That voyage was a real adventure, and a time out of time. I remember peeling hundreds of potatoes in the galleys for the Spanish cooks. I didn't realize I was doing their job for them. I remember an eruption of glittering flying fish, leaping at the prow in a golden sunset. At night we would sneak out of bed to watch the grown-ups dancing. The ship lit up with laughter and music and lights as it throbbed across a changing sea. From the heat of the tropics, we passed into the cooler Atlantic Ocean and sailed past Spain into the English Channel. Then, as Marmie had warned us, the temperature began to drop so much that we had to run around the decks to keep warm. Lester thought we were about to crash into an iceberg, thanks to some story he'd heard in Trinidad about the cold in England, and his agitation only increased as we got closer to Southampton.

On our last night at sea, there was a huge party which went on late into the night. The final hours on board were agonizingly slow, and it was hard to be patient. We woke up in port on the morning of the 2nd of September 1960. We all washed carefully, and put on the special arrival outfits Auntie Olive had given us. I plaited my hair and Sandra's in a stylish way, and decorated it with ribbons, as Marmie used to do. No prince or princess could have felt better. Everyone wanted to look their best when they first set foot in England, so we emerged onto a deck crowded with luggage and people dressed to the nines. The men wore trilbies and wide-shouldered suits with baggy trousers. The women were all in hats and gloves and colourful dresses puffed out with full, starched petticoats.

The docks were bewilderingly huge – a great mass of cranes and rail containers and iron-roofed sheds, and hundreds of people, some busy working, some recently disembarked themselves or about to set off on voyages of their own, others anxiously looking for loved ones. I gripped the rail and shivered, wondering how we'd ever find Marmie.

Chapter Six

Suddenly we spotted her. All four of us waved frantically until we could see that Marmie had also found us with her eyes. I'll never forget the way she beamed with joy, and clutched at her bosom, looking up at us like an angel. Her whole body seemed to sigh in relief. She turned to the man beside her – mysteriously, not Dardie – and pointed us out to him, then gestured to us to stay where we were. As if we could move! We were hemmed in by other passengers, and so excited now we could barely draw breath. It seemed an age before the ship was docked. The man who'd stood with Marmie disappeared from sight, and reappeared by our sides.

'I'm your social worker,' he explained. 'Your mother isn't allowed on board, and my job is to look after unaccompanied minors.'

I wasn't sure what all that meant, but the important thing was that he was taking charge and taking us to Marmie. He grabbed our grips, swept everyone away and we eagerly followed in his wake. No rope ladders this time, but a big metal gangway. My heart began to pound loudly as I rushed towards Marmie, who looked more beautiful than I'd ever seen her. We raced to be the first to be clutched in a bone-breaking hug. I never wanted to let go again. Marmie smelled beautiful, just how I remembered. She sounded beautiful. She was beautifully turned out. Nothing had changed.

'Where's Dardie?' we asked, when we could speak. 'And Junior? And Cynthia?'

'Your dardie's at work, so you'll see him this evening. Junior and Cynthia are waiting with a friend in London. We have to get a train home now. But first I have something for you. I thought you might be a little cold here.'

She gave me a powder-blue Marks and Spencer knitted cardigan, embroidered with yellow flowers, my first present from England. Nothing could have been more magical to me. I felt I'd been sprinkled with fairy dust.

There was a station at the docks then, long gone now, so in no time we were standing on a platform, amazed to see the lines of criss-crossing metal tracks. As Marmie shouted a warning to us to stay away from the edge, a loud snaking green monster came rushing towards us, hissing and grinding and panting. I'd never seen a train like this before.

We had trains in Trinidad, pulled by steam engines. We used to take one to go to the beach at Couva or Chaguanas, sitting on wooden slatted seats with our picnic packed, passing the strange buildings of the oil refinery and its lake of pitch, and then chugging slowly through sugar cane plantations and paddy fields and coconut groves. When musicians came aboard and played, there'd be dancing in the aisles. When we passed through the bird sanctuary, huge flocks of salmon-pink ibis rose in the air, disturbed by the commotion.

This train was very different. As I climbed on board with the others, and we all sat down on the posh velvet-covered padded seats, I felt as if I were in a film. Nothing seemed quite real. And yet it also felt so familiar. I looked out of the window and as we raced towards London, I saw not a strange land but green fields, and cows and sheep, just like ones I'd seen on postcards or in pictures in my schoolbooks. But now I was part of the picture. Thinking back to it now, that journey seems like a bridge of pure joy from one world into another. It was a safe haven and an adventure. We felt completely protected again, living out a dream in the care of our beloved Marmie. She was always very open in her emotions, so her happiness was as obvious as our own. Her world had knitted back together. It felt as though something that had become loose was now fixed firmly back in place. We were a family again.

We thought we could just carry on where we had left off.

'Junior and Cynthia are waiting for you,' Marmie told us. 'They are so excited to see you all. Cynthia has so many pictures for you. She's drawn everything, to show you how England is. Oh, she has turned into a great artist, ya little sister.'

There was no danger that they could have forgotten us. Marmie and Dardie had kept us alive in their minds, painting pictures in their imaginations all the time we'd been parted.

'And do you know, she even drew pictures of all four of you for the policemen, and told them your names and everything!' Marmie could laugh about this now, but what a shock it must have been when Cynthia had set off one day on an adventure all of her own, walking out of the front door and down the road towards Shepherd's Bush. A passer-by had picked her up, and not knowing what else to do with this independent little girl, had taken her to the police station, where she entertained the officers with her stories and drawings. 'She told them all about you.'

London was expecting us!

And then the train pulled into Waterloo station.

Marmie was a very forthright, no-nonsense sort of person,

always a bustler. She hurried us all off the train, saying, 'Come on now! It's rush hour, so you'll have to keep close to me.'

Rush! Rush! Rush! How could I ever keep up? I was feeling so bewildered by the scale of what we'd stepped into. I'd never seen anything like this grand building before, with its great high ceilings like a palace or cathedral, and the light flooding in, and so many numbered platforms, so much harsh noise and movement. My ten-year-old mind could make little sense of any of it: all the trains arriving and departing, and all those people rushing here, there and everywhere, so determined to get where they were going. Everyone in such dark, drab clothes, as if they were going to a funeral, all those men with almost identical coats and bowler hats, carrying briefcases and long black umbrellas.

On we rushed, through one barrier and then another and then we were at the top of a huge staircase with big wooden ridges on the steps. As I edged onto it, I realized that the stair-case was moving. Utter terror struck me. I thought we'd been caught in an earthquake. I had experienced one in Trinidad five years earlier, this trembling dread: the whole world shook, and the ground cracked, and the lights went out and everything went black. So, when we set foot on that escalator I thought this was happening all over again.

'It's all right, children. Nothing to be scared of.' Marmie tried to calm us down and comfort us. 'Hold on tight.'

Where were we? What kind of place was this? We hurried on through blackened tunnels, more crowds, and onto the underground platform and all at once there was a great rush of wind, and a tremendous racket and roar, and I was confronted with the first tube train I'd ever seen in my life. The doors slid open all by themselves! Was this some kind of space machine? The overpowering mass of intense sensations and impressions left me petrified and speechless. I suppose we must have had to

42

change trains again. And then we reached the stop called Turnham Green and emerged into light and more people and more noise. What next? We had no idea. Now we faced a cacophony of cars and buses and lorries, and the startling sight of shop windows, one after another, and bright red pillar boxes and tall, glassed boxes with telephones inside. Our first hard grey pavements. I felt we were in an urban jungle.

Marmie kept talking and telling us what everything was, reassuring us in our terror.

As I stared around in shock and wonderment, I noticed people were staring at us too. Admiring my smart dress and pretty new cardigan, I imagined at first. But I soon realized it wasn't admiration in their eyes, but something unfamiliar. A harsh, disapproving look I'd never really seen before.

'Nearly there,' said Marmie briskly, as we turned into Mayfield Avenue.

Our house was number 1. Built of red brick, it had one floor on top of another and was joined to the house next door, and seemed very solid and substantial. We followed her up the path, and Marmie unlocked the brown-painted front door. But then she led us up the dark narrow staircase, and we saw all the doors inside the house were firmly shut. On the landing she used another key to open another door.

'Welcome to your new home!' she said.

This was it? This small dingy room crammed with furniture – a double bed for the six children, a sofa for my parents, a table and some chairs? We had come all this way to live in a single room, all eight of us, sharing a cooker on the landing and an outside toilet with all the other tenants in the house?

Disappointment and exhaustion overwhelmed me. I burst into tears.

Chapter Seven

'If I have to live in a chicken coop, my children will live in that chicken coop with me!'

Cooped up must have been exactly how Marmie felt in that room, even after Dardie had set off early on his bicycle, heading for work on the production line at a car factory nearly ten miles away in Colindale. Marmie wasn't prepared to wait around until things were perfect in London before she sent for us. She had seen how things were here and made her decision. She knew some Black families stayed in one room for years, paying over the odds for their rent, unable ever to earn enough to escape the poverty trap, never sending for the children they'd left behind. These weren't the stories you ever heard back in Trinidad. Few people ever went back to the Caribbean once they'd left for England. It was too shameful to admit that the streets weren't paved with gold, that maybe the life left behind had been a better one after all. So, the cycle was perpetuated.

My main memory of our first few weeks in England was playing wildly in that little room, all six of us excited beyond belief, winding each other up into a frenzy.

'Be quiet, all'a'yuh!' Marmie would finally say. 'This is not a savannah, you know! Keep the noise down, or the neighbours will complain!'

Our mother made it completely clear to us that we children were more important to her than anything else in the world. She taught us how to manage our new existence by example, never wasting effort or energy dwelling on the negative aspects of life, but managing to find the best in every situation. Right now, the wonderful thing was that we were all together again. And the next most wonderful thing was that we were eating Marmie's cooking again.

In Trinidad my parents had always insisted that the key to success was schooling. Nothing could be more important, and it was exactly the same in England. A new school year was just beginning and I was very excited and keen to learn as much as I could. Sandra was old enough to go to the local secondary school, so we were separated for the first time. I started primary school in Chiswick with Lester and Ellington, setting off confidently, looking forward to the experience. Junior and Cynthia were at nursery.

Marmie left us at a typical late-Victorian school building with high wire fences, a grey tarmac playground and echoey green-tiled corridors that smelled of disinfectant. When we first arrived, lots of the children took turns to rush over and touch me quickly – my skin, my hair – before running off giggling. At first, I imagined they were being friendly. I couldn't have dreamed what would soon happen.

Lessons were the first surprise. The other children didn't seem to care very much about learning. And compared with the work we had done in Trinidad, everything seemed very easy. I understood the tasks perfectly, although the teaching methods were very different. There was much less discipline and less reciting facts parrot fashion. Yet whenever I answered the teacher's questions, she screwed up her face and made me repeat my answer. She clearly thought I was an idiot. Eventually I realized: she couldn't understand my accent. I don't remember any other Black children in the school. I suppose she'd never heard how people talk in the Caribbean. She behaved as if I wasn't speaking English at all.

In the playground it was even worse. I was completely mystified. I knew all about England – her history, her geography and her national anthem were part of my very being. Yet the children I met in London seemed to know nothing at all about me, and nothing about where I came from. They'd never even heard of Trinidad. My experience in the last school when we were living with the horrible auntie had taught me not to let my discomfort show, so I tried to answer these children's questions, hoping that I'd soon be asked to join in the familiar clapping games and hopscotch.

I'd come with such high expectations. I had love and friendship to give in abundance. All I wanted was to make friends. But when break time came, it was like being thrown into the lion's den.

'What are *you* doing here?'

I had no idea how many times I'd hear those words.

A colourful bullseye was painted on the brick wall of the playground. But I was the real target. I'll never forget being backed up against that wall, the bullseye behind me, hemmed in by a circle of taunting boys. And the name-calling began. I couldn't understand the words they were hurling at me. I'd never heard them before in my life. I won't repeat them now. What the words were and exactly what they were supposed to mean doesn't matter. What really hurt was the emotion behind them, and the feeling of rejection they gave me. The children's body language and faces told me more than their incomprehensible words. They told me that my kind wasn't welcome. I didn't *belong*.

I stood with my back to the wall, clenching my fists and digging my nails into the palms of my hands so hard that it nearly drew blood. I would not let it show. They would not make me cry. I could not let them get the better of me. I looked the other children right in the eye, upset and confused but knowing better than to let anyone see they had hurt me. Why didn't they treat me with respect and dignity? I was baffled. But I managed to hold my ground until they got bored and left me alone.

As soon as I got home, I told my mother what had happened.

'They kept saying "your kind". What did they mean, Marmie?'

I remember her body language as vividly as I remember that of my bullies. She looked completely deflated. I saw tears well up in her eyes. The realization that she had let her children down by not warning us about the deep-seated prejudice against Black people in Britain hit her very hard. Why hadn't she told us what we were in for? I still don't know. My guess is that she imagined vicious and unthinking racism of this kind was something that only happened to adults. She thought – or hoped – that children couldn't be so cruel. Cynthia and Junior had been too young to experience insults of this kind. Yet in our playground, racism was absorbed and repeated by children my age.

I remember how she comforted me and then called all the others over. She always made sure that when something important like this came up, we all heard what she had to say, all six of us together. This was a conversation no parent should ever have to have with their children.

'Sit down, all'a'yuh. I want to tell ya something you need to know. We're living in England now. And some people aren't going to like you. They're going to hate you just because of the colour of your skin. But I want you all to go to school and be

47

strong and to learn. And if you do that, one day you'll be great. 'Cos education is your passport to life.'

She hugged us all to her, enveloping us in her comforting Marmie-ness.

'And remember that Marmie and Dardie love you.'

I looked down at the back of my hand, rubbed it as tears ran down my cheeks and wondered why people were going to hate me. It was a terribly, terribly painful realization: I was different and there was nothing I could do to make the other children accept me for who I was. In the world outside our joyful home, I wasn't Floella any more. I was no longer regarded as a person, an individual with thoughts and feelings and aspirations. I was a colour. That was the day I lost a certain innocence and I too would see a person's colour and wonder whether he or she would hate me.

However often Marmie repeated the fact that she loved me, this couldn't take away all the anger and worry and fear I began to carry around with me wherever I went. I had to be on guard constantly. I had to look out for myself, and my siblings too. Having to be continually alert would take its toll.

As I've said, Marmie was always beautifully turned out, and she made sure all her children were too. She had a real flair for fashion, whether she was running up clothes on her sewing machine or rummaging in a church hall for bargains. Marmie thought a nice suburban neighbourhood would have the best jumble sales. By Christmas we had moved to Penge, in the London Borough of Bromley. The fact that it was a very White area didn't bother her at all.

Now we had two rooms. The kitchen/living room also served as a bathroom, and we washed in a tin bath, taking it in turns to hop in while Marmie poured warm water over us.

A curtain in the middle of the bedroom divided our parents' sleeping area from our own. The house was owned by an African man and his White English wife, who often insulted my mother and us.

'Keep your animals quiet!' she would tell her.

Our new primary school – St John's in Maple Road – was a little kinder than our last one, and I started to make a few friends. One of them was Norman, who was the heartthrob of the class and lived on our road. I had given him a black eye when he kissed me during a game of tag. I'd never heard of kiss chase, so was surprised. But he forgave me and we often walked home from school together. When a girl called me names one day as we stood by the cloakroom pegs, I slapped her so hard that my palm print was left on her face. That stopped her. I quickly learned how effective it was to retaliate to insults with force.

In Penge we felt more settled, so Marmie, who was missing her habitual churchgoing, decided it was time to find a suitable congregation to join. She dressed us up in our Sunday best, complete with hair ribbons for the girls, and shirts and ties for the boys, and we set off for the nearest church.

We were surprised that nobody said hello or introduced themselves when we came in and sat down. The service seemed very sedate compared with those we were used to in Trinidad. No noisy 'Hallelujah' or 'Praise the Lord' here. Nobody was moved by the spirit.

But we were all too familiar with the looks we were getting. Those unwelcoming, unfriendly stares. The question in their eyes we'd grown to expect, but not in a church:

'What are you doing here?'

We sat through the service quietly, our behaviour as impeccable as our fine outfits, and filed out at the end, wondering if perhaps the vicar would come and talk to us then. He didn't say a word. He didn't even seem to want to look at us, although it was impossible he could have failed to notice our presence. We were the only Black family in the congregation. And then we heard these words, spoken loudly and deliberately, and punctuated with a disapproving sniff:

'I see they're letting *their* kind in the church now.'

We never went back again. Sometimes we'd go to Salvation Army meetings because Dardie liked the music and played in the band, but these took place in a very plain hall. I stopped going to church that day because a church should be a place where you practise good, and that comes from the heart. It made me realize that Christians don't necessarily go to church and people who go to church aren't necessarily Christians. No true Christian would treat another human being like that. We were ostracized. It's little wonder that a lot of Black people at that time started up their own churches.

What are we doing here? I spent four years asking myself that question. Sandra and I were desperate to find some way to return to Trinidad. At night we secretly plotted and schemed and fantasized, but in our hearts we knew we were stuck. There was rarely any going back.

Marmie had several jobs and often worked early in the morning or evenings, doing the laundry for a school called Dulwich College which took boarders, and also cleaning offices in Victoria. I sometimes helped her with that during the school holidays. I'm still an excellent cleaner, and always take care to chat to any cleaners I meet to this day. Marmie was saving hard again, this time for a deposit on a house of our own.

She used the same method she had used to raise the price of our fares to England: an informal saving circle called a 'sousou' in Trinidad, or a 'partner' in Jamaica. These were common at the time as banks often refused to lend money to Black people, so it was the most efficient way to save, although obviously there was no interest. Every month ten friends would contribute five pounds each to the pot to make a hundred pounds. One after another, each person took it in turns to go home with the whole pot. And once everyone had had their hand, they started again, in reverse order. A very kind woman unexpectedly gave her hand to Marmie. Suddenly she had a hundred pounds, 10 per cent of the price of the house.

Our new address was not very far away. Number 47 Ridsdale Road, Anerley, belonged to a widower who could not bear to be in the house after the death of his wife, so he walked out and sold not just the house, but all its contents to my mum. So, all at once we not only had three bedrooms, and a sitting room and dining room, but all the furniture we needed too, from carpets and curtains to cutlery. I still have a few plates from that house. What a relief, we all thought. Somewhere of our own again, with space to breathe and play. A retreat from the relentless hostility that faced us whenever we stepped outside.

Except we had hell there.

Some of our neighbours were watching us. They tended to come at night. They must have known when Dardie was away on tour. He was having more success with his sax by then, picking up jobs in Archer Street, a narrow Soho back street where musicians traditionally gathered in hope of work. So, he was fulfilling his dream, but that meant sometimes travelling around the UK or further afield for three or six months at a time.

Our first warning was an ugly message in paint daubed on the wall of our house.

'GET OUT, W***'

Scrubbing it off was humiliating.

One evening there was a knock on the door, and we heard Marmie scream when she went to answer. Someone had shoved dog mess through our letter box. Another time they put a hosepipe through our door and flooded the hallway. An anonymous busybody even called the NSPCC and complained Marmie was mistreating her children. Really, it was our neighbours who were cruel to us. Yet nobody seemed to care.

When the inspector came and met Marmie, he said he wished all parents had the same standards of strictness and discipline.

You didn't mess with my mum.

'Yes, Marmie. Whatever you say.'

You showed respect. You never answered back. You knew her word was law. And her wisdom was boundless.

Marmie often used to give us a list of food she needed and send us to Penge to do the shopping. We knew from experience that there was no point in coming home unless we had bought everything she needed.

'Go back until they serve you!' Marmie would say if we ever came back empty-handed, complaining of our treatment, that others would get served but not us. 'They'll have to in the end, if you just stay put.'

And I found out this was true. I reckon that my mum's wisdom gave me my staying power all through my life. If you don't give in, everything comes good in the end. That's true for the big things as well as the small ones. So, I learned to stand my ground in the shops. That taught me resilience.

But anything could happen on the long journey to get there.

On the streets of London in the early 1960s, if you were Black, anyone could insult you at any time. You had to be prepared for this and you had to be strong. Nothing can describe that feeling of uncertainty and anxiety every time you set out into the world, knowing that at some point, one way or another, you'll have to decide how to deal with the cruelty coming your way.

So, you'd see someone approaching you and your mind would start whirring.

Is it this person? Is it this person? Are you ready for them? Ready to fight? Ready? Is it going to happen now?

And when they passed by without comment, your whole body flooded with relief.

Oh . . . It didn't happen this time. Thank goodness for that.

Until you saw the next person coming towards you.

Is this going to be the one? Yes, it is. Get ready to fight, fight, fight.

All the time you had to stay alert and keep reading the situation: reading the body language, reading the face, reading the walk. Smelling, smelling that person up ahead of you, a potential threat who was coming closer and closer. Knowing what might happen, and preparing yourself to strike. So, you were always ready.

Because strike I did. My anger had turned to rage. My rage had turned to violence. I had become a fighter.

Fighting physically was the only way I could feel better about the injustice of my treatment. What had I done to deserve these daily humiliations, this endless spewing out of spite? An innocent young girl was such an easy target. Groups often attacked adults, but it tended to be people on their own who abused children in this way. They were nearly always men.

It was a very draining experience. Perhaps as an adult it's easier to rationalize, but when you're a child, it's impossible to see any answer or explanation for this kind of behaviour. All you know is that complete strangers who know nothing about you are being horrible to you for no reason at all. It left me feeling hurt, disillusioned and very disappointed about Britain. I'd felt I was the luckiest girl in the world when I arrived. How could this be happening in my own Mother Country? How could the land I'd grown up loving care so little for me and my family?

Chapter Eight

For four years I was angry.

I was angry when I was called names and people spat at me.

I was angry when I went to the shops for Marmie and the shopkeeper pretended not to see me.

I was angry when a neighbour threw a bucket of icy water over me when I came out of our outside toilet.

I was angry when a grown man lifted up my skirt as he passed me on the street and asked, 'Where's your tail, monkey?'

I was angry when I was waiting on a station platform with Sandra, and some men in a passing train opened the window when they saw us, unzipped their flies and, laughing, tried to spray us with urine.

I was angry when I saw Lester's white shirt turn red as he lay on the pavement outside school with blood streaming from his face after fellow pupils had beaten him up.

By the time I joined Sandra at Penge Secondary Modern School for Girls in 1961, I had learned to fight back with my fists. I was always very strong and tough, and I was also fast. A really good runner. I was determined to give as good as I got. I was never scared. If you show fear, you've lost.

When I saw what the four boys at his new secondary school had done to Lester, I ran after each one in turn and punched them back. After that they mostly left Lester alone, as they had left Sandra alone after the fight in Trinidad. The following year Ellington moved up from primary school too. He and I had much the same approach to protecting our siblings.

Being a girl gave me the element of surprise. Nobody expected me to whip off one of my second-hand Clarks school shoes and give them a whack back with its hefty leather sole. They were shocked when I retaliated with a quick, sharp kick. The terrible thing is that I began to enjoy beating up my enemies.

I never lost a fight. My competitive streak used to kick in instantly, and winning these fights gave me a rush of pleasure that became quite compulsive. It was so satisfying to come out on top. I felt as though I were developing my own special force, a secret weapon, almost a superpower. I could smell out trouble even before it arrived, and when I went on the offensive, nobody could beat me. I enjoyed hurting the people who hurt me. Even today I can point out the exact spots where I triumphed in my most vicious fights.

For four years, outside my home, the rage boiled ever more furiously inside me.

Inside was another world: safe, joyful, and full of love and noise. We had each other and we were self-sufficient in our relationships. We didn't need friends. We had so much fun together.

Marmie was determined we should get to know our new city, so at weekends and in the holidays she'd make us all a big packed lunch, and we'd set off for a day of adventures all over London. Sometimes she'd drive us, but sometimes we'd have Red Rover bus passes, so we could hop on and off any Routemaster we liked. We heard the chimes of Big Ben and saw the

Houses of Parliament, and the Tower of London, the Christmas lights of Piccadilly Circus and Oxford Street. We roamed round the zoo, marvelling at all the animals. We gazed at Buckingham Palace, hoping for a glimpse of the Queen.

We never felt fear with Marmie there.

One day, when I was about fourteen, my mum sent me shopping as usual, but alone. It was half an hour's walk down to the shops in Penge and half an hour to walk back again. I was very fit from doing that walk all the time, and carrying all the bags too, as well as from all my running and fighting.

I knew it would happen at some point on that long walk on that steep hill. It always did.

As usual, when I left the wonderful safe environment which was home to go through the streets, I was on the alert, as well trained as any soldier on patrol. I was waiting for it. I was ready.

By this time I believed I was actually a skinny Black version of the Incredible Hulk. I'd come to imagine that I could cope with anything. *Bring it on*, I told myself.

And sure enough, just outside the church on Anerley Road, I saw a boy coming up the hill towards me, sucking a lollipop, and he had that look about him. He was an easy one to read. He didn't even have to think about it. As soon as he set eyes on me, he started up with his taunting. It was automatic behaviour.

Nehhnahhhnenehhahhh. On and on he went. All the usual stuff.

And do you know what? I felt great. Because I had the upper hand. Force of gravity. I was coming down the hill. I knew what I was going to do and he didn't. *Ha ha!* I thought. *You don't know what you're in for. You really don't know.* As soon as he got close enough to me, I reached out and shoved that sticky lolly down his throat. *There!*

I stood over him, and his eyes bulged at me, wide with shock. He started to choke. He started turning blue. And suddenly it was as if the whole world stood still. And I heard an ethereal voice:

'Floella! Floella! What are you doing? Because of this boy's prejudices, his ignorance, his stupidity, you're going to get yourself into trouble. Stop it! Stop it now! You know who you are.'

Who was speaking to me like this, gently, firmly, so lovingly?

'You know your Marmie loves you and your Dardie loves you. Start loving yourself the same way, Floella. Start showing the world who you really are.'

It sounds mystical, but I think it must have been the voices of my mum and my dad, in my head, voices I'd carried with me all my life but which I had forgotten to listen to. It reminded me of all the important lessons they'd taught me throughout my life. It told me to think of who I was, to think of my pride in my African heritage, to think of where my parents and grandparents had come from and what I'd learned in church.

'Why are you doing this?' the voice continued. 'You have the power to do anything you want to do. You can't change the colour of your skin. And if this boy has a problem with the colour of your skin, then it's his problem. Not yours. Start loving who you are, Floella. Find the right way to go through life.'

'Oh yeah!' I found myself saying.

It was like a revelation. An epiphany. I saw the world clearly again, and I had a vision of myself moving forward with no hatred in my heart, no anger, no anxiety.

'Call me what you like!'

Did I say this out loud, or just think it?

I have a power that can cut through anything that happens to me now.

I pulled the lollipop out of the boy's mouth, and said, 'Yes, so what?' He gasped and spluttered and ran off. And that was it.

The whole magical episode must have taken seconds. A feeling of pure exhilaration swept through me. I went on to the shops with a new spring in my step. If they refused to serve me, I was ready to smile sweetly and say, 'I'll wait. It's OK.'

And then I found that I did get served, because people could see that I was perfectly content. I wasn't looking pathetic, or sorry for myself, or angry.

'I'll just wait,' I said calmly.

How could anyone resist?

That's when I learned to smile, and not carry anger in my heart.

I'm so grateful that this happened to me when I was four-teen and not forty. Think of the damage I would have done to myself: to my self-worth, my heart, to my whole being and my attitude to the world. I would have got more and more angry, and started to believe that I couldn't win in this world.

I did have a force, as I imagined, but I was using it in the wrong way, and trying to fight something that couldn't be defeated in that fashion. It wasn't that the problem was impossible to solve, but I began to understand that true satisfaction comes from making somebody see something differently, not from hurting them. True change can't be forced. If somebody can't see and feel for themselves that their behaviour is wrong, or cruel, or misguided, they can't truly change. I was fighting a losing battle. Maybe the people I fought with would leave me alone next time, because they were scared of me, but their racism wouldn't go away.

At fourteen, I had won a spiritual battle. Now I knew who I was, where I was going, and the purpose of my life. What a turning point. I knew what I was doing here.

That was the day I stopped fighting with my fist and started fighting with my brain. That's the day I realized that education truly was my passport to life, education in the widest possible sense. It was almost as if I graduated that day, having absorbed the philosophy my parents taught me. Everything came together in that instant, my first spiritual moment.

It's so important to listen to the voices in your head, but you need to stay in control, and make sure you're always listening to the good voice, and not the bad one. Both are often there, fighting it out between themselves. You have to be mindful so that you can hear them quite clearly, and feel the magical sensation of doing the right thing.

Even today, I talk to myself, and listen. If you know the sound of your voice saying something, you're not afraid to say it out loud to other people.

Hear it. Feel it. Breathe it. Then *you* can be in control.

And so my smile became my armour. Nothing can penetrate it. It also allowed the world to consume the goodness I felt pouring out of my soul.

Wherever I go now people talk about the power of my smile.

'Your smile! I love your smile!' one person will say.

'Your smile makes me feel comforted,' another tells me.

'Your smile makes me feel safe.'

'Your smile makes me feel happy.'

Well, that was the day I got my smile.

> *Smile, though your heart is aching.*
> *Smile, even though it's breaking . . .*

Chapter Nine

During those years in Anerley, I lived in two cultures, continually switching between Caribbean at home, and English on the streets and, of course, at school. I lived a double life in lots of ways. Home was like a safe, noisy nest. It was often a cacophony, since every one of us gave as good as we got, and Marmie regularly complained about the racket we made together. Yet we all knew that the teasing and jokes and laughter came from a place of love.

I'd always enjoyed lessons and loved school more than ever when I went to secondary school because there was so much more to learn. But, desperate for everyone to love me, I imagined that the best way to do this was to make people laugh. So, when I wanted to be the class 'entertainer', I'd use my broadest Caribbean accent.

'Go on, Floella! Say some more!'

They thought my accent was so funny. Everybody would laugh uproariously. *I'm in there*, I convinced myself. *I'm definitely in there.*

One day we were having a poetry lesson with Mrs Thomas, my English teacher. Now, she was a very proper sort of person indeed, who wore a twinset and pearls and looked down her nose at anything she didn't approve of. She wanted the very best for her 'gals', as she called us, rather like Miss Jean Brodie. She wanted every one of us to excel, and she was one of the strictest teachers in the whole of Penge Secondary Modern School for Girls.

That day she summoned me to the front of the class.

'Come and recite a poem for us, Floella.'

So I decided to recite 'The Beggar Maid'. Knowing how popular my Caribbean accent was with the class, I performed the poem exactly as I would have done in Trinidad. Hugely confident, I threw back my head, and set off at some speed:

'"Her arms across her breast she laid;

She was more fair than words can say . . ."'

I hadn't got two lines in when I was interrupted. Mrs Thomas was horrified.

'Floella Benjamin, you *guttersnipe*!' She spat the word out. 'If you want to remain in my class, you will have to learn to speak the Queen's English!'

I was devastated. Hot tears sprang from my eyes. She had insulted me in front of the whole class. What would they think now? Of course, what I hadn't realized at the time was that the other girls were laughing *at* me, not *with* me. There's a big difference.

'Stop that snivelling, you *guttersnipe*!' Mrs Thomas ordered.

That word again. I didn't know exactly what it meant but I could tell from her tone that it was something very terrible and disgusting. It was a word she used quite freely to express her disapproval.

'Now, get into detention.'

My embarrassment and shame were complete.

I rushed home that afternoon to tell my mum of my humiliation, longing for comfort.

'Marmie, Marmie! Mrs Thomas called me a *guttersnipe*. She told me I had to learn to speak the Queen's English.'

'Eh, eh.' Marmie shook her head. 'I didn't bring you to England for a teacher to tell you off like that. You mad? You crazy? You go to school and you learn to speak the damn Queen's English, you hear me?'

That was a shock. I'd thought she'd jump to my defence.

'Yes, Marmie,' I whimpered, chastened.

'Education is your passport to life,' she reminded me.

So, I went back to school, and I learned to speak the Queen's English. I listened carefully, and copied Mrs Thomas's precise pronunciation and careful vowels. I made myself sound like a BBC presenter.

'Bravo, Floella!' said Mrs Thomas when I recited the poem as beautifully as any 1950s radio announcer. 'Bravo!'

Mrs Thomas brought out the performer in me. By stopping me in my tracks at that tender age, and making me realize I had to pay attention to where I was and to whom I was speaking, she taught me how to communicate better. She had no doubts about my ability to do this. She was simply angry that I hadn't worked that out for myself. So, I learned how to read and understand a situation and respond appropriately. Now, wherever I go in the world, I tune in to the culture and to the people around me.

This was an important lesson at an important time in my life. I'll always be grateful that my mother didn't rush off to the school and complain about my treatment. Some islands have stronger accents than others, and the way people spoke when I was growing up in Trinidad was perhaps less pronounced and we used fewer dialect words than elsewhere in the Caribbean. So maybe it was easier for me to adapt when I needed to. Maybe I simply had a good ear for voice as well as music. But there were certainly other Black children who didn't realize the consequences of speaking in the same way at home and at school, and sadly suffered for this. They were treated as 'backward' or 'slow' by teachers who couldn't understand them and who made little effort to do so. Many were put into classes for children with learning difficulties. Other Black children were moved to so-called 'special' schools: schools for the children categorized as 'educationally sub-normal'.

A pernicious and widespread practice in the UK at the time, this only came to light because of campaigning by the Black community. It wasn't until 1970 that the Grenadian teacher and writer Bernard Coard wrote the paper which became an influential book *How the West Indian Child is Made Educationally Sub-normal in the British School System: The Scandal of the Black Child in Schools in Britain*. In 1963, I simply understood that my best chance of getting on at school was to stop playing the clown, and to learn how to communicate with everybody as effectively as possible. If I didn't take myself seriously, nobody else would. If my teachers didn't want to teach me because they couldn't understand me, I would be the loser, not them.

My mother felt that learning to speak the Queen's English when I needed to would only be a benefit. It certainly didn't take anything away from me. I wasn't denying or hiding my identity. I can still go back to Trinidad and speak like a Trinidadian. It might seem Mrs Thomas's words were cruel, but they built me and made me a bigger person. Everything happens for a reason. Not many years later, Mrs Thomas's words would save me from a dangerous situation.

I was very lucky in my secondary school. The head teacher, Miss Bowles, was a stout woman of vision, and extremely 'proper'. She often dressed the same way, wearing neat lace-up shoes, a pale pink or white short-sleeved blouse and a grey skirt with a clean hanky permanently tucked into the waistband.

What an air of authority she gave out! Her face was jolly, her eyes sparkled, and I never, ever saw her angry. She used to call me 'the girl with the big smile'.

She believed in her girls with a passion, and she wanted us to aspire to great things. The intrepid Miss Bowles exposed us to so many different adventures and experiences which were practical, fun and mind-broadening. We learned ballroom dancing from Latin and formation dance star Peggy Spencer, the choreographer well known from TV work for the BBC's *Come Dancing* and much more, who had long been famous in Penge for running the maple-floored Royston Ballroom. Years later, when I was the subject of *This Is Your Life*, Peggy said she had spotted me on the dance floor that day, and knew I would 'be something' from the way I moved. The local tennis club came to give us tennis coaching. (But I was asked to sit out, because I hit the ball too hard for anyone to return.) Miss Bowles took us to see the first computer in an air traffic control tower at Heathrow and to listen to orchestras rehearsing at the Royal Festival Hall at the South Bank on Saturday mornings. She even got the local driving school in to give sixth-formers driving lessons on the netball court. Most of the girls there were White, so it meant an enormous amount to me when one year she chose Bernice, a tall thin girl from Trinidad, to be the head girl.

Having discovered my purpose in life thanks to my lollipop epiphany, I applied myself enthusiastically and was good at motivating other girls. This in turn made me popular with my teachers. I was a special favourite of the deputy head, Miss Roberts, who was in charge of sports, and the choir mistress also, who loved the way I could enunciate my words when I sang. Dardie had always encouraged me to put my heart and soul into singing, and Sandra and I certainly did when we sang the blues around the house, making up lyrics to accompany our cleaning and polishing and – in my case – clothes-washing, which I had to do by hand with an old-fashioned washboard over the bath, and hated.

One year, when I had a solo slot in the Christmas concert, unable to decide whether to sing, dance or act, I decided to do all three. Inspired by one of the films Dardie had taken us to – probably *Annie Get Your Gun*, or *Calamity Jane* – I dressed up country and western style, wearing a checked shirt, jeans, boots, hat and spotted necktie, to perform 'She'll be Coming Round the Mountain When She Comes'. I'll never forget the sensation of the part I was playing taking over my body when the piano started, the energy that coursed through me as I danced and sang, or the enthusiastic roar of applause that brought me back from the Rockies to the world of school. I truly believed I was that character, and as a result, I'd at last found admiration and respect. Finally I was no longer a colour, but Floella Benjamin, performer extraordinaire. I had touched my audience in a special way, and the cheers were just as loud when I did an encore.

Only two teachers didn't believe in me. I couldn't do art, according to my short-necked art teacher, 'Bulldog' Burton, and I couldn't swim either. When we had swimming lessons, the teacher told me to stay in the shallow end.

'You stay there. Coloured people can't swim so you don't have to try,' she said.

She genuinely believed this. It was a widespread myth, and maybe still is. People thought we had an extra bone in our heel! So, she didn't bother to teach me.

However, my running went from strength to strength, and when I became school captain, I hoped with all my heart we'd win the coveted inter-schools competition cup again. I knew from previous years that the captain traditionally took the cup home for the weekend, before it was displayed in a glass cabinet at school. I longed for this moment, and often used to picture my family's pride at such a glorious achievement. My parents would be overjoyed. My brothers and sisters would be in awe, inspired to aim ever higher themselves. If one of us won something, all of us had won.

'Look what we've achieved!' I'd say, triumphantly placing the gleaming trophy on the big wooden Blue Spot radiogram, or maybe on the mantelpiece.

Wow! I always thought, whenever I saw the captains who preceded me receive their trophy. *That'll be me one day.* My name was already in gold on the house boards for winning other events, but that silver cup was what I aspired to. I was in Elizabeth Fry House, whose colour was yellow. Nowadays many schools across the country are choosing my name for their houses – who would have thought?

At last the day came. We were competing on the huge playing fields of another school, Langley Park. It was a hot summer's day, and we did brilliantly.

The winners were announced. My dream was coming true. In a blur, I went up to the podium, still wearing my spikes, navy bloomers, white aertex polo shirt and Afro hair. A local dignitary was handing out the trophies, I shook their hand, took hold of the trophy, and was soon surrounded by the other team members. They crowded round laughing and cheering, as ecstatic as I was. Wow! What a day! I held the cup up in the air to show everyone, and hugged it to me.

And then, without warning, one of the teachers simply put out her hand.

'We'll take care of the cup, Floella,' she said, taking hold of it.

I was too surprised to resist. There was no time to argue.

But trudging back to Anerley, I cried all the way home. How would I tell Marmie? What on earth did the teacher imagine? That we would steal the cup? Sell it? That it couldn't be safe in a Black family's home?

But when I told her the whole story, once again Marmie's wisdom strengthened me.

'You've got to take the joys of life, and you've got to take the disappointments,' she reminded me. 'Don't let those disappointments upset you. We know you're the *victrix ludorum*. Nothing changes that, and we don't need a cup to prove it. Just knowing is enough joy for us.'

If things don't work out this time, they'll get better next time you try, but it's no use giving up if you fall at the first hurdle. You have to pick yourself up, dust yourself down, and take a run at the next one. This is a great philosophy to have in life, though it's hard to practise. It might take a day, a week, a month to succeed sometimes . . . It took twenty years when I was campaigning for there to be a Minister for Children in government. Maybe I didn't get to take home the cup that day, but now I'm the special guest invited to school celebrations the length and breadth of the UK to present cups and trophies to young athletes, not to mention academic prizes, and giving new generations that special feeling of success and achievement.

'Don't you ever forget,' said Marmie, 'Every disappointment is an appointment with something better.'

Chapter Ten

I was about thirteen when a postcard arrived from West Africa. I was captivated. That image of a beautiful African woman dressed in traditional clothes, wearing her hair in long plaits decorated with bright red and white beads, was something completely new to me. Perhaps she was a Fulani woman? I've no way of knowing, but whoever she was, I can tell you that she's stayed firmly in my head ever since, and maybe even changed my life. In the 1950s and early 1960s, as Black girls, we grew up having our hair prettily plaited in lovely cane row braids when we were children, decorated with ribbons for special occasions, but we just knew that on becoming a woman, we'd either have to start straightening our hair with hot combs, or wear a wig. Natural African hair was hardly ever seen in South London.

One day, I thought to myself as I gazed at the stunning photograph that had landed on the doormat out of the blue, *I'll plait my hair like that*. I longed to know more about my African roots. I didn't want to hide my origins. I wanted to celebrate them, just as our dad had always encouraged.

It was Dardie who'd sent us that postcard. He was on tour again, travelling ever further afield now, as the rise of pop music (which he hated) made it even harder to find work in the

UK. This trip was with a top-billing group called The Mohicans, who'd once been supported by the Rolling Stones, and it had taken him to Monrovia, Liberia. This must have meant a great deal to Dardie. The Republic of Liberia was established as a colony early in the nineteenth century by free-born and freed people of colour, mostly from the United States, but some from the Caribbean. Its name means 'Land of the Free'. In the early 1920s, Marcus Garvey had high hopes of mass African-American settlement in Liberia.

But when Dardie got to Liberia, he found injustice and inequality. Always something of a frustrated politician, he was shocked at the terrible treatment of ordinary workers, and so he encouraged those he met to stand up for themselves, to form a union and demand their rights. One night after a show, he was woken by a terrible crash. Some men had broken down the door of his hotel room. They proceeded to beat him up, and when he recovered consciousness he found himself in prison, in a small, roofless, white-walled cell. The midday sun was beating down on him. Then his night visitors returned and told him:

'If you want to spend the rest of your life here, keep talking.'

Dardie knew he couldn't abandon his wife and six children. What good could he do to anyone from a prison cell in Africa? Fortunately, this was just a dramatic warning. He was released, but came home labelled a troublemaker.

To his frustration, his jazz career was not reaching the heights he dreamed of. And Marmie had other ambitions. She wanted him to settle down to a steady job with a dependable income, so that we would all see more of him. As she explained, if he started his own band, he'd still be able to play at weekends and evenings, at local events around London. She wasn't asking him to give up his music altogether.

When Marmie told you what was what, you listened. A little reluctantly perhaps, Dardie gave up his travels, and got a weekday job as an accounts clerk at British Rail. At the same time, he formed a jazz combo with some other musician friends: the Roy Benjamin band. They didn't earn much, but every little helped, and he enjoyed the gigs at working men's clubs, pubs and weddings.

One day he announced that they needed a girl singer for the band.

'I'm going to audition you two, Sandra and Floella. So, you'll need to learn this song.'

'The Lady is a Tramp'. That was one we already knew very well from listening to Ella Fitzgerald and Sarah Vaughan over and over again. Off we both went to practise until he called us down to sing with him.

Sandra went first and got off to a shaky start. She was always shy, and after missing her first cue, her sweet soprano voice trembled and soon died away altogether.

Then it was my turn. I was named after Ella, wasn't I? Now it was time to turn into her.

Dardie played the intro on his saxophone, and I began to click my fingers in time. Bursting into enthusiastic song, I imagined the whole of Duke Ellington's orchestra accompanying me.

'"*I never bother with people I hate
That's why the lady is a tramp!*"'

I bowed to tumultuous applause – at least, that's what I heard in my head when all my family clapped and cheered.

'You're quite the showgirl!' said my proud father. 'You're hired!'

We had fun practising together, and my first public performance drew near. It was a spectacular West Indian wedding, which filled the grey Victorian town hall in Anerley with a riot of flamboyant colour and finery, a delicious feast of curry, rotis, chicken, rice and rum-rich wedding cake, and a party of guests ready to show off their most stylish dance moves.

Singing up on stage with the band made me feel as if I were soaring through space to another planet. I was in my element. On top of the world. I couldn't wait for our next engagement.

Within a few years Lester and Ellington joined the band on drums and piano, and our weekend bookings became family events, with Marmie in charge of the gigs, keeping an eye on all of us. She drove us everywhere, from Wormwood Scrubs prison to Chelsea Town Hall, with the car piled high with instruments and performers, and Lester's drum kit strapped to the roof. When she got bored she joined in, playing the maracas. When Dardie had too much to drink, and started pontificating, she called a halt to the fun and whisked us back home.

'Roy! You've had enough. Now shut up.'

She had power over all of us.

Although I was busy singing at other people's parties at the weekends, as long I was still at school Marmie didn't approve of me going to my own parties, and certainly not on my *own*. She had one worry above all, which I discovered the day I started my periods – my monthlies.

The blood was a complete shock to me. I was always tall and skinny, straight up and down, and I must have matured earlier than Sandra, who was more petite, because she certainly hadn't been able to warn me.

'Marmie! Marmie! Something awful's happening! What's this?'

With a serious face, she sat me down for one of her talks. But this time she didn't gather all my brothers and sisters around her.

'Right. You're a woman now. That means you don't go playing around with boys or let boys go playing around with you.

71

Because if you do, you'll get a big belly, and I don't want anyone round here coming home pregnant. So keep your legs crossed.'

And that was it. Of course, I had no idea what she meant. But she'd put the fear of God into me. All I knew was that I had to make sure boys stayed away from me. I took the task seriously. Nobody was going to mess with Floella Benjamin.

The first test came when my best friend Janice turned fifteen. Janice was one of the most popular girls in the school, and I was so proud that she had chosen me to be her best friend. We promised each other to stay friends for ever. Janice was blonde, pretty and seemed incredibly sophisticated.

However, it took some persuading on my part for Marmie to let me go to her house after school on her fifteenth birthday. It was my first ever party invitation, and I was thrilled. Although I was friends with other White girls at school, I never saw them out of school, or went to their homes.

'I'll be home soon after seven,' I told Marmie when I left that morning.

As soon as we got to Janice's house, and her mother opened the door, I recognized that look on her face. I'd seen it so often before, and I see it still sometimes to this day. Her lips smiled, pulled up at the corners like stage curtains opening, but her eyes didn't. They flicked quickly up and down, taking me in with that 'What are you doing here?' look. Nobody else would have noticed, but I was perfectly sure she didn't approve of me. Not because she knew me, or because of anything I'd done. Simply because of the colour of my skin.

After a splendid tea and fancy birthday cake, Janice's mother went out for a while, to my relief. But no sooner had she gone than we heard a knock at the door, and three or four boys turned up. With much giggling, everyone began to play a teenage version of blind man's buff, with the boys all blindfolded, and the girls running away – or not – from their kisses. I panicked.

Of course, I wanted to be part of all the fun, but Marmie's warnings about boys were still ringing in my ears. I dashed upstairs and leapt into a wardrobe, where I hid in darkness until I felt safe to emerge, and slink home.

Marmie remained extremely protective of us all. After our ill treatment in Trinidad in her absence, she felt she couldn't trust anyone with her children, and wouldn't even let us join the Guides or Scouts. Evening 'gallivanting' without her was quite out of the question. She went ballistic when I asked if I could join my best friend at a local disco, and wouldn't let me go. I was disappointed, because I loved dancing so much. But as usual, Marmie had her own solution.

The following Saturday, we both dressed up in our best clothes, took the train together to Victoria, then the tube to Hammersmith. Where was Marmie taking me? Then I saw the crowds and the lights: 'PALAIS–DE–DANSE' spelled out in big neon letters. Inside, the dance hall was like a glorious dream world, a real palace. With my mum as my partner and protector, I whirled around the floor for hours, lost in the all-encompassing music of Joe Loss and his big band, who played live on stage all night. I couldn't have been happier. That was the first of many nights at the Hammersmith Palais. And Marmie always made sure I was tucked up in bed by midnight.

Chapter Eleven

Although I still loved school as much as ever, and was doing well, there wasn't enough money coming in for any of us to stay on to do A levels. At sixteen, we were each expected to start making our contribution to the family finances. Any further qualifications had to be acquired at evening classes. I wasn't surprised or disappointed. I knew how things stood. I'd already spent a year earning money from a Woolworths Saturday job. Most of that seventeen shillings and sixpence went to Marmie to help out, and she saved enough of it to pay eventually for the Hotpoint washing machine which relieved me of my most-hated chore. Of course, Sandra was already working, handing Marmie her wage packet every week, so that our mother could decide how much Sandra needed to live on, how much should be saved, and how much was needed to help support the family.

Fortunately, by the time my turn came round to consult the school's careers officer, Mrs Barratt had got the measure of Marmie.

Their run-in at Sandra's interview is legendary in our family.

Sandra had set her heart on working at the Wellcome Laboratories, an important pharmaceutical research centre not far away in Beckenham. Her dream was to be a research technician. When she quietly explained this, Mrs Barratt was sympathetic but categorical.

'Oh, I'm sorry, dear, but that's quite impossible. They don't take coloured people there. How about a job as a nursery nurse?'

Britain was on the eve of the first Race Relations Act (1965), but even when this passed, it only banned discrimination on grounds of colour, race or ethnic or national origins in public places. So, shops, boarding houses and above all employers could actually still legally refuse to give you a job because of the colour of your skin. The second Race Relations Act covering employment only came into being in 1968, and it was so weakly enforced that not a single prosecution ever took place under its legislation. In 1965, if you weren't White, few other avenues beyond public transport or the NHS were open to you. Girls like us were automatically expected to take menial factory jobs, or work as a cleaner or carer.

Yet Marmie exploded at Mrs Barratt's suggestion.

'Eh, eh. Are you crazy? I didn't bring my children to England and educate them and they didn't study hard for a professional career for you to tell me my daughter can't get a job where she wants to because of the colour of her skin. Nothing and nobody's going to stop any of my children finding a career doing whatever they set their minds to. If they have the ability to do it, they'll do it.'

Back at home, Marmie made Sandra dry her tears and write an application to Wellcome. When Sandra was invited to an interview, Marmie made her a beautiful suit and accompanied her to the appointment. It was just as well, because when they first arrived, a man directed them to a building where they were interviewing cleaners and bottle-washers. What else could a young Black woman be doing there? When they eventually found the right place, the very same man was Sandra's interviewer. It simply hadn't crossed his mind that she might be on his list of fifty candidates for the trainee technician job. Most unusually, Marmie went into the actual interview room with Sandra, but when she started to answer his questions for her daughter, the man insisted that Sandra had to speak for herself.

After that, it was a long wait. We wondered what the point of an education could be if you still couldn't get the job you wanted. Weeks and weeks seemed to go by, while the whole family began to lose heart. Except for Marmie, of course, who counselled patience. 'No news is good news!' she declared. But at last the letter arrived, bringing the good news that Sandra had got the job. This sent us into a frenzy of celebration, and gave Marmie the final word at Speech Day that summer, when fate – or maybe not? – seated her next to Mrs Barratt.

With great satisfaction, and a beaming smile, she greeted the careers officer:

'Hello, Mrs Barratt! Sandra got a job at Wellcome, you know.'

Mrs Barratt's eyes were opened. The dynamics between the pair of them shifted, and of course, it was another story altogether when Marmie and I sat down to discuss my career. She was all ears. 'So where does Floella want to work?'

Initially I'd wanted to be a teacher, but I knew that would be difficult without A levels. But being good with figures, I thought working in a bank would be a good plan. I could work towards the qualifications I needed for teacher training college in the evenings.

'Do you have any idea which bank you'd like to work for, Floella?' asked Mrs Barratt.

'Barclays!' I replied eagerly. I was absolutely sure of that, because I had another motive. My best friend Janice was preparing for a career at Barclays, she'd told me. Devastated at the prospect of being separated when we left school, we'd hatched a plan to get jobs in the same bank. How else could we keep our pact to stay friends for ever?

'Leave it to me,' said Mrs Barratt. 'I'll arrange an interview. Let's try some other places too, just in case.'

Of course, I'd pictured myself behind a glass window, dealing efficiently with customers. But until the Race Relations Act of 1968, only White people were ever employed as cashiers. Nearly all office jobs for Black people were out of sight, behind the scenes. There was an opening in the chief accountant's office at Barclays, we learned. I'd work my way up, I innocently imagined. Surely, I'd get there in the end.

The day of the interview dawned, and Marmie took me to the bank's City headquarters in Lombard Street. This time she waited patiently outside the office door. Everything rested on this interview, I felt. If I didn't make the right impression, Janice and I could be parted for ever. I have never been so nervous about anything before or since. I wanted this job so badly.

Stomach churning, I sat down at a vast desk, opposite a woman in a neat navy suit. I remember nothing of her questions now. All I can remember is the thumping noise which quickly filled the room. Something very strange had happened to my right leg, and there was absolutely nothing I could do about it. An uncontrollable nervous reflex was making it twitch violently, banging hard against the desk above.

Thud. Thud. Thud.

The more embarrassed I felt, the louder it got.

Smile, I told myself. *Just keep smiling.* The noise continued, but I smiled away, the woman smiled sympathetically back, and whatever I said must have been the right thing, because a few weeks later I learned that I'd got the job, as well as the three or four others I'd applied for. I was over the moon. I rushed to school to tell Janice the wonderful news.

Instead of the squeal of joy I was expecting, I received a cold stare.

'Well, I've decided to go and work at Lloyds instead,' Janice told me, matter-of-factly. As if we had never made our promises. As if she hardly knew me. 'My mother thinks it's best. See you later.'

I don't think we ever spoke again.

That betrayal devastated me. Janice broke my heart that day, and destroyed my trust. Perhaps I had been naive, for I knew what her mother thought of me. And my own mother had hardly approved of Janice. She worried my best friend would lead me astray, with her discos and boyfriends. In fact, all my family were often shocked by the way some White children took their education for granted, instead of applying themselves to their studies. But I had pledged undying loyalty, and our friendship was one of the most important things in the whole world to me. How could it mean so little to Janice?

I felt upset and confused for a long time. Were my White friends at school just pretending to like me? It was a hard way to learn that, in the wider world, friendships between races were generally despised, and mixing cultures socially unacceptable. After leaving school, it seemed impossible.

Determined not to let this setback crush my confidence, I enrolled for A levels in History and Geography at evening classes at Brixton College, and set a new course for my life. Never again would I let something like this happen to me, I told myself.

It was daunting at first, heading off alone into the City with all the other commuters, all dressed in dreary black or grey or navy blue, except for me. I'd walk from London Bridge to Cannon Street, where I worked on the ninth floor of a huge office block called Queensberry House. Hidden from any customer's view, I sat in an enormous open-plan office, sharing a large table with seven young women and men, all of us operating hulking great adding machines. Made of grey metal, these mechanical monsters had big buttons with numbers on the top, a bit like an old-fashioned typewriter or cash machine, with a lever at the side.

Just one person in my department ever showed me any hostility at work: that podgy assistant manager. Despite him, I adored the work so much that I revised my ambitions and decided to work my way up to become the first Black woman bank manager instead of a teacher, although there were no other people of colour in my office. I little imagined that ten years later I'd be drawn to working with children in a way I could never have pictured then. In 1966, alongside my A levels, I began to study for a banking diploma at Wandsworth College.

After work I was always busy, because if I wasn't studying, I was running with the bank's athletics club, regularly winning the 100 yards races, hurdles at all distances, and usually placed in a number of other events. Once again I was the *victrix ludorum*, never losing a race for the head office team at the championship meetings. Running was another kind of performance for me, and winning gave me a sense of achievement and success, which felt almost addictive. *I am a winner*, I told myself, when I looked in the mirror.

Most of my training was running up and down Anerley Hill to catch my train, but one day at a competition a coach advised me to commit more time to it. With proper training, she suggested, I could one day represent Britain at the Olympics.

Perhaps I should have followed her advice, but I didn't like the way my thigh muscles had already bulked up just from the amount of running I was doing. My figure wasn't exactly womanly. I had big staring eyes, big teeth, a great big nose. And my face was often covered with spots like buttons, so many that my siblings used to tease me I could sell them to the Singer's sewing machine shop. So, I stuck to running for the bank, earning respect and admiration from my boss, the chief accountant, and enjoying the applause at the races. And on Saturday nights, I partied.

Chapter Twelve

Sandra and I always went out together, often communicating in a made-up secret language nobody else understood. People on the tube probably thought we were speaking 'African'. A lightweight when it came to alcohol, which made me cry or feel sick or fall asleep, I didn't drink, and I didn't smoke either. At the age of seventeen, I felt intoxicated with life. I had a permanent smile on my face. And how I loved to dance.

Our social life initially revolved around the West Indian Students' Centre in Earl's Court. This was a place we knew quite well already because Dardie's band played there. So Marmie felt it was a good, safe place for us to go on our own.

'You'll meet only decent, intelligent young people there,' she assured us.

And indeed, it was eye-opening: one of the few places we could go out in London to enjoy ourselves, find out more about the world, and be confident that nobody would give us odd looks, ignore us completely or call us names. We felt valued and respected there. WISC's home was in an imposing late-Victorian building in ornate red brick on the corner of Collingham Road in Earl's Court. It was open from ten in the morning until eleven at night, and had a lounge, a library and a bar as well as rooms for billiards, games and watching television, and plenty of space for lectures, debates, meetings and social events of all kinds. There was even a sprung-floor ballroom. Funded by the various governments of the West Indies, WISC was a lifeline for students and young people from all over the Caribbean, a melting pot where we discovered that as West Indians we had much more that united us than divided us.

Learning about other Caribbean islands and nations that lay hundreds of miles away from Trinidad, I also came to appreciate the dangers of judgement without understanding. Back in Trinidad, I'd probably absorbed the unthinking prejudices of my island. Of course, Trinidadians were better than Grenadians! Meanwhile, in Grenada, Grenadians thought they were better than Barbadians, or Antiguans or whoever it happened to be easiest or closest to feel superior to. Here in London, thousands of miles from where we were born, we could develop new shared identities.

I was on a true voyage of discovery in a world that was changing fast. The first efforts to gain independence in the British-controlled Caribbean in the form of the short-lived West Indies Federation had collapsed in 1962. There would never be a single unified state of all the island groupings in both the Greater and the Lesser Antilles, as Trinidad's Prime Minister Eric Williams had once hoped. But one by one, the former colonies in the region were becoming independent in their own right, starting with Jamaica and Trinidad and Tobago in 1962, then Barbados and Guyana in 1966, and followed in the 1970s and early 80s by the Bahamas, Grenada, Dominica, St Lucia, St Vincent, Antigua and Barbuda, Belize, and St Kitts and Nevis.

In 1967, I joined the organizing committee of the West Indian Students' Centre, and soon became chair. Dedicating myself to the centre's social events, I arranged everything from seaside coach trips (surprising the residents of Margate) to

82

beauty contests, cocktail parties and the annual Carnival celebrations. Here I had my first experience of standing on stage to
introduce important speakers with half my mind trying to keep
on top of all the practical arrangements behind the scenes – had
I prepared enough cheese-and-pickled-onion sticks? Had the
special guest arrived? So I didn't always get a chance to listen
to all the eminent visitors who came to give talks, which ranged
from Caribbean High Commissioners and visiting politicians
to well-known and emerging artists, writers and thinkers,
such as C. L. R. James, George Lamming and Edward Kamau
Brathwaite.

In that exciting era, soon after the assassination of Malcolm
X, the Black Power movement was developing fast in Britain.
At home my father lectured us about Michael X, the controversial Black revolutionary who was born Michael de Freitas, in
Trinidad and Tobago, and came to London in his twenties in
1957. Stokely Carmichael was another of Dardie's heroes. He
too was born in Trinidad, but emigrated to the United States
when he was eleven, in 1952. Jailed as a Freedom Rider at the
age of nineteen, he soon became one of America's most prominent civil rights leaders. Marmie was far less militant than
Dardie, and preferred the peaceful approach to change taken
by Martin Luther King Jr.

When Stokely Carmichael came to the centre during his visit
to London in July 1967 to speak at the Dialectics of Liberation
congress, it caused a sensation. A charismatic, almost mythical
figure in trademark sunglasses, he electrified audiences wherever he went. His call for Black people to come together 'to
fight for their liberation by any means necessary' was erudite
and inspiring. Carmichael was an international celebrity, and it
was like having a rock star in the building.

To be honest, though, I've learned more about him since
that day than I knew at the time. As usual, I was too

preoccupied organizing everything necessary to make such an important event a success to be able to listen to his speech. I certainly didn't realize that Stokely Carmichael was followed wherever he went in London by Special Branch agents – some say there was an *agent provocateur* in the audience that evening, trying to provoke a riot. Carmichael was effectively kicked out of the country soon afterwards.

But I was absorbing his message about the power of self-determination in other ways.

'Say it loud: I'm Black and I'm proud!' sang James Brown in 1968, the year Tommie Smith and John Carlos raised their black-gloved fists at the Mexico City Olympics as 'The Star-Spangled Banner' played. We sang along with Brown, committing every word of his song to heart. We'd had more than enough of other people's derogatory names for us. Black was what we wanted to call ourselves. 'Black is beautiful', we proudly affirmed.

Once Lester had left school to begin an apprenticeship as an electrician, the family had three extra wage packets coming in. Marmie wanted an upgrade. She set her sights on a bigger house, with a garden where she could grow the flowers she loved, in a better neighbourhood. One Sunday afternoon we left Dardie practising his sax, and set off after lunch in our trusty Ford Zephyr to view the semi-detached property she'd chosen in affluent Beckenham.

The street was wide and peaceful, with houses on a much grander scale than we were used to, all surrounded by well-tended gardens. We could see the 'For Sale' sign at the gate, and raced up the path to the front door, which Marmie opened with the key she'd picked up from the estate agent. We rushed wildly around the house, inspecting every one of the huge empty rooms. After the garden-less semi in Anerley, this place seemed like a palace.

Our laughter came to an abrupt end when we heard an enormous commotion outside. *NEEE-NAW-NEEE-NAW-NEEE-NAW* . . . Sirens and flashing lights heralded the arrival of several Panda cars and police motorbikes, and even a Black Maria van.

There was a sharp knock on our door. A policeman in crash helmet and goggles stood outside. Marmie greeted him with her most charming smile.

'Yes, Officer. What can I do for you?'

With an air of great authority, he turned to his colleagues, and assured them that he could handle this alone. To our relief, they soon vanished. The lace curtains in the houses opposite continued to twitch. The policeman explained that the neighbours had reported a large group of coloured people had broken into the house and were stealing the fixtures and fittings. As soon as this policeman saw us, he understood the situation. His own wife, a Ghanaian doctor, had experienced exactly the same thing when viewing the house where they now lived, a few streets away. Both she and her husband became good family friends after we moved in, and he shared some horrendous stories of police racism, which eventually made him leave the force in disgust.

Of course, Marmie was not deterred, and stood her ground. An Italian family next door were very sympathetic, as they had suffered similar racial prejudice. Eventually, most of the hostile neighbours moved away, and Marmie and Dardie lived happily in that house for the rest of their lives.

I decided I needed a car of my own. It was mainly for coming home from parties on a Saturday night. I was still always sober at the end of each night, and always unkissed. In fact, I'd begun to despair that nobody ever asked me to dance when the music slowed. I always had to sit out the final number. Even my parents were secretly wondering why I didn't have a boyfriend. Sandra was never short of dance partners. There must have been something unapproachable about me. My confidence? My body language? Everything about me said so clearly 'don't mess with me'.

I sometimes regret never having had that experience of being young, and seeing a man cross the room to ask, 'Can I have this dance?'

But if the price was independence, that suited me.

Having saved up the thirty pounds I needed for a sky-blue second-hand Austin A35 which Dardie helped me choose from the pages of *Exchange and Mart* and then drove home for me, I realized I couldn't afford driving lessons. Dardie had no patience, so Marmie bravely took her life in her hands and began the difficult task of getting me through my test.

'Child, you trying to kill us?' she asked me, after I'd mounted the kerb in a particularly hair-raising incident. I found it hard to tell left from right and had a habit of accelerating like a rally racer. So, it was fourth-time lucky when I finally passed.

What a liberation it was. One Saturday morning, the car began to misbehave. I'd have to get it seen to if we were going to get home from our party that night. Everyone was depending on me. I couldn't face Sandra and Lester's disappointment, never mind my own. At last I found an open garage in Gypsy Hill, where a mechanic promised to have the vehicle fixed for me by five p.m. That afternoon I returned to the forecourt, delighted to see my car sitting waiting for me. However, the garage looked firmly shut, and there was no sign of the helpful man.

My heart sank. Maybe he hadn't gone yet. I knocked on the metal door, calling out hopefully, rattling the handle. At last it opened.

'Thank goodness,' I said. 'I thought you were gone.'

'No, I've been waiting for you,' said the smiling mechanic, and he ushered me into the back of the garage to his tiny office, assuring me the car was fixed.

I sat down cheerfully, and got out my chequebook.

'What do I owe you?' I asked.

'You.'

The chilling note in his voice made me look up in alarm.

'Pardon?'

I played for time, pretending not to hear or understand. But I knew immediately that I was in danger.

'I want you,' he said, beginning to unbutton his flies.

I was completely trapped. There was nowhere to run. Nobody to hear me if I screamed for help. I was on my own.

But without panicking, from the depths of my soul and before his very eyes I morphed myself into my old English teacher, posh Mrs Thomas. Channelling all her propriety and imperious disapproval, I sat up straight-backed in my seat, crossed my ankles and clasped my hands firmly in my lap.

'Now, now, my good man,' I began haughtily. 'Don't be foolish.'

He faltered a little, perhaps not expecting me to go on the offensive, and began to plead.

'Please let me have you. I've never had a coloured girl before.'

Then I let him have it:

'If you dare to touch me, you *guttersnipe*, my three six-foot brothers will come and break every bone in your body and teach you a lesson you'll never forget. So, pull yourself together, you *guttersnipe*, and tell me how much I owe you.'

I held my breath. It was a battle of nerves that I wasn't going to lose. I stared at him, unafraid, and I won. The dirty little man looked shamefaced as I paid, but I wasn't taking any chances, and haughtily insisted that he lead me back to my car so that I could keep him in my sights. It took for ever to get through that dark, smelly building, never knowing if he might suddenly turn on me.

I sobbed out loud with relief as I drove home, and the fear I'd repressed seemed to take over my shaking body. I realized Mrs Thomas making an example of me four years earlier had saved me, and helped me to deal with the situation. Marmie was right. Every adversity happens for a reason. All my difficult teenage experiences had built up my resilience to a point where I could hide my true emotions perfectly. I had learned how to put on a mask, take charge of a situation and act with perfect confidence, no matter what. My spirit was unbroken. I was stronger than ever.

Only once did I ever let my guard down again, and I'll always regret it.

I had reached a point of being completely happy in mind and body. So happy that I allowed myself to relax too much. One Friday night, I was out with a White male friend I'd met at my evening class. We went to a Croydon bowling alley, a place full of Victorian gilt and red velvet and bouncers in suits at the big glass doors. I was probably the only Black person there, but I was used to that.

What's she *doing here?* people must have been thinking, but I didn't notice. My competitive spirit had taken over, and I was delighted by my success, laughing and jumping for joy each time I made a strike. I didn't even notice that I was attracting attention, or that we were surrounded by White faces, until suddenly, as we were on our way out, I felt myself being hoisted into the air and launched forward, like a puppet. Attacked from behind, in the most cowardly way, my friend and I were bundled through the entrance and both of us beaten up brutally while the bouncers turned away and didn't intervene. It was five years since I'd last had a fight. My old powers refused to be summoned. My piercing screams only provoked more violence.

With a stream of racist abuse, my attacker punched me in the face so hard that blood spurted from my mouth and one of my large front teeth shot out to the back of my throat. By some miracle, I instinctively did the right thing and shoved it back into place in my gum, pressing as hard as I could. Someone must have called an ambulance for us, because at last we heard a siren and the men ran off, leaving us battered and bruised almost beyond recognition.

The attack made my family angry. More than anything I was angry with myself for allowing myself to be lulled into a false sense of security. *How could I have let my defences down like that?* I thought, as we were patched up in hospital. I could never allow it to happen again. We knew the police wouldn't be interested, since we had no witnesses. When my father tried to tell a local paper, they laughed at him. 'Tell us something new,' they said to him. Nobody cared. Attacks like that happened too often to be newsworthy. In April 1968, the Conservative MP Enoch Powell had condemned non-White immigration into Britain in his poisonous and incendiary 'Rivers of Blood' speech. Enoch Powell and his supporters made racist violence seem acceptable. The National Front, a new neo-Nazi party, was on the rise.

Yet we weren't even immigrants. We had moved from one part of the British Empire to another, at the invitation of the government. We were never made welcome.

That night at the bowling alley would be the last time I'd let anyone get the better of me, and the last time I'd ever lower my guard. From that moment on, I've always stayed alert to danger, no matter where I am. My personal radar is finely tuned to spot trouble coming. My sixth sense is always switched on.

At the bank I was making more headway with revolutionizing dress codes than I was in my career. My Marmie-made mustard-coloured trouser suit with matching floral blouse had caused a stir. After that, many of the women in the office dared to wear trousers too and I'd even persuaded some of the men to wear coloured shirts. But how long would it take to become a manager? Everyone in the senior positions of the bank looked ancient to me. Ancient, male and White, of course. And for some strange reason, I'd convinced myself that I didn't have long to live. I had a premonition that I would die at the age of twenty-one. This didn't frighten me, for I've never been scared of death. But it did make me think I should get a move on, although my dream of becoming a bank manager was beginning to look more like a fantasy than a reality.

This sense was catalysed by a run-in with that assistant manager which convinced me that he was out to get me.

'Floella, take these papers to the Bank of England right away,' he ordered one afternoon.

I was very surprised.

'That's not my job,' I told him firmly. There was a pool of messengers who had responsibility for deliveries like this – a great team, with whom I often chatted and laughed. No other accounts staff would ever have been asked to do a menial errand like this. Clearly the banking diploma I'd recently acquired meant nothing to him. All he saw was my colour. Furious at the way he tried to put me down, I remained defiant.

'I suggest you pick up the phone and call one of the messengers to collect the papers as usual.'

More than ever, I wondered how I would manage to break through so many corporate barriers and make a success of a banking career. A few weeks later, I opened the evening paper on the train home and an advertisement leapt out at me.

'Singers and dancers wanted for a national musical tour. No theatrical experience necessary. Open auditions to be held at the Shaftesbury Theatre for one week.'

Zing!

I knew immediately what I had to do.

PART 2

WHICH WINDOW SHALL WE LOOK THROUGH TODAY?

Chapter Thirteen

I slid out of my outfit in the ladies' toilet, packed away my wig and slipped back into my seat in the chief accountant's office before anyone could ask me where I'd been. Secretly, I felt as if I'd been on an adventure like Dardie's. Confidently rocking up to the stage door an hour earlier, I hadn't imagined for one moment that I'd get the part, after telling them my terms and conditions. I certainly hadn't thought ahead to the consequences. So, when the phone call came from the theatre later that afternoon asking me if I'd take the job, I replied without thinking.

'Yes,' I said.

How could I possibly refuse? I didn't even remember to check the pay. I suppose I just thought it would be thirty pounds a week as I'd asked for. What now? I literally had no plan. But I knew I had a battle ahead.

Of course, Marmie exploded. Not for nothing did Dardie call her 'Molotov', instead of her real name, Veronica.

'I didn't bring you to England to go gallivanting on a stage with naked people! You mad? You crazy? You're going to give up a proper job in a bank, a job for life, good pay, singing with your dad at weekends? You're going to give up all that, and bring shame on all our family, for *this*!'

I was crushed. There could be no pretending about *Hair*. I had ended up in the touring version of the West End hit almost through chance, intrigued by a newspaper ad, but everyone knew all about this new 'tribal love-rock musical', already a Broadway hit – or at least they thought they knew. When the first British production had opened the previous autumn in London's West End, the very day after Britain's two-hundred-year-old theatre censorship laws were lifted, the media went wild. Newspapers (inaccurately) reported orgies on stage and unheard-of profanity, suggesting scene after scene of debauchery. 'Makes *Marat/Sade* Look Like *Peter Pan*' boasted the original poster.

It's hard to imagine now, but in the era when *Hair* was first scandalizing theatre audiences, even White men got abused in the street for wearing their hair long. That could mean simply down to their collars.

'Get your hair cut, hippy!' people would yell, disapprovingly. Long hair represented rebellion, and used to infuriate the strait-laced older generation. And of course, you had to get your hair cut when you went into the army. So that was the story behind the title of the musical.

For Marmie, the show epitomized all the evils she feared most – nudity, sexual freedom, drugs, lawlessness. In her eyes, I was hurtling headfirst into everything she'd brought me up to avoid. Orgies aside, she had practical concerns too.

'Why you want to leave home? Where are you going to live? What's going to happen to you?'

She knew from Dardie's experience how precarious a career in show business could be. No pension. No security. No idea where the next pay cheque might come from. Out of the blue, I had presented a fundamental challenge to her plans for her children. These had been going so well. Our success was the fruit of her investment. She always put us first – except that one time when she left us behind in Trinidad, something she always regretted.

Of course, I was devastated by her disapproval. She was the family boss, and if she said no, there was no way I could do it.

Yet I couldn't help thinking, as I always do, that there had to be a way. The next day, I went to see my boss at Barclays. Luckily, the head of the chief accountant's office liked me because I always made the head office proud with my triumphs on the sports field. I'd been awarded *victrix ludorum* at the annual August Sports Day for three consecutive years by then, and also twice in the Club Championships.

'Mr Sharp, I need to ask you something. I've been offered this job. It's not a proper job, and it's only a six-month contract, so I was wondering . . . Could I have six months' leave of absence and then pick up where I left off when I come back? I promise I'll be back for Sports Day.'

'Yes, of course,' he said, without hesitation. I was taken aback at his readiness to give me what I wanted, but perhaps the prospect of being associated with show business promised to bring some excitement to his life.

Then I went home and talked to Dardie. He'd always loved my spirit, and my singing and dancing, and he was also convinced my moral compass wouldn't let me down. He knew I wasn't the type to be easily led astray. And although he had been more disappointed in his ambitions as a performer than he liked to admit, there was no reason why his daughter shouldn't now shine. By the end of our conversation, I was convinced he'd back me up when I put my case to Marmie again. Dardie didn't want me to spend the rest of my life regretting passing up such an amazing opportunity.

'Please, Marmie. Please let me take this job. Mr Sharp says I can have my job back afterwards. It won't make any difference to my career. I can still be a bank manager.'

She shook her head firmly.

'No.'

Then it was my dad's turn to beg on my behalf.

'Molotov, let the girl do it. Let her fulfil her dream. It's just for six months. She's not going to lose anything. She'll only gain from the experience. Let her go.'

Silence.

'Marmie, I promise I won't take my clothes off. I promise I won't take drugs. I won't drink. I won't smoke. I'll be a good girl, always. Please, please, please let me do it.'

There was a funny expression that came over Marmie's face when she knew she was beaten. Her shoulders would go back. Her lips would turn down. No way would she look at you. And then I heard her say the best I could possibly have hoped for.

'Hmpphh.' Pause. 'Hummpphhh.' Pause. 'Please yourself.'

So, she was giving in. I wasn't completely happy, because more than anything, I wanted my mum's approval. But I never got her blessing. Oh no. There was none of that.

'Please yourself,' she said, shrugging her shoulders. 'You make your bed. You lie on it. You know what I think.'

Rehearsals started in January 1970. In the touring cast, we were all starting from scratch. Like me, most of the rest of the chorus were completely new to professional theatre work. Working in the provinces was one of the most popular ways to get an Equity card in those days, and without membership of that most powerful of closed-shop unions, you couldn't work in the West End.

We had no idea how radical this show would prove to be, or that it would come to stand for a new era of freedom in theatre history in so many different ways. *Hair*'s progressive themes dramatically challenged the status quo. The musical glorified sexual freedom, exposing environmental pollution, mocking religion and blind patriotism and above all promoting an utterly contemporary anti-war message, while the Vietnam War raged. The producer opened multiple productions at once in the US because he really wanted the musical to influence public opinion, and bring the fighting to an end.

Hair also drew on the experimental theatre movement of the time, using an open, abstract set design, with no curtains and everything exposed to view. The live band was on stage, not in the orchestra pit, which was very unusual. As actors, we had to use improvisation in rehearsals, change characters, and at times mingle with the audience to break down the 'fourth wall'. And at a time when miscegenation laws had only just been overturned in the US, the show celebrated interracial relationships with a great passion.

'Black, White, yellow, red. Copulate in a king-sized bed!' we chanted. Of our cast of about thirty or more, twelve of us were Black, Asian or mixed race.

I played one of the young hippies in the 'tribe', so most of our dancing was quite free and pretty crazy. We could really express ourselves. The majority of the time, we wore our own clothes, and you could choose whatever style you wanted. I still have one part of my favourite outfit, a gorgeous Indian velvet waistcoat in red, orange and white, covered with embroidery and mirror glass circles. It glittered wonderfully under the stage lights. Typically, I'd wear it over a tie-dyed T-shirt and shorts or bell-bottom jeans, with a floaty scarf for a belt. I looked pretty cool! Many of the boys wore headbands, and I usually favoured an Afro hairstyle.

But for my biggest number, 'Black Boys/White Boys', I had to learn some chorus-line-style choreography. Three of us, all Black, dressed up in Supremes-style wigs and blue sequinned dresses, appeared with toes pointed identically, hips bouncing, and singing '*White boys are so pretty/Skin as smooth as milk*', while we were rolled down the heavily raked stage on a trolley. Meanwhile the Black boys in the cast were dancing with the White girls, who sang in a kind of competition: '*Black boys are delicious*'. On the word 'Momma', we three released the fabric we'd had pinned between our thighs to reveal we were all wearing not individual dresses, but one large one. Surprise! That always got a big reaction from the audience.

Of course, I held fast to my promise to Marmie. In the infamous thirty-second scene in which everyone appears naked from below a sheet, chanting 'beads, flowers, freedom and happiness', I was the only member of the cast still dressed, except for Claude, the dead soldier on the floor, a part played by Paul Nicholas, who was one of the few established professionals in the touring company. I would hide under the sheet and close my eyes. 'I'm not looking!' They kept trying to get me to change my mind, but I had laid down my boundaries, and nothing would budge me. Choreographer and director David Toguri was extremely persuasive, and never gave up asking me.

'You'll never know freedom, if you don't try!' he used to say. But I was happy with my choice.

I had a lot of singing and dancing all through the show, and precisely two words to say:

'*Oy vey.*'

Woe is me. And how I put my heart into those two Yiddish words. I knew I was only in the chorus, yet I was determined to give my tiny part as much as I would if I were a leading lady. Even if you're not the star, you can believe you are.

This issue of the hair on your head has always had a very particular significance for Black women. Even today, after decades of hair torture, messing around and burning ourselves with hot irons, or dangerous chemicals, always trying to look more European, a natural Afro represents freedom and pride in our own identity. Role models like feminist and philosopher Angela Davis led the way in the 1960s. Black American singer and actress Marsha Hunt, recently arrived in London, became known as the star of the West End production of *Hair* despite the fact that she had only two lines of dialogue. It was her face, surrounded by her giant candy-floss Afro, that was used for the show's iconic poster.

Indoctrinated for so long, I kept wearing my pageboy wig on stage at first, now firmly pinned, but within a few weeks I'd got rid of it. I loved that liberation. By this time, I'd started to copy that wonderful postcard my father had sent me from Liberia, experimenting with plaits and beads. The following year, I auditioned for a deodorant modelling job for an African women's magazine, and I imagined this would be the perfect style.

'Oh no!' they said when I turned up. 'You look *tribal*. Our magazine is for sophisticated African women.'

And they made me put on a bubbly wig for the shoot: straightened hair with bouncy, black curls.

It's incredible to think, more than half a century later, that Black women are still battling to take full charge of their identity in this respect. As recently as 2018, Viola Davis spoke of how empowered she felt when the director Steve McQueen encouraged her not to wear a wig or straighten her hair for her part in the film *Widows*. That was revolutionary.

We had three months to learn the ropes before we went on tour, and David Toguri took rehearsals during the day at the Shaftesbury Theatre, where the West End cast performed every night. David instilled in us the importance of projecting right up to the gods, so that the real fans in the cheap seats would hear every word. If you aimed down at the stalls, your words would be lost.

One afternoon, great excitement filled the theatre. Gerome Ragni, one of the writers of *Hair*, was flying over from New York to give his approval to the national touring production. Were we getting everything right? Had we properly understood the ethos of the show? The cast was all fired up, eager to get his blessing.

We were about halfway through the rehearsal, and I was standing stage left, projecting away to the upper circle and beyond, when a handsome long-haired young man walked in and was ushered to sit down right in the middle of the empty stalls. The houselights were up so we could all see him clearly, and a ripple went round the chorus as every one of us, myself included, tried our best to impress our visitor. He sat down confidently, legs crossed and arms spread over the back of the seats on either side of him, taking up plenty of space. Clearly a somebody, we all thought. What fascinated me most were his clothes: a grey polo neck sweater, leather jacket, crushed velvet mushroom-coloured trousers and brown patent leather shoes. *How extraordinary*, I thought. *Here's someone who dresses just like me.* Because *I* had mushroom-coloured trousers too, and also brown patent leather shoes. *We must be kindred spirits*, I told myself, deliberately wandering downstage so that I was dancing right in the front line.

We watched as Bob Gabriel, the company manager, rushed up to the handsome stranger, all charm.

'Oh, we're so glad you've come.'

'Thanks.'

'We're so excited to see you. Did you have a good flight?'

'Flight?' the newcomer said. 'I've only come from Covent Garden. John Barber sent me over from the office.'

'John? You're not Gerome Ragni? Who are you?'

It was Keith Taylor, who'd been working nearby as a stage manager at a West End nightclub; the producers of the cabaret show there were also the producers of *Hair*. His bosses, John Barber, Frank McKay and James Verner, were transferring him to the touring show of the musical as assistant stage manager. I wasn't at all disappointed to learn that this stranger wasn't actually the show's writer. By then I was curious about Keith himself. But of course, I had no idea how important he would soon become in my life.

Chapter Fourteen

In March we went on tour. Since I was supposed to be coming back to the bank, I hadn't enjoyed a big send-off, but my colleagues had clubbed together to buy me a suitcase. Our first stop was the Palace Theatre, Manchester.

My sister Sandra came up for the opening night. She loved the show. It was a great relief to her to see right away that she'd be able to go home and tell Marmie and the rest of the family that I was still the same old Floella. I hadn't changed or been corrupted by my glitzy new life. In fact, my habits at home proved hard to break, and I'd quickly taken on the part of mother hen or big sister to many in the company.

There were no big stars and people came from all walks of life. Many were starting out on their stage careers, like the actor Richard O'Brien, who was writing *The Rocky Horror Show* while we were on tour, and used to try the songs out on us. There was also Paul Barber, who played Hud, and became famous in the 1980s for his roles in *Only Fools and Horses* and *Boys from the Blackstuff*, and later starred as Horse in *The Full Monty*. He'd had a tough life growing up as an orphan in a care home and was working in a department store when he auditioned for *Hair*. Others were originally singers, or worked in nightclubs. One started life working in a factory, and another as a painter-decorator. Whether actors or stage management, we all happily threw in our lot together, sharing digs and looking out for one another. I treated Paul Barber and Trevor Ward, a fellow member of the tribe, like my little brothers, and often ran up clothes for other friends on the sewing machine, which also gave me a useful bit of extra money.

The show's infamy meant that the police were convinced that we were all drug-taking hippies ourselves. But this couldn't have been further from the truth. We knew the theatre could be raided at any time, and the slightest hint of illegal substances would get the show closed down. Keith had the job of keeping everything drug-free, scouring and sniffing the dressing rooms for any signs of dope-smoking, or worse.

Life suddenly became very glamorous. We were given VIP treatment wherever we went, with open invitations from all the nightclubs, and – for the White cast members only – free styling from local hairdressers who wanted to cash in on the notoriety of the show. What freedom! No Marmie to go home and report to. Interviews with local papers, photographers snapping actors and crew alike, open doors everywhere. Everyone wanted to know you. Everyone wanted your autograph. It was a whole new world for me.

After the first night in Manchester, we all went in a party to a nightclub called Explosion, one of the new 'discotheques'. It was full of girls in tiny hot pants and long suede over-the-knee boots. Sweeping in, the whole company together, we felt like stars.

The next morning, we eagerly read the 'notices' – the theatre reviews. To my great thrill, I discovered I'd been spotted. 'There was a young girl on stage who said "oy vey"', wrote one critic. 'I don't know who she is but she's going to be a star.'

*

From Manchester we opened in a couple of other cities before we went to Bristol in August. This time, not just Sandra, but Marmie and thirteen-year-old Cynthia were in the audience for the opening night. I remember rushing out to meet them as soon as I could. I looked at Marmie, the great unspoken question on my face.

'Yes,' she said. *Yes*, I thought.

'I like it,' she said. She saw I was respected and happy and had made lots of friends. She didn't feel uncomfortable about anything I was doing up on stage. She could see I'd found my true self. At the bank, I'd been trying to force myself into a system which didn't suit me, and didn't look likely to take me anywhere special. At last, I had Marmie's blessing. This meant the world to me, even if I couldn't tempt Dardie to see the show.

In those days, every town in Britain had much more of its own character, and like Dardie before me, I was excited to get to know all the big cities. Of course, our reception varied. In Liverpool, the Church was very worried about the morals of the show, and the Anglican bishop had to come and see it before we were allowed to go ahead. In Aberdeen, which was a ghost town then, before the oil boom, they gave us tea and cakes in the theatre between the matinee and the evening show. Everything there shut at nine, and instead of an opening night party, we ended up in a Greek-owned fish and chip shop, ravenously hungry, but the police arrived and closed it down before we had a chance to eat. My landlady made us kippers and porridge for breakfast and put a warming pan in my bed to greet me after the show. Our biggest excitement in Scotland was being invited to go on board a Royal Navy destroyer for drinks. I was experiencing things I never imagined possible, and only ten years after my arrival in Britain.

In Newcastle Keith found a group of us digs in a big empty house, but we all felt it was haunted and one by one we left for less spooky lodgings. By September we were in Leeds, and Sandra brought up a rich and delicious rum fruitcake made by Marmie for my twenty-first birthday. Sadly, the mice in our digs got to it before we could. But I've still got the sapphire ring Paul Barber and Trevor Ward saved up to buy me.

Because so few of the cast were professionals, there was quite a high turnover. After a few months, the company began to hold open auditions, which Keith organized. Usually, people would stumble onto stage, blink at the lights, sing a few lines of The Beatles' song 'Yesterday' and be instantly dismissed.

'Next!'

In Birmingham, a young Black singer with a beautiful Afro made everyone sit up right away. Her voice was extraordinary – rich and deep – and she ticked all the boxes. Keith told Bob Gabriel, the company manager, about her. He immediately sent her to London, and she got the job. Her name was Joan Armatrading.

Joan was very, very shy, and when she came and joined the touring company I thought I'd better take her under my wing. I asked her if she had anywhere to stay.

'My landlady has an extra room,' I said.

And so she moved into my digs. One morning, over breakfast, we were chatting about our families. She was also a child of the *Windrush* generation and she had come to Birmingham from St Kitt's at the age of seven, after four years apart from her parents. But her mum was from Antigua.

'Oh, that's funny,' I said. 'My dad's from Antigua. What's your mum's maiden name?'

'Benjamin,' she said, never having noticed my surname. 'Marge Benjamin.'

'Benjamin?! Like me! My dad's called Roy Benjamin.'

And we realized that we both had the same grandfather. Her mum and my dad were half-siblings, but while he'd gone off to

Trinidad and married, Marge had moved to St Kitt's and started her family there. Over the years, the siblings had lost touch. They'd had no idea they were both in Britain now, and our meeting paved the way for a family reunion. Completely by chance, I'd found my long-lost cousin.

It was some years before I discovered quite how many children Grandad Leonard had brought up. It seemed he was bewitchingly charismatic, and every woman he met fell head over heels in love with him; even when he was on his deathbed he invited a young nurse to join him under the sheets. At one point, two women went into labour with his babies simultaneously. But he insisted that all his children lived with him, even if they had different mothers, and he made sure all of them had a good education and inherited his views on life. My father's mother's parents were furious when their respectable, virginal daughter, a teacher no less, succumbed to his charms not once, but twice. Tragically, my grandmother died giving birth to Dardie's only full brother, Cheers, who eventually went to live in America. All Leonard's children adored him. Growing up, I'd heard all about Dardie's siblings, including my two uncles who'd been killed in the Second World War, fighting for Britain, and a third uncle, Campbell Benjamin, who settled in the Motherland after coming to Liverpool to help the war effort, and who was a Labour councillor for over three decades before becoming Mayor of Bolton. So, politics were very much in my family DNA.

My cousin Joan quickly got friendly with another cast member, Pam Nestor, a free-spirited young woman who came to England from Guyana in 1961 and revelled in *Hair*'s hippy philosophy. They soon began to write songs together – Pam wrote the lyrics, Joan the music. She discovered her own voice, and left the show, but we've always admired each other's work, and kept in touch, and our paths have continued to cross.

Although the whole company was very sociable and friendly, my closest friend was Keith. We had an immediate, unspoken bond and often think we must have been destined to meet at some point. When he was about ten, he came to London from Ashton-under-Lyne in Greater Manchester with his mother, whose husband had left her when Keith was only a year old. The same year I came from Trinidad, Keith and his mum were tramping the streets of Victoria with a suitcase, looking for somewhere to live. He was alarmed by the forbidding signs in boarding house windows: 'No coloureds, no Irish, no dogs.' A few years later Keith, aged thirteen, left his mum too and never returned to her. He ended up living not far from me in Norwood, in a London County Council children's reception centre, called Wood Vale, on Elder Road.

Like me, he left school at sixteen, and went to art college before starting his first enterprise, making gemstone jewellery which he sold to boutiques in King's Road and Carnaby Street. He then learned the craft of stage management in a Soho nightclub called the Latin Quarter, after spotting a job ad in a newspaper. Keith and I had both spent time over those years in Crystal Palace, Chiswick and Earl's Court so we must have already crossed paths in our lives so many times without us realizing. But we'd never knowingly met till the day he walked into the Shaftesbury Theatre and was mistaken for the musical's writer.

Keith would often drive down to London in his MG sports car on a Saturday night after the show, offering a lift to anyone who wanted to share the cost of petrol. One weekend, I asked to join him. It had been too long since I'd seen my parents.

Halfway down the motorway, Keith decided to stop at a service station to get something to eat.

'What?' I said. 'No need for that. I've got a flask of coffee. I've got garlic sausage sandwiches.'

I kept feeding him as we drove. He later told me he knew I was different because nobody had ever done that before. He was very handsome and stylish, funny and amusing too, and above all completely trustworthy. I felt so relaxed in his company because he never tried anything on. A lovely best friend. He looked extremely dashing with his long hair and his peppermint-green suit. He always carried himself with great confidence, and it was only when I really got to know him that I realized he was actually quite a lost soul at that time, never having had the security of a loving family.

Chatting, laughing and eating away, we reached Hyde Park Corner in what seemed like no time.

'Out you get. See you back here on Monday,' he said. His flat was in Earl's Court.

'What do you mean?' I replied. 'I don't live here. I live in Beckenham.'

'Where's that?'

'I'll show you.'

When we eventually reached my house Marmie opened the door. Keith always says she knew right away there was something between us, even though we didn't know ourselves. Not that she said anything to me.

Complete soulmates, we both felt safe and protected with each other from the moment we met. We used to talk late into the night and into the next morning too, and stayed great pals not just all through that year when we were on tour together, but afterwards too. By that time I had my Equity card, and I'd been invited to join the London production of *Hair*. Performing in the West End was quite different: suddenly, I was a small fish in a big sea. Keith was still touring the show but we kept in touch, mainly through messages left with stage door keepers, and every so often I'd dash off to see him, in Birmingham, or wherever he was that week, often driving so fast I'd be stopped by the police. I could usually talk my way out of being charged. Marmie had taught all her children to deal with the police with charm and humour!

With Keith, there was no sudden romantic moment. We grew imperceptibly, inescapably, closer. It felt like fate. I think it was, since there's nobody in the whole universe like Keith for me. Once we'd found each other we didn't need anything or anyone else.

'No matter where you are in the world, if you need me, I'll come,' we've always said to each other.

I never went back to the bank, and never looked back. In 1972 I was invited to audition for the chorus of another controversial but ultimately record-breaking musical, which went on to run for eight years. *Jesus Christ Superstar* opened on 9 August at London's Palace Theatre, with Paul Nicholas starring in the title role. Originally a concept album, Andrew Lloyd Webber and Tim Rice turned it into a rock opera telling the story of the last seven days in the life of Jesus of Nazareth. It was their first professional show together. Religious groups condemned it for blasphemy at first. Christians thought the character of Judas was too sympathetic, and protested there was no reference to the resurrection.

It was a very different kind of show from *Hair*. Everything had to be perfect, and the musical director Anthony Bowles used to shout at you if you got a note wrong. Luckily, I found the dance routines easy to pick up. But one was particularly torturous because we had to walk downstage on our knees on a raked stage made of Perspex blocks with metal ridges between them. Fifty years later, my knees are still suffering. Fortunately, King Herod's big number, sung by Paul Jabara, challenging Jesus to walk across his swimming pool and turn water into wine was a lot less agonizing: dressed like flapper girls in gold lamé, we came on stage on a large waterbed and danced the Charleston around Jesus.

After a few years as great friends, spending most of our time with each other, Keith suggested we find a place together, so in 1973, we bought a wonderful maisonette in Herne Hill where we spent six very happy years. Our moving-in present from Marmie was the Hotpoint washing machine I'd bought with my Woolworths money ten years earlier, which was still going strong. I was always talking about my mum, and spending time with her; Keith and Marmie had taken to each other the moment they met. But I'd never met his mum, or heard anything about her.

'Why don't you ever talk about your mum?' I asked him one day.

'I don't like her,' he replied. 'We don't get on. We never have. I don't want anything to do with her.'

'What are you talking about? Everyone loves their mum! Why don't you give me her number and I'll call her up and arrange for us to go and visit her.'

So, I phoned her up.

'Hello, Mrs Taylor! I'm a friend of Keith's . . .' And we had a very friendly chat. She seemed like a lovely woman to me, so I made a plan for Keith to go and have tea with her. Off he went, very reluctantly, hoping it might shut me up.

'Your girlfriend sounds very nice,' she told him. 'And what a lovely name she has . . . Floella. Very unusual.'

'Oh yes, she's from Trinidad,' said Keith.

'You mean she's Black?' she said, horrified.

When Keith came back and told me how outraged she was by the colour of my skin, I simply couldn't believe it. She had been so friendly on the phone. And from what Keith had told me, she'd always brought him up without any sign of prejudices. When they were living in that shared house in Victoria with neighbours from Mauritius and other distant countries, she'd given him the impression she simply thought foreigners were interesting and exotic.

A few months later, she fell ill, and Keith got a call to come and see her in the old Westminster Hospital, then in Horseferry Road.

'I'll come with you,' I insisted. We took some grapes for her. We found her ward, sat down by her bed, and I started chatting away in my usual friendly style, asking her how she was and so on. But every time she spoke, she addressed herself only to Keith. She never once looked at me. Never acknowledged me. Never responded to a word I said. We didn't stay long.

But afterwards she phoned Keith.

'How could you bring a Black woman to the hospital with you? How could you embarrass me like that? What must all the other people have thought of me, being visited by a Black person?'

So, foreigners were all right, in her eyes, as long as you didn't have anything to do with them.

'I don't believe it!' I said to Keith when he told me. I suddenly understood his feelings about his mother. She was a two-faced racist. She had also lied to him. Not long before I'd met Keith, he'd learned another disturbing truth about his family, after going to see his uncle in Ashton-under-Lyne in Manchester where they both grew up. His uncle was getting married, and at the wedding he told Keith, very upset, that he'd just found out that he wasn't Keith's uncle at all, but his half-brother. His father had been a US airman stationed in England during the war, but when it was discovered that he'd got an English woman pregnant, he was flown straight back to

America, and denied all contact with his son. Their mother's mother, a wonderful Scottish woman called Ada MacDonald Barnes, had brought him up as her own son. Keith loved his grandmother, a great cook who was the catering manager at a big factory, who managed to keep the whole family together for as long as she was alive. Without her, both Keith and his half-brother might have spent their whole lives in an orphanage.

Their mum had lied to them all their lives. So, both her sons hated their mother for what she'd done to them, and refused to have anything more to do with her than they had to.

I never met her again.

We tried as hard as we could to track down Keith's father, following every avenue we knew, but Taylor is such a common name. It really seemed an impossible task.

One bright spot in Keith's childhood was his dog Rocky, a golden Labrador who had been his true friend and companion. Rocky's death had broken Keith's heart. When we made our home together he thought having a dog would make it complete. We had seen a magnificent Doberman at a dog show, and decided it was the breed for us. We searched for a dog of good pedigree and found Arrow, whose lineage was impeccable. Everyone who saw him admired his regal appearance. You could see instantly that he came from a show-winning family. Our wonderful, loyal, handsome Arrow instantly became the centre of our lives, looking after us as devotedly as we took care of him.

For some years we both regularly worked nights. Keith was back managing the famous Latin Quarter, the Wardour Street cabaret club, which had been the scene of a gangland fight in 1970, where David Knight (brother of Barbara Windsor's husband Ronnie) was stabbed to death. His killer was gunned down in a revenge attack four years later in a Soho amusement arcade. Keith had some sensational experiences at the club.

Ever since *Hair*, I'd found myself in a world full of celebrities. *Jesus Christ Superstar* had also had lots of publicity, and everyone wanted to be associated with anyone connected with the show. I was invited to go to David Bowie's Christmas party by a friend in the cast who was one of Bowie's backing singers. I was terribly excited as we got ready after the show. With my hair in plaits arranged like a crown on my head, and wearing my favourite outfit – a long, floaty Biba dress in white muslin – I really felt like a princess.

After the show we headed off to his big four-storey house in Oakley Street, in Chelsea, the heart of swinging London since the sixties. Bowie had recently retired his Ziggy Stardust character, and was at the height of his fame. Although this was before that house became famous as the 'Coal Mine' – it wasn't till the following year that he painted the walls black out of sympathy with the striking miners – it already had a reputation for wild gatherings and general decadence. When we arrived, I was immediately taken aback by the sight of a Christmas tree, upside down in the front garden. It was whispered that Bowie and his wife had had a row, and she'd hurled it out of the window. It was like walking into a hall of fame. Every pop star you'd ever seen or heard of seemed to be there at this party. Up the painted stairs, we found ourselves in a huge living room with a circular sunken floor with seats scattered with cushions all around it. I felt like Alice in Wonderland. Stargazing, looking round in disbelief, I spotted first Mick Jagger, then Cat Stevens, Marc Bolan . . . *What am I doing here?* I thought.

When David Bowie walked into the room, slim and charismatic, all eyes were drawn to him. He looked amazing, his aura in the flesh like nothing I could have imagined. He came straight over to me and bowed.

'May I have this dance?' he said.

To my astonishment, I suddenly found myself heading for the dance floor with David Bowie himself. Everybody around was watching and whispering. Though I don't remember the song, I remember that it was a slow number, he held me close and I've never forgotten the way he moved. He was the best person I've ever danced with, his body so in tune with the music and with my own it was mesmerizing.

'You move so rhythmically,' I said to him, very surprised. 'How come?'

'It's because I was born in Brixton,' he replied. 'I know all the Brixton moves.'

I was having a wonderful time, chatting and dancing, and he asked me about myself, and then the record changed. After that first dance, I sat down again, and Mick Jagger came and sat next to me, trapping my dress. I tried to tug it from under his thigh.

'Excuse me. You're on my dress.'

'Sorry, princess.'

Being singled out by Bowie had drawn the party's attention to me.

It all felt completely unreal, as if I'd gone to sleep and woken up in a Fellini movie. Everyone else seemed to know each other, and they were perfectly relaxed and at home in this strange 'anything goes' atmosphere. Of course, I was stone-cold sober as I still hadn't started drinking any alcohol at that point in my life, because it made me feel ill. I didn't take drugs. I didn't smoke. To be honest, this exciting new world was all feeling a bit too out-of-control for my liking. I always liked to be in control.

Then Mick Jagger started gyrating with a girl, so sugges- tively that his wife Bianca marched over and slapped his face in front of everyone. George Melly, who was sporting his trademark fedora hat, offered to take her home, and she waltzed off. The next moment, Bowie was coming over to me again.

'Would you like to come upstairs with me?' he asked. 'I want to offer you the world. You can have anything you desire.'

What did he mean? I had no idea but I knew that if I left the room with him then, I was effectively saying 'yes' to anything he had in mind. Perhaps it was a perfectly innocent invitation, but I wasn't going to take that chance.

'No, thank you!' I replied with my usual big smile. There was safety in numbers. Or so I thought, until I went downstairs to the kitchen to get a glass of orange juice, to find Angie Bowie hanging out with a few female friends. She watched me float into the room and then she announced:

'Well, I've now seen my New Year's present!'

I began to feel very vulnerable. This wasn't my scene at all and I didn't want to get sucked in. Whatever anyone might think from the way I looked, I wasn't that kind of girl, and I didn't want anyone to take advantage of me. I've joked ever since about the night I turned down David Bowie!

Luckily, I'd already made an arrangement with Keith for him to pick me up after finishing at the Latin Quarter and take me home to Herne Hill. I ran out of the house into the cold December air to wait for him on the street corner as we'd agreed. I could still hear the music from the party. *Come and get me. Come and get me, Keith.* I was so relieved when I saw our car coming round the corner, dead on time. I knew I'd always be safe with my Keith. Like a knight in shining armour, he'd always come and rescue me. In our little blue Hillman Imp.

Chapter Fifteen

If you were Black, there were only two theatrical agencies who would take you on in the early 1970s. Trinidad-born Pearl Connor was the first. I was taken on by the second, Oriental Casting, run by Niall Toland and Kristopher Kum. But Niall was constantly working against the prejudices of the day. He got me an audition once for a very lucrative advert, and I was thrilled when the director wanted me. But the client flatly refused to have a Black person touching their product. I had never expected to be called for the role, so missing out wasn't a huge surprise or disappointment.

You hardly ever saw a Black person advertising food. Or cosmetics. Or holidays or houses or furniture. Definitely not washing powder. Too many White people seriously believed that Black people's skin was dirty, and would rub off on whatever we touched. So, we were the last thing any detergent brand wanted associated with their product. You could do certain types of chocolate or coffee adverts, and eventually I did get a Marvel milk commercial. But generally speaking, Black people were only used to promote products that were seen as exotic, such as tropical fizzy drinks like Lilt. We were rarely seen doing ordinary, everyday things, within ordinary British homes.

I soon started to ask why. Oh how different the advertising world is today where diversity is a priority.

Meanwhile, although I was thoroughly enjoying being in another groundbreaking West End show, my ambitions were widening beyond both commercials and musicals. I longed to break into TV drama, but it seemed impossible without any experience. How did you get the experience in the first place? And of course, I had no training. So, every time I went for an audition, I'd hear the same thing:

'Where have you trained?'

'I'm a natural,' I'd say enthusiastically.

'Next!'

One day, when I was discussing this problem with another girl in *Jesus Christ Superstar*, she gave me some very practical advice.

'You just have to tell them you trained at such-and-such, and this is what you've done.'

She mentioned some examples.

What? Just make things up?

'Yes! It's the only way.'

My friend then coached me carefully, telling me exactly what to say for all the usual questions that came up. So, the next time I went along to an audition, I gave it a go.

'Where have you trained?' the director asked, as usual.

This time, I said airily, 'Oh, I trained at Mountview.'

'And what have you done?'

'I've done this, and I've done that . . .' And I reeled off the names of the television series and dramas that my friend had advised me to mention. Of course, in those pre-internet days it was much harder to check the truth.

But then the director suddenly sat up and said, 'That's funny, because I directed that last thing you mentioned and I don't remember you at all.'

I looked him straight in the eye.

'Fair cop,' I said. 'I had to make this up because otherwise I'd never get a chance, but if you give me a chance now, I'll show you just what I can do.'

'You're so convincing. I believe you,' he said, and he gave me the part of Barbara, a sixteen-year-old shoplifter, in a hard-hitting women's prison drama for London Weekend Television called *Within These Walls*, created by David Butler. It starred Googie Withers as the radical new prison governor, and went on to run for five series.

At the first rehearsal I sat down with the script at the read through. Something wasn't right.

'Excuse me,' I said to the writer, an academy-award-winning playwright called Rosemary Anne Sisson who usually special-ized in period dramas and plays. 'I don't think a sixteen-year-old Black girl with this background would speak like this. She just wouldn't say these lines.'

'Oh, what would she say? Tell us and we'll change them!' she said, cheerfully. So, I did just that.

Because I had made her seem so real, the character of Barbara appeared in five episodes in all. One day I was in the canteen with the senior producer, and we got into conversation.

'So why is it that Black actors are always cast as thieves or prostitutes or bus conductors?' I asked him. 'Why can't we ever play professional roles, like lawyers, accountants and doctors?'

He almost laughed.

'Oh Floella, that wouldn't be realistic, would it?' he said, dismissively.

I was stunned. This wasn't how I saw the world at all. Most of my siblings already had professional careers, or were heading in that direction. Sandra worked as a lab technician at Wellcome Laboratories, Lester was a London Transport elec-trician, Ellington a quantity surveyor, and Roy Junior was then at Aberystwyth University, the first in the family to go straight from school to higher education. He was an RAF cadet pilot, and the undefeated British and Irish universities boxing champion. Cynthia always wanted to get married and have children, and did so at the age of seventeen, but she promised Dardie she'd continue to study the piano, and later became a classical pianist and teacher. All my friends from the West Indian Students' Centre also had serious ambitions in life. Yet on television, almost the only Black characters you ever saw were criminals or drug addicts, nurses or transport workers. Something had to change. So, it was back in 1974 I first vowed to make that happen.

Within These Walls came out on a Friday. The Monday morning after the first of my episodes, my agent's phone started to ring. My TV career was launched. Soon Niall was inundated with requests.

First it was the producer of *Crown Court*. Then I was asked to join the popular hospital soap *Angels*, and numerous other dramas, including, in 1979, *Waterloo Sunset* directed by Richard Eyre, and *A Hole in Babylon* by Horace Ové. I also appeared in a Joan Collins horror film, *I Don't Want to Be Born* (1975). In the US this was released under several alternative titles, including *The Devil Within Her*, *The Monster* and *Sharon's Baby*, and later became a camp cult classic. I played a nurse in this too, appearing wide-eyed and innocent at Joan Collins' bedside, while her devil-possessed, bloody-nailed baby drooled gore. Interestingly, Joan spoke up on my behalf when we were filming this, criticizing the direction I was given. She was right, of course, and got her way, which made me look better.

Still working nights at the club, Keith was around at the end of a phone more than I was during the day, so he started taking messages, and soon became my manager. Yet my options still seemed to me to be very limited. Although I was never afraid to broach this with producers, I felt this wasn't good enough. Why shouldn't I have the same opportunities as a White actor? I was sick of playing nurses or call girls.

So, whenever I went to an audition, I'd look down the script carefully before reading. I just wasn't interested in playing one Black stereotype after another. If I was down to try out for yet another clichéd character, I'd simply say no.

'Can't I play this part instead?' I'd ask. I never got angry about it. If you get angry, you waste your energy, and you're less likely to get what you want in the long term. I just wanted to see change. I kept my calm and began to speak out more and more. I wasn't afraid to challenge producers and directors.

'Why?' I always asked. 'Why is it like this? Why can't it be different?'

For many years I felt a lone voice in the wilderness. In the mid-seventies I was often told by producers to shut up if I ever wanted to work again. But I refused to let it rest. There's no change without challenge. It was the beginning of my lifelong campaign for diversity on screen and off.

News travelled by word of mouth in the West End, for both actors and stage managers. I was excited to find out about a new show called *The Black Mikado*, an almost all-Black version of the 1885 Gilbert and Sullivan operetta. It was set on a Caribbean island instead of Japan, and the score was adapted to a mix of reggae, rock, blues and calypso. Director Braham Murray liked my beaded hairstyle when I auditioned, and I was one of the first to be cast.

American actors were often cast as leads in West End musicals, particularly Black ones, because it was thought they'd bring in the crowds, and the Mikado in this production was played by an African-American actor called Val Pringle. He taught me a lot about how much tougher it was to succeed as a Black person in theatre in the US compared with Britain. In London, it was actually possible to be an overnight success, and be treated with great respect. Yet there were far fewer parts available, and, as I wrote to Equity, almost no starring roles for Black British musical actors.

In *The Black Mikado* I played an extremely feisty Pitti-Sing, one of the 'Three Little Maids from School'. Norman Beaton played Nanki-Poo, Derek Griffiths was Koko, while Michael Denison, as Pooh-Bah, was the only White actor in the production. Michael was my dancing partner, and a perfect gentleman. I remembered him as a matinee idol when I was a young girl, starring in films like *The Glass Mountain*. I'd never dreamed that one day we would be acting together.

The choreography was incredible, and my dance routine the most challenging I'd ever done – so fast and energetic that I discovered parts of my body I hadn't known existed. I picked it up quickly, but could hardly walk after the early rehearsals, and felt as if I were crawling home. For six weeks before we opened, at the Cambridge Theatre in London's Seven Dials in April 1975, we toured the country, continuing to rehearse during the day.

'No, no, no, no, no!' the choreographer, Amadeo Barrios, used to shout, impatiently, clapping his hands. 'Do it like Floella! Do it like Floella!'

That was the worst thing he could possibly have said. Before I knew what was happening, I was seeing stars, and my bare foot was in agony. Another girl, who seemed prepared to do anything for a chance to play a part, had jumped with all her weight on my foot, driving it into the wooden floor. But what she didn't realize was that I do not give up. Ever. I refused to have a night off. They gave me a cortisone injection and I went on stage during the show with my foot throbbing and bound up in a bandage, dyed brown. Even now, I'm still sometimes in pain from that injury. Yet the memory of what she'd done must have given the girl who did it still more pain. When we had a chance encounter in a shop where she was serving in New Bond Street decades later, she begged me for forgiveness. She'd become a born-again Christian by then.

After that, Michael Denison held me up with his hand, supporting me like a rock in our dance routine together, much more than I realized. But one night he was off, and without thinking, I leaned on his understudy, expecting the same support, and immediately collapsed to the floor.

I believe everyone needs guardian angels to help see them through life, and I've been lucky enough to have a number of these during my lifetime. Michael Denison was one of my first. He looked out for me in so many different ways, and always made me feel good about myself.

'You remind me of Audrey Hepburn!' he used to say.

When we were playing Leeds, the production money suddenly ran out. At the end of the week, when we queued up at the company office to pick up our brown envelopes of cash, we found there were no wages for us. Obviously, we all had rent to pay, and needed to eat. We didn't know what to do. It was Michael who paid us out of his own pocket, tiding us all over until the producer finally came up with the cash.

While we were in Leeds, Michael took me and some of the company to visit his friend Lord Harewood, at Harewood House. It was a glorious day out, wandering around the house and picnicking in the garden. Lord Harewood's Australian wife amazed us by setting up a barbecue in an old oil drum. It never occurred to me that this extraordinary Yorkshire country house and estate had been built long ago by a slave owner, funded by the profits from his West Indian plantation. I wonder if he had owned any of my ancestors? He owned the

great-great-great-great-grandparents of the actor David Harewood, who confronted the present Earl of Harewood about his
family's brutal past. Maybe I should have asked questions
myself back then.

The Black Mikado also introduced me to Derek Griffiths,
the most mischievous actor I've ever worked with. We laughed
and laughed and laughed, for he was a terrible practical joker.
I couldn't find my dress one day, and he'd hung it out of the
window on a long hanger, swinging it like a flag. One evening
I was talking to fans at the stage door, signing autographs,
taking compliments, and Derek passed me, calling out:

'Night, Floella!'

'Night, Derek!

And he just took out a banana skin and smeared it on the
windscreen of my pride and joy – my White Triumph GT
sports car – knowing I'd completely lose my cool in front of
my admirers and go haring down the street after him.

But I got my own back.

Like most actors, Derek always had a bit of an obsession
with checking the zips on the flies of his skintight black satin
trousers. Well, nobody wants to expose themselves on stage by
mistake. In one scene, he and Michael and I had to stand in a
huddle, plotting some bit of business on stage, so one night,
while Michael was talking, I whispered to Derek:

'Your flies are undone.'

He couldn't look down to check. But he did panic! Instead
of replying to Pooh-Bah, Koko turned on his heel and marched
off the stage, leaving us to ad lib the rest of the scene.

I can't even share most of the jokes he played on people, for
they were far too outrageous, but Derek still makes me laugh
without fail, we remain great pals and I've always kept the
bottle of Chanel No. 5 he bought me for Christmas in 1975.

Derek was then already well established as a beloved *Play*

School presenter. I'd watch during the day, and talk to him about it at the theatre. It looked so enjoyable, I thought. How I'd love to do it. Being with Derek was such fun, because of the kind of person he is and the way he moves his body like an elastic band. Naturally I was convinced that doing the show would be just as much of a pleasure as acting with him. I was also drawn into this happy place by presenters like Carol Chell, who had such energy about her, approaching everything she did with a delightful smile, her body language and little giggle perfectly communicating her great sense of fun. Here was a place you could be yourself, I was certain. You could perform for children with no inhibitions, simply embracing joy and love.

'Go for an audition!' Derek told me. 'Just write in and ask them.'

Eventually I did. But first I wanted more theatrical experience. And I was looking for another change of direction.

In 1976 I asked Niall to put me up for some straight theatre acting, and he got me an audition for a substantial role: the saucy French maid in *The Husband-in-Law*, a Feydeau farce adapted by Christopher Hampton and directed by Patrick Garland. Afterwards, I felt quite anxious. I really, really wanted the part. I remember sitting on the grass in Hyde Park in a green maxi dress weeping my eyes out, certain I'd blown it. What if I never moved on from musicals? I wanted to be taken seriously. I didn't want to be pigeonholed.

I couldn't believe it when I got the job. My wish had come true. I'd be working with some of the great names in theatre – Kenneth Williams, Peggy Mount, Bryan Pringle, Gerald James. Unimaginable. They were all so big, and suddenly there was my name up on the billboard with them!

Kenneth Williams was very tough on anyone who tripped up in rehearsals. He had already made it clear that he had all the power in that production. Everyone was kept on their toes, anticipating the wrath of his tongue if they accidentally fluffed their lines. One day, when I messed up my entrance, he exploded.

'Ohhhhhhh,' he groaned, in the way only Kenneth Williams could, with his extraordinary vowels. 'Where did you get her from?'

I flipped.

'Listen, you. I don't care who you are, but I won't have you speaking to me like that. Do you understand?'

The whole room went silent.

'Hmmmm,' said Patrick Garland, gently, in his understated way. Nobody ever answered back to Kenneth, or crossed him in any way. But Marmie always told us to demand respect from others, and show the same in return. This felt a moment to do exactly that.

Somehow, I mustered enough presence of mind to call the stage manager for my prompt.

'Nancy! What's the line?' I demanded.

And I carried on.

A few moments later, Kenneth dried up completely. He sashayed over to me to apologize.

'Floella, I should never have talked to you like that. Will you please forgive me?'

'Only if you promise never to do it again,' I demanded.

It was a deal. And after that we were the best of friends. So, we had a great time on tour together. I continued to wear my blue beads, covered up on stage by the bubbly wig, and I think Kenneth was as amused as I was when I overheard the landlady of my digs in Nottingham tell her friends about her exotic new lodger:

'I've got an African princess staying, who wears all her jewels in her hair!'

I had nightmares about someone creeping in and cutting my plaits off as I slept.

Kenneth and I often had tea together while we were away from home on tour before opening in London, and he'd tell me delightful stories about working with Noël Coward. For ever after, he wrote me regular notes to congratulate me on any new work I did. Unforgettably, he also taught me important elements of stagecraft: how to work an audience, how to make them laugh, weep, and show their appreciation.

'Watch me!' he'd say.

I learned that after a big number a subtle sweep of your own hands, a single almost inaudible clap can act like a punctuation mark and set off a chain reaction of applause. His comic timing was impeccable and I quickly came to appreciate his true mastery of the well-timed pause. Kenneth really took me under his wing that year. We had huge mutual respect, affection and admiration, and the live theatre skills he taught me have served me well for ever.

Chapter Sixteen

A house – with a door.
Windows: one, two, three, four.
Ready to play? What's the day?
Yes, it's Play School.

At last I had a letter from *Play School*, inviting me to come and meet the producer. It was the beginning of the very hot summer of 1976, and *The Husband-in-Law* was now in the West End, renamed *Signed and Sealed*. I could not have been more excited. *Play School* had really changed the face of children's television, and its influence was huge. I loved watching it myself, I'd seen what fun Derek had on the show, and I wanted to be part of it. From watching the afternoon repeats before I went off to work at the theatre, I'd seen how imaginative and innovative the programme was. The presenters were free of inhibitions.

In 1964, when *Play School* started, the very first programme ever shown on the newly launched BBC2, the fact that it actually used on-screen presenters whom children could see and get to know and love was a great step forward. Other novelties included having live musicians in every episode, the familiar but varied line-up of toys and pets so that every child could have their favourite, the fact that it was filmed in colour, and, of course, the educational content, directed specifically at the under-fives. The first producer, Joy Whitby, had originally devised *Play School* to help parents cope with the shortage of nursery school places. It meant that infants at home, whether rich or poor, could start learning how to tell the time, and establish other basic concepts about shape and size and so on. By 1976, the three windows which led to the daily film sequences – round, square and arched – were already iconic.

For my initial interview, I decided to cover up my hair beads with the bubbly wig I wore on stage with Kenneth Williams. That seemed safe. It's the BBC, I thought. Staid and respectable. It didn't seem the right time to take a risk.

Dressed in a checked shirt and jeans, I sat and waited outside a relatively small office on the fifth floor of the East Tower of White City. I had some experience, which was essential, since I knew from Derek they didn't want beginners. I wanted the job very much. But what unique qualities could I bring to the programme?

Anne Gobey, the producer, called me in. She was a tall and slender woman, very pretty, in glasses, a brown jacket and a blouse with a frilly high neck. Her lovely smile immediately put me at ease, and before long, her girlish laughter was ringing out encouragingly. Full of enthusiasm, I told her what I'd been doing, and about my varied work in musicals, theatre and TV dramas, and slowly she began to lean back in her seat.

Hmmm. I'm not impressing her, I thought to myself. I had learned by then to read every situation in which I found myself, and something about her made me feel I was losing her attention. I knew I only had one chance to prove myself. But something wasn't working. So, I leaned forward.

'Oh, by the way, I don't really look like this, you know.'

She giggled, uncertainly.

'What do you mean?'

'This is what I really look like.'

I swept off my wig, shook my head, and my long plaits threaded with hundreds of blue beads rattled out around me. At last I was completely myself.

'Oh, my goodness! That's amazing!' said Anne. She'd never seen anything like it. 'How fantastic! We must give you a camera audition.'

They fixed a studio date for a Tuesday afternoon in June, a few weeks later, so that I could audition on the *Play School* set after they'd finished recording the week's programmes. They'd send me a mini script to learn in advance. I was thrilled.

But on the very morning of my screen test, our dog Arrow disappeared. Keith and I had taken him for a walk in Brockwell Park, near our flat. He came out of the main gate ahead of us to wait at the zebra crossing, looked around carefully as usual, and set off. In front of our very eyes, a car suddenly sped by so fast that it hit him. Stunned and disoriented, Arrow limped off out of sight, too fast for us to catch up with him. It was so uncharacteristic of him. A perfect dog, he'd been part of the family for three years by then. We adored him. Everyone who ever met him loved him.

We searched in vain. Feeling ever more drained and wretched, I wondered whether I should cancel my screen test. But Keith persuaded me to go, and assured me he wouldn't give up the hunt for Arrow.

I thought I'd better explain my situation to Anne Gobey as soon as I arrived.

'My dog got hit by a car and ran away. He's still missing. I'm devastated.'

The mood immediately changed, and everyone was sympathetic, but I knew I had to put on a brave face, keep going, and do my best.

The studio was vast, with three cameras and camera

operators waiting. The famous *Play School* windows were re-assuringly familiar. I forced myself into the right mood for the tasks ahead of me. There were no autocue or 'idiot-boards', so I had to do a 'make', sing a song and read a story, with all the appropriate voices, all from memory. A 'make' could take all sorts of forms: perhaps making a model out of junk, creating wooden spoon puppets, painting a picture using a clever trick. The main thing was that it could easily be done at home with a parent or carer and didn't need special equipment. Glue, sticky tape and pipe cleaners often featured, along with toilet rolls and empty cotton reels.

The whole afternoon was something of a blur. Outside, I was bright, bubbly Floella, talking to every child as if they were right in front of me. Inside, I was broken-hearted. Even now, I can't remember what I had to sing or make – perhaps a bus, out of a cardboard box? I do recall that the story was about Chicken Licken, who thought the sky was falling down. I impersonated all the different farmyard birds with great vigour.

My smile gets me through life to this day, as it always has done, and helps me overcome every bad thing that happens. Even if I'm not completely sure of myself, I smile by habit, and this gives other people confidence. *If she's smiling, it must be all right*, they think. But, strange though this might sound, it's still a genuine smile, because I mean it. But when I left, I felt very sombre. Late that evening Keith heard a knock on the door. To our great delight, we learned that someone had found Arrow, and traced us through his collar tag, and brought him home. Our reunion was ecstatic. We couldn't stop petting him, and vowed never to let him out of our sight again. A few days later, a letter arrived to say that I'd got the *Play School* job. I'd start as soon as my current theatre run came to an end.

The weeks went by and Britain got hotter and hotter. The theatre was completely stifling, and in my thick costume and heavy wig, under the blazing lights, I felt I was melting. Few West End venues had air conditioning in 1976, and it was a disastrous season for many companies. The record-breaking temperatures had a terrible impact on our audience figures too, and by August, the inevitable happened. The show had to close. So, I was able to start with *Play School* sooner than I'd anticipated. That's when I started to believe that when one door closes, another opens.

My first show was broadcast the week beginning 26 September 1976. The executive producer, Cynthia Felgate, who was a production assistant on the programme when it began twelve years earlier, always encouraged her team of presenters to do other work around *Play School*'s schedule, to keep us fresh. Most of us had started in theatre, and had comedy experience, and, of course, music and songs were an essential ingredient. We'd each record a full week of shows in just two and a half days. Although people often tell me they remember me being on every day in their childhood, in fact each presenter only appeared every six to eight weeks. Each week had a different team assigned: a co-presenter, a producer, a director, a prop person, musicians and an assistant floor manager and so on. (Most of the technical staff were men, because until a damning report in 1973, the BBC refused to employ women as camera operators or assistants, floor managers, sound engineers, dubbing mixers or lighting assistants.)

I could hardly have been luckier with my first co-presenter, the magical Johnny Ball. He was the very best, and he taught me so much. For example, he taught me how to consider the camera operator, and ensure that every shot of you is delightful for the young viewer.

If you're sitting down, encouraging the child at home to do

some kind of activity with you, and you need to stand up, you have to take your time, instead of leaping up right away. As you're talking, you bend your body forward, and gently get to your feet, so that the camera can ease back, and slowly move up with you. Everything looks smooth and easy.

How do you talk to a camera when you're 'doing a make'? You have a close-up camera on your hands, while you're speaking to a second camera. (I hated my hands when I first saw them in close-up. 'AaaaRGHHHHH!' I screeched at the sight of my bitten nails. I never bit them again.) You can lose your eye connection if you look down at whatever your hands are doing. Johnny taught me the technique of just glancing down very quickly when you needed to. It all has to look effortless and magical. Whether you're making a model or doing a painting, you always try to involve the children.

'Can you guess what I'm painting?'

Back at school, Miss Burton had put doubts in my mind about my artistic talents. I still painted with more enthusiasm than skill, so guessing wasn't easy.

'It's got wheels. And it's got a roof, see. Hmmm . . . Windows!'

And I'd see the cameraman looking really confused, and wondering, *What is it?*

I believe this gave the viewers time to create pictures in their own heads as they tried to imagine what I could be making for them. Because my paintings were childlike – matchstick people, simple trees, perhaps a house with a roof like the *Play School* house – the children at home recognized what they represented, and could appreciate the life and vigour in them. They were creative, not perfect! That was the important thing. If you look at children's paintings, they're very creative, and in fact I can look at one and know a child's state of mind and mood from what they've painted. It's the doing that matters, and the confidence and joy with which you wield your brush. I showed children how to enjoy whatever they were making.

Although I was Auntie Flo to my family by then, I didn't especially think of my little nephews and nieces when I was performing. Communicating with small children came very naturally to me, by instinct. I was childlike in the way I enjoyed the world and liked to get the best out of it, but not childish.

Cynthia Felgate, a woman of great insight, gave me some important advice at the outset:

'You have to imagine there's only one child watching you. Not hundreds or thousands or millions.'

'Hello,' I always said. And then I'd wait. 'Are you all right?' Another pause, for the child's response. 'Well, what we're going to do today . . .' Suspense! And then I'd tell them. All the time giving each individual breathing space and thinking time, so they could imagine, feel, anticipate and react. A careful rhythm for a very natural process, at a pace so beautifully delivered that it stayed in their heads and hearts for ever.

You have to have the measure of the pulse of what you're doing. You take them up and you gently bring them DOWN . . . And then UP again, a surprise this time, and then carefully down. That way, when you end the programme, you've made them feel that you've spent precious time with them. And although you have to go now, you'll be back. *Don't worry.*

'Bye-bye. See you next time!'

So, you leave them with that feeling of anticipation, and security, knowing they were cared for, and always would be. You didn't just slam the door of the *Play School* house and disappear.

Unlike today, when instant gratification is the norm, children had to wait for you to return the next day, or in the afternoon repeat, and that was a good thing. They knew that it would happen eventually. *Play School* would be back again.

We worked with child psychologists on the programme, to help us understand the different moods and situations of the different youngsters in our audience. Maybe a child was watching us in a palace. Maybe in a housing estate. Their needs were identical. As I knew so well from my own experience, every child needs to feel love, a sense of belonging and appreciation, and something regular in their lives on which they can always depend. Continuity is terribly important for children. With unconditional love in our hearts, we offered something that they knew was just for them.

We explored lots of different emotions on the programmes, expressing a range of feelings in a safe way.

'What's it like to be happy?' we'd wonder, with them. 'Can you make yourself happy by tickling yourself?'

And then we'd sing a happy song.

'What's it like to be sad? Have you lost something you love?'

We'd encourage the children to act out those feelings.

Or be angry. Grrrrrr. Or frightened. Or excited.

But my very first week, after the Thursday programme had been filmed but not broadcast, Cynthia came to tell me that someone high up at the BBC was rather concerned about my beads-and-plaits hairstyle. The public may not like this, they decided. The next day I was due to come in to record the final programme of that week, the Friday programme.

'So, for this last programme, could you put on that bubbly wig you wore for your audition?' Cynthia asked. 'We want to show the public that you have another side.'

I was a bit taken aback, and, frankly, a little disappointed. The rest of the team all seemed fascinated by the beads and thought they looked great on the screen, although the sound person had been confused at first.

'What's this clicking noise I keep getting on the microphone?'

he'd asked. Unfortunately, they didn't bother to tell me the problem, so took ages checking everything, until finally working out that it was the clatter of my beads as I moved, and then they got used to the sound.

'Oh. OK. If that's what the BBC wants, I'll change my hair.'

We recorded the Friday programme with me wearing my bubbly wig.

The following week when the programmes were broadcast, it seemed I was a hit.

'Who is this smiley girl with the beads?'

Children and parents alike loved how the blue beads and plaits flew in the air and made a noise when I sang and danced. The publicity was fantastic.

But what happened? Why had the beads vanished by Friday? Lots of people didn't realize I was wearing a wig, and they were worried I'd taken out the plaits they loved. There was a protest, and people wrote into the BBC. 'We like the beads. We want the beads back.'

So, the wig went out of the window, and I quickly became widely known as the Lady with the Blue Beads. At one personal appearance I made, about fifty blind children who wanted to get to know me better touched my face, carefully feeling my plaits and beads to work out what made them rattle and click. I closed my eyes, and hundreds of fingertips brushed over my skin and hair. It was an extraordinary sensation, which became almost electrifying as their sense of recognition communicated itself to me. *Ah, that's who she is.* I also met deaf children who imagined I could sign, or might even be deaf myself, because I was so expressive with my hands. I became patron of the charity Friends of the Young Deaf and have always believed that all children should learn to sign, starting with their nursery rhymes, so that they can communicate no matter what the circumstances. The important thing for me was for all children to feel included, and that each one should feel I was talking specially to them, and that they could see themselves in me, however different we might look.

My sparkly glitter shoes also went down well with the kids, and I always wore my heart necklace. This had been my very first present from Keith, a symbol of his unconditional friendship and devotion which he'd given me in 1971. A heart within a heart, he designed it and had it specially made for me to represent our two hearts. We are like two peas in a pod, born just two days apart in the same month in the same year. I've treasured that silver heart and worn it ever since. So, I also became known as the Lady with the Heart.

'When you were on TV I thought you were a magical lady, and that if I could rub your heart, magic would happen,' people still often tell me. And then they ask if they can rub my heart necklace now.

I was also known as the Kissing Lady. Apparently, boys and girls used to rush up to the television when they saw me, and kiss the screen. Grown men still tell me I was their first love, the first lady they ever kissed.

People always seemed to want a hug when they met me at events or even spotted me in the street. Perhaps that's why I started to hug strangers too, quite instinctively. I was once walking down the pavement near Piccadilly Circus and a little boy of about four or five saw me, rushed over to hug my legs, and said:

'Mummy! Mummy! Let's help Floella! She's escaped from the television.'

I had to reassure him that I was fine, and I didn't really live in the television set.

Children have never been afraid to run to me and give me a hug, because they know I love them. The power of my sincerity, the sense that I would always put children first, seemed to

Above left My beloved mum Veronica, who we called Marmie, aged twenty in Trinidad, 1946.

Above right My handsome dad Roy, who we called Dardie, aged twenty in Trinidad, 1946.

Marmie, who was six months pregnant with my brother Ellington, and Dardie together with (*from the left*) Sandra aged four, Lester aged two and me aged three, 1952.

Marmie and Dardie
in England, 1962.

The intrepid
Miss Bowles, my head
teacher at Penge Secondary
Modern School, 1963.

Inside our first house in
Anerley, 1962. (*Back row, left
to right*) Ellington, Sandra,
Lester and me. (*Front row*)
Cynthia and Roy Junior.

School photo of me, aged fourteen, smiling after my first spiritual moment.

A family musical affair at Chelsea Town Hall, 1967. Dardie is playing the saxophone, Marmie is on maracas, Lester is on drums in the background and I'm singing.

Me as compère for an event I organized at the West Indian Students' Centre in 1968. Sandra, sitting far left, was on the judging panel.

Keith, aged twenty, when he joined the stage management team of the national tour of *Hair* and was mistaken for the writer of the show.

Me, aged twenty, in the pageboy wig I wore for my national *Hair* audition, 1969.

Some of the cast members of the national *Hair* tour, including (*front row*) Pam Nestor, Trevor Ward, (*middle row*) Richard O'Brien, Joan Armatrading, (*back row*) and Paul Barber. I'm far left.

In my favourite Biba muslin dress, which I wore to David Bowie's party in 1973 and to the Cannes Film Festival in 1977. I still have it!

Keith and me in Brockwell Park, Herne Hill, 1974. One of our favourite photos.

Kenneth Williams and me on stage on tour in *The Husband-in-Law*, 1976.

Left I revealed my famous blue-beaded hairstyle during my *Play School* audition.

Our magnificent well-bred Doberman, Arrow, who was loyal and loving.

Some of the *Play School* presenters and toys. (*Back row*) Bruce Allen (holding Hamble), Fred Harris, Delia Morgan, Chris Tranchell, Johnny Ball, Derek Griffiths, Carol Leader (holding Little Ted), Ben Bazell, Chloe Ashcroft (holding Jemima) and David Hargreaves. (*Front row*) Carol Chell with Big Ted, me with Humpty and Sarah Long.

Brain Cant and me promoting the new series of *Play Away* in 1983.

My guardian angel Cynthia Felgate.

In *Playabout*, my production for BSB, with the puppet Grandad, 1990.

At the Cannes Film Festival 1977, arriving in an open Cadillac for the premiere of *Black Joy*, along with the other stars of the British film entry: Norman Beaton, standing next to the producer's friend, me, Trevor Thomas and Paul J. Medford.

break through the screen and penetrate people's hearts. However difficult their circumstances, they knew somebody was there for them.

I still get letters and messages from adults telling me I was everything to them. Perhaps they were in a dark place in their childhood, with nobody else to love them. Perhaps they lived in a children's home. And I spoke directly to them, listened, and made them feel special. I'm still there for them today: they are my '*Play School* babies'.

Chapter Seventeen

I felt so privileged to be able to go in and have such fun at work. At the time, I didn't know how far-reaching and long-lasting the effects of *Play School* would be, both on its young audience and on my own life. I simply understood it was my duty to do my very best to give the children the strongest possible foundations for the future. Carol Chell, Chloe Ashcroft and others had a unique gift of making viewers feel happy, each in their own special way. I'd watched them do that. And now it was my turn. Each person's gift was different because we could all be ourselves. My only ambition was to make *Play School* as fun as it could be for the children.

We had one day to rehearse the five programmes of each week we did, and we got our scripts a couple of weeks before filming. We had to learn everything so we'd be word perfect on the day, songs and stories too. Then we had forty minutes to record a twenty-five-minute programme. That's not much leeway to make mistakes!

As soon as the scripts arrived in the post, I'd go straight to look at the story. Is it from a book? That would mean illustrations would be shown on screen, so you might be able to glance at a script while you weren't visible to the audience. A story to camera was more challenging. Thanks to all that quick learning practice, I developed something close to a photographic memory. By the time you came to recording the Thursday and Friday programmes, it was harder and harder to remember lines and links and transitions.

Wednesday was always Pet Day. A Dr Doolittle-like woman called Wendy Duggan and her husband Ron looked after all the animals in their Putney home, bringing each one into the studio, sometimes travelling by bus with them. There was Katoo the cockatoo, who was always eyeing up my beads, sliding along the perch in his cage and trying to make a sly grab for my hair. I had to be careful with him, as he could be quite vicious. The rabbit was gorgeous, and there was a guinea pig and some mice too. I used to wear Polo mints as earrings, hanging through my sleepers, and lots of animals loved those and tried to get hold of them. I even once had an elephant put its trunk round me at the zoo, after my Polos. The mints fascinated children too. It was so important for the children watching to have pets on the show, as many could never hope to have a pet of their own, and it was a great way to engage them.

There'd always be some sort of activity. You might pretend to be an elephant. Or a giraffe. How do they move? Wearing a stripy dress, I remember stretching my neck up, walking gracefully and slowly, chewing my leaves, and looking over the wall, just like a giraffe. A few days later I was in Covent Garden and I heard a stranger's voice saying:

'I'd know that giraffe anywhere!'

It was a man who'd watched the programme that week, and told me how much he'd enjoyed it.

Another time I had to be a caterpillar, crawling along a leaf, singing a song, waiting to turn into a butterfly:

'Caterpillars only crawl!'

After that a surgeon wrote to me to say that he found my

141

performance so mesmerizing that he had begun to sing that calming song every time he was doing an operation.

I was always surprised how many adults watched the programme, and what it brought alive in them too.

Play School was a mini culture show. We had one particular director who loved ballet, so we did a lot of classical dancing with him. We also learned to do mime. There was poetry on the programme too. William Blezard, known as Bill, was one of the most important pianists on the programme in creating the sound of *Play School*, with his improvisations and accompaniments. Very proper and very old school, he had worked with Joyce Grenfell, Marlene Dietrich, Noël Coward and Laurence Olivier, and he was very precise and strict with us. Very little was ad libbed, except for the voiceover during the film shown after going through one of the windows. Nothing was slapdash. We had to get things right. To me, it was the perfect children's programme.

The biggest chunk of the twenty-five minutes of airtime was taken up by the story. This was always introduced by the clock. A model under the clock would give the audience a little hint of what the story would be about. But first, we looked at the time.

'Where's the long hand pointing? It's something o'clock. Where's the short hand? Today it's pointing to the number . . . four. Today the clock says four o'clock.'

The clock was once the cause of a terrible kerfuffle when it stopped working and one of the prop team tried to fix it, and the electricians went wild. They immediately called for an all-out strike. The unions were incredibly strict in the 1970s, and without electricians, we couldn't record the programme. The producers were all set to put out a repeat.

All was finally resolved, and the show went on.

Once we'd told the time, always giving the child plenty of time to guess, and to glow with a sense of achievement if they got it right, then a tiny model on the clock base, which was a clue to the story, would spin round to music. And the presenter would sit in the story chair. This was my favourite part.

Even if you made a mistake, you couldn't stop. I once wrote a story about a little Caribbean boy called Jason, who went down the hill to the market, and then came up the hill again with a big bag of rice. But I realized as I was telling it that I'd left a big chunk of the narrative out. What had he seen on his journey? I had to backtrack on the spot and just keep going, very naturally, without letting on that I'd made a mistake. *Play School* taught me never to panic, but just keep going confidently, with a reassuring smile on my face.

So, there was very little editing before each programme was broadcast. There was no time for that. It had to be seamless. The discipline was extraordinary, but we took it for granted. At the very end of a recording, we might redo a few things. The forty minutes we had for filming was needed for the cameras to get from one end of the studio to the other, from one presenter to another. We were rarely in shot together.

The windows were terribly important to everybody in the country, adults included. Grown men gambled on them. I once visited a British army base in Germany and they told me they all used to look at the shape of my mouth to work out which window it was going to be. Here all the pauses didn't just build suspense and excitement in the children, but also gave the cameras time to move in and defocus to the enchanting harp music before the film was shown. These films were designed to take the audience out of the familiar environments of home and the programme into the wider world beyond. As a presenter, you only saw each film for the first time at the studio rehearsal, and then you had to decide what your commentary would be.

For anyone who grew up with *Play School*, the toys were as beloved as the presenters. We had knockabout rehearsal versions, who sometimes came on public appearances with us, and also the real things, the show versions, who were fiercely protected, locked in a box and wheeled out only for filming.

How I loved Humpty, with his green plush face, white pom-pom nose, a smiley red mouth, a little topknot of hair and matching magenta collar, feet and hands. He was my saviour.

By the time I got to recording the Thursday programme, it would be after seven p.m., and having already done three in such a short time, my brain was scrambled. There were times when I was on camera and halfway through I'd go completely blank. But if I had Humpty cuddled on my lap at the time, he could come to the rescue.

'So, Humpty, what's next?' I'd say, counting on the fact that the camera would have to move to Humpty's friendly reassuring face for his close-up. The children at home would definitely want to know what he thought. And then I'd have a second or two to gather myself and my thoughts. When you squeeze Humpty, you feel instantly comforted.

He was my favourite to take with me when I was doing personal appearances. I used to do lots of these, meeting children face to face all over the country, and signing autographs. You could just sit him down beside you and everyone would go 'Ahhhh! Humpty!'

I'd ask each child their name, and when it was their turn I'd throw Humpty to them, because he's so soft and huggable. I did this once on a visit to Wimbledon, and only when Humpty fell to the floor did I realize I'd thrown him to a child with thalidomide-impaired arms.

'Now, come on, Humpty!' I said quickly. 'What do you mean falling about like that? Have another go now. Are you ready now? You might need to help Humpty this time.'

So, I threw him again, in a way the child could catch him.

Strangely enough, at that very same event I was confronted

with a little boy of around six who did not look happy to see me.

'I hate you,' he told me when he got to the front of the queue. 'Because you're a . . .' And he used a racist word.

'What?!' I said.

He repeated the word.

'But I love you,' I replied. 'And so does Humpty. We both really love you. Come and give Humpty a cuddle.'

I looked up and saw his dad watching. Clearly, he'd told his son to go over and say this to me. So here was a child growing up with hatred in his heart, hatred he couldn't even understand, but which his parents were programming into him. It brought home to me how important it is to expose children to diversity from a very, very young age, and combat the indoctrination of some parents. Nobody is born to hate.

I was the last presenter ever to go on tour with the toys, so I still have the rehearsal versions of two of them: Humpty, with his lovely green paisley pattern on his bottom half, rather than the checked trousers he wore on the show, and also Jemima.

Jemima was really everyone's 'It' girl, a real supermodel, and probably the first love of many boys' lives. She has long brown wool hair, tied up with a big red bow in a jaunty ponytail, perfect pink circles on her cheeks, and long legs that go on for ever. Her dress is covered with daisies, and she has lacy sleeves and matching white bloomers. Again, she has an endearingly friendly smile.

But she was a lot more wayward than Humpty, and could be a real pain to work with because she kept falling over. You'd have to put a ruler or a wire coat hanger up the back of her dress to make her sit up straight, or prop her up with her arms.

'Come on now, Jemima! Sit up!'

Because if she flopped forward, the children would write in, worrying about her. And it could be terribly distracting.

Luckily, she came into her own for action sequences. Her long floppy limbs made her a perfect dancing partner, and she was wonderfully animated when you were telling stories with her, flicking her hair and marching up and down on command, like a little Avenger. She was always the belle of the ball, the star of every picnic, the one you'd want to take out on an adventure with you.

The teddy bears didn't have a huge amount of character, and they weren't very mobile, so they were much harder to interact with. Big Ted always looked after Little Ted. They were just very sweet, and, of course, most children had a teddy so they could identify with them.

And then there was Hamble.

Humpty and Jemima had been specially made for the programme. But at some point, one of the producers decided the programme needed an extra doll, so she just went to the shops and picked Hamble off the shelf. She might even have come from Woolworths. Solidly plastic and not at all cuddly, Hamble just sat there, stiff and inexpressive. She had lots of dark hair and an odd expression, but she still had her fans. Maybe we should have made a bit more effort. I tried to include her, but I fear she was always a bit jealous of Jemima and her free spirit.

How I wish we could bring Hamble back into the fold, and let her know you don't have to be beautiful to be loved!

One day in the mid-1980s, Hamble was quietly replaced by a new doll from India, called Poppy. Dark-skinned with shiny black hair, she sometimes wore a beautiful sari, and sometimes blue stripy dungarees, and she's now on display at the National Science and Media Museum in Bradford with most of the other show toys. But whatever happened to Hamble? She simply vanished. Did someone take her home and treasure her? Was she dumped in a skip? The mystery of her disappearance has never been solved.

Chapter Eighteen

It didn't take me long to notice that whenever we did a story on *Play School*, all the illustrations were White. No Black children were pictured, ever. No Asian children. No disabled children either. So, one day I pointed this out.

'Cynthia, darling,' I said, 'can't we have some Black and Asian and Chinese faces in the pictures? Does every child have to be White?'

'Oh?' she said, a little shocked. 'We hadn't noticed.'

That was a turning point for me. I realized that part of the problem was the fact that the people with the power to create programmes, or books, or toys, or whatever they were making, had never looked at what they were doing through anyone's eyes but their own. They automatically recreated their own rather narrow worlds. It wasn't necessarily a deliberate exclusion. It certainly wasn't in Cynthia's case. But she had simply never noticed what wasn't there. That afternoon the illustrations were changed.

The author Shirley Hughes said exactly the same thing to me. I used to love her Alfie stories, but until I mentioned this to her, all her characters were White.

'Goodness, Floella. I hadn't noticed.'

And from then on, she was careful to include all races in her books.

Helen Oxenbury was another fantastic children's author and illustrator, famous for *We're Going on a Bear Hunt*, who realized how important it was for all young children to see themselves represented. From the 1980s her pioneering baby board books even featured Black babies on the cover.

If you've never experienced racism yourself, it's harder to imagine what it's like to live in a world which judges you by the colour of your skin.

Millions of people from all walks of life watched *Play School*, parents and children. I realized that when my young White viewers watched, they saw me only as a person they could relate to, not the colour of my skin. I was struck by one letter that said, 'I love you, Floella. I want to be you.' And the girl had sent me a photo of herself with plaits and blue beads, but she had ginger hair and freckles and white skin. But children who weren't White had few chances to see themselves in the programme beyond presenters like me, Derek and actor and barrister Paul Danquah, star of *A Taste of Honey*, who was the first Black host of any children's TV show in 1965.

I once met a family from Iran who told me that they used to sit with their little daughter and point to me.

'You see, *she* made it. You can make it too.'

I have heard similar stories from children from Nigeria and Ghana, India and China . . . so many children who looked different in some way found they could relate to me. Back in my Trinidad childhood, Harry Belafonte, Dorothy Dandridge, Lena Horne and Sidney Poitier had been role models for me. I was proud to do the same for a new generation of children looking for someone they could relate to on screen.

Once the light had dawned for Cynthia, she made sure that everyone else working on the programme was equally aware of the importance of representing children of every colour and culture, so that all viewers felt their lives and experiences were reflected. This was important to keep the programme fresh and lively, always a priority for Cynthia. Poppy's appearance was part of this endeavour.

In about 1982 I was asked to write a foreword for a new children's book. I felt very honoured and was excited to look through the proofs. But I had to decline the invitation. I didn't see a single face illustrated that wasn't White.

'I'm very sorry,' I told the publisher. 'I can't do it. There are no Black, Asian or Chinese characters in this book.'

'But this story is set in a fantasy land, Floella!' she argued.

Black people aren't allowed in fantasy worlds? Or an all-White world is a desirable fantasy?

Two years later, the reading charity BookTrust asked me to chair the Smarties Book Prize. I made a speech about diversity and belonging. I thought it was my duty to make all children feel inspired to see themselves in books, and to appreciate different cultures. One of the broadsheets published a headline: 'Floella says Snow White should be Black'. This was definitely a phrase I had not used. It was made up by them.

Change has taken so long. For decades commercial publishers continued to believe that a Black face on the cover of a book meant it wouldn't sell. Some bookshops had special sections for Black books. Only in the last few years have publishers really sat up and taken notice of recent surveys analysing inclusivity in children's books. Back when I was on *Play School*, I was trying to educate the people who were creating the books.

I feel very proud to have played such an important role in ensuring that diversity became a fundamental philosophy in children's television. Even if the published books weren't out there, producers and presenters could make up their own stories and illustrations, and, increasingly, we did. A lot more children's programmes than adult ones had presenters of colour, perhaps because by instinct, children don't see prejudice. They have to learn it. Sadly, it took even longer for television to become aware of the need to represent disabled people too, but here again children's programmes led the way.

Cynthia tended to pair me with new presenters and new directors on *Play School*, so that I could show them the ropes, teaching them all the tricks Johnny Ball had once taught me. Although I wasn't the only Black presenter, for some reason they rarely scheduled two on screen in the same programme. So, I never had the fun of presenting a show with my friend Derek. Although I must confess that when I asked Anne Gobey about this she told me that putting the two of us together would have been madness. We would have misbehaved like schoolchildren, giggling non-stop, she said.

Not long after I got the job on *Play School*, Peter Charlton, the producer of *Play Away*, the Saturday afternoon sketch and music show, asked me to audition for this too. A knockabout programme led by Brian Cant, it was full of jokes, sketches and terrible puns and plenty of dressing up in hats and wigs galore. At the audition, I made the team fall about with my exaggerated impersonation of the Queen.

'You're just what we're looking for,' Peter said as soon as he heard my voice. 'A perfect alto pitch.'

Derek was already a regular on *Play Away*, which I joined in 1976, five years after it was launched, but we never worked together on this much sillier programme either. *Play Away* suited my own exuberant sense of fun perfectly. It was a bit like an old-fashioned variety show, but for a family audience, and quite challenging for actors. We had to bring so many characters to life at such speed, one after another, sometimes ten or twenty in one show, always with very quick costume changes and all in front of a live audience. One moment I was an angel, the next I was the Queen of Sheba or – uniquely, it transpired – a female Sherlock Holmes: Shirley to Brian's Watson. I used my Trinidadian accent for quite a few sketches and developed the character of Reggae Rita, who was such fun to play, and brought a Caribbean flavour to the show. In March 1984 I recorded a song about her for a popular BBC album made with Brian Cant called *Singing in the Band – Songs from BBC TV's Play School and Play Away*, which won a gold disc and was released as a single. Brian and I had great rapport, and we worked with lots of experienced guest stars too. Tony Robinson, Julie Covington, Anita Dobson and Jeremy Irons all made appearances on *Play Away* before they became household names.

It was lovely as an actor to get an instant reaction from an audience of children right there in front of you. You knew straight away that something had worked from the roars of real laughter.

Keith used to write a few sketches and visual gags for the show:

'Doctor, doctor, I feel like a bridge!'

'What's come over you?'

'A car, a bus and a lorry!'

Or:

'What do you call a woman who climbs walls?'

'I don't know. What *do* you call a woman who climbs walls?'

'Ivy!'

At this point, although I thought *Play School* and *Play Away* were enormous fun, they didn't take up all my time, and I didn't for a moment see them as 'proper' jobs, or imagine how much *Play School* in particular would shape my destiny. The guaranteed repeats were a great perk for us, thanks to the excellent daily repeat fees, and even better for the youngest children who'd watched the morning edition and could then eagerly tell their big brothers and sisters which window it would be that day when they watched again together in the afternoon.

But little by little, my work on these programmes began to change my entire vision of the world. One day, quite early on, I had to voice a 'through the window' film about dustbin collection. So, there I was, making up what I thought was a suitable commentary. And without a word of criticism, Cynthia Felgate, who was another of my true guardian angels, asked me to go to visit a primary school in Ealing.

'Floella, I want you to watch the children watching you talking about the rubbish collection film. Just go and see them.'

'OK,' I agreed, without much thought. It seemed an odd request, but I knew Cynthia always knew what she was doing.

I listened to the boys and girls watching and talking, and it was like being reborn. I saw the world as if for the first time. Nothing was a given. No knowledge could be taken for granted. Everything was interesting in a new way.

'I wonder what it smells like.'

'How do we make all that rubbish?'

'What do those men do with it all?'

'Where's that rubbish going?'

Oh my goodness. How that experience of being with those children in Ealing opened my eyes. I can't tell you how joyful it made me. I learned there and then never to make any assumptions about anything or anyone, or bring any preconceptions to a situation. To look at life freshly all the time, and to view the world through the eyes of others as a matter of course. This is a habit I've carried through life ever since. It's a wonderful feeling, and I think of it as a blessing.

Chapter Nineteen

I've always used my time productively, and I was constantly looking for creative ways to supplement my income. Since Keith and I both worked in the theatre in the evenings, and often had spare time to fill during the day, and since I liked sewing and he liked designing things, we decided to open a shop. Covent Garden seemed a great place to start: it was in the heart of Theatre Land, and very much on the up at the time. A vigorous local campaign in the early 1970s had managed to overturn a terrible plan to flatten the neighbourhood, and regeneration was just beginning to transform the area – the piazza where fruit, veg and flowers were once sold would re-open as Europe's first speciality shopping centre in 1980. We found premises at 46 Monmouth Street, close to the dojo where we'd started taking karate classes, and tried to get people to invest. But everyone said no. What did we know about running a shop? So, we sank all our savings into the venture, bought an industrial sewing machine, and went ahead on our own.

We named the boutique Doberman, after our beloved Arrow, and he was often in the shop with us, and very popular with customers. Doberman was a great meeting place for actors, who regularly dropped by after auditions and rehearsals, stretched out on our chaise longue as if settling down for psychoanalysis, and shared their sorrows or successes over a glass of bubbly. As he mentioned in his famous diaries, Kenneth Williams often came in for a cuppa and a chat after visiting his accountant, who was two doors down. One actor, Roger, ended up working for us whenever he didn't have a theatre job.

Sometimes, for fun, we pretended that the clothes we sold were made by an imaginary designer called Louis Doberman, and this story actually got into the press. Sometimes we even heard people claiming to know him, which made us laugh. In fact, our stock came from all sorts of places. I made some clothes – mostly trendy dresses and tops – and we found someone else who created gorgeous knitwear, and we also bought other garments from up-and-coming designers on sale or return. Keith designed jewellery and themed novelty badges for the stars of shows to give as presents to other company members – smiley faces, musical instruments, birds. And, for added glamour, we had a glass display case of beautiful Cartier-style watches on the counter. After a while, we began to sell sexy underwear too, almost by accident. There weren't many places to go even for ordinary bras and pants in those days, and we couldn't believe how quickly they sold out. Suspenders always had the best sales after Benny Hill had been on television the night before, and corsets and basques after a Kenny Everett show.

We were good at striking bargains with wholesalers who traded in cheap dresses made out of designers' offcuts, fabric waste known as cabbage. Most of the cash-and-carry garment traders off Oxford Street were Jewish, and they assumed I was Jewish too because of my surname, Benjamin, and always gave me a good deal. But one day I made it clear that I wasn't Jewish.

'See you next Thursday,' I said to one of our regular suppliers in Great Titchfield Street – a man called Nick.

'What?!'

I hadn't realized that the following Thursday was Yom Kippur, the most important Jewish holiday of the year. Clearly, I wasn't Jewish, despite my surname. But we were great customers, and Nick still always gave us lots of bargains and tip-offs about other suppliers.

Around Christmas, when actors are really busy and can't get out to buy their presents, if I was on a programme like the *All Star Record Breakers*, with Roy Castle, Sarah Greene, Ben Thomas and all the other favourite children's presenters, I'd bring a suitcase of shop clothes into my studio dressing room and sell party dresses and mohair star-sign jumpers to the other performers.

Marmie was very proud of Doberman, and we always encouraged her to pick any clothes she liked for herself when she came to visit us there. She dropped by one day when Roger was minding the shop, and she spotted a shoplifter trying to make off with the fancy watches. So, she threw herself across the door, and said:

'You're not leaving here. Put those watches back. My daughter's worked hard to build up this business and you're not getting away with this. Roger! Call the police!'

The thief took one look at Marmie, handed over his loot, and scarpered. You didn't mess with my mum.

One time when I was alone in the shop, I was surprised by a young man who suddenly pulled back the changing room curtain to reveal himself with the leather trousers he was supposed to be trying on around his knees. He wore nothing else at all.

'Oh, rather small!' I said, meaning the trousers.

He grabbed his parts.

'They all say that!'

'Now, you realize you're going to have to buy these

trousers,' I said sternly. 'There's no way I can sell them to anyone else now.'

He left the shop, thoroughly chastened.

Keith used to design window displays to rival Harvey Nichols, and took great pride in them. But on Christmas Eve 1979, his spot-lit leather-jacketed mannequin – sprayed black by Keith, and surrounded by diamanté – proved too tempting. A more successful burglar smashed the glass with a paraffin roadworks lamp and nearly set the whole shop on fire. That break-in broke our hearts.

I'd only been doing *Play School* for about three months when a leading role in a feature film came up. *Black Joy* (1977), with all Black stars, was based on a play by the Guyana-born writer Jamal Ali, who was then running the Black Theatre of Brixton, the first professional multicultural radical theatre company in Britain. Ali had co-written the screenplay with the writer and director Anthony Simmons, who directed *The Optimist* starring Peter Sellers in 1973.

Now known as the UK's only blaxploitation film, *Black Joy* is a gritty story of a young and innocent new arrival from Guyana called Ben (Trevor Thomas), who turns up in London with his little suitcase – his grip – and nothing but a slip of paper with an address in Brixton. Norman Beaton, my fellow cast member from *The Black Mikado*, later famous for the sitcom *Desmond's*, played a Caribbean con artist, Dave, out to dupe the newcomer, with the help of a little boy. Lots of people take advantage of Ben, but eventually he becomes streetwise. A real piece of history, with a soundtrack to match, the film shows exactly what Brixton and Stockwell were like in the 1970s.

'I've seen your work, and I think you'll be perfect to play

Miriam,' Anthony told me when we met. He was a lovely man. 'I know you've got depth. You can show the various sides of her and bring the character alive.'

I told him I wasn't going to take my clothes off. That was still very important for me, and I never compromised. I'd looked at the script, and I'd seen what it said: *Miriam and Dave are in bed making love in the nude.*

'If I do that scene, you'll see me in my nightie and I'm not even going to give the impression that I've got no clothes on,' I said.

Anthony agreed. He really wanted me to play this part.

Can you imagine how I felt at that moment? I'd already got my dream job on *Play School*, and now I was going to star in a demanding role in a really heavy drama. An actual feature film! I thought I'd made it.

Miriam is the single mother of the sassy little boy Devon, a little hustler played by Paul J. Medford. And she's the lover of Norman Beaton's Dave, a manipulative ne'er-do-well who can persuade her to do anything. He's such a charmer that she keeps falling for him, hook, line and sinker. But in one fiery scene of domestic violence the tables are turned. She's discovered she's pregnant again and tries to finish with him, telling him she's had an abortion.

'What? You mean you killed the child without telling me nothin'. And here is I looking to be a father.' Dave hits Miriam violently. 'You little wretch.'

When we filmed the scene, I was so caught up in its passion that I improvised instinctively. Unscripted, I grabbed a pair of scissors, and came back at him, blades in hand, jawline set, eyes bulging with fury, intense rage animating every part of me. I didn't feel like Floella. I was Miriam.

'You good-for-nothing b******! You're nothing but a ponce. You got no pride . . .'

It's a hard, uncompromising scene. I scream at him to get out before I draw blood, telling him that I'll spend the rest of my life in prison if he hits me again. You can feel the vibration of my heartbeat, the anger and frustration of this woman. Everybody on set was so electrified by my performance, they spontaneously clapped.

That year the film became the first Black film to be chosen as an entrant for the Cannes Film Festival. My portrayal of a woman incensed by the man who was ruining her life made the audiences there gasp too.

At Cannes, we stayed at the Carlton Hotel, that grand Belle Époque palace with two famous domes which dominates the seafront. This is where all the most prestigious movie stars in history have always stayed, where Grace Kelly first met Prince Rainier III of Monaco and where she'd filmed *To Catch a Thief* with Alfred Hitchcock. Ava Gardner, Kim Novak, Jane Mansfield and Gina Lollobrigida had stood on those balconies in front of adoring crowds. Greta Garbo, Picasso, Errol Flynn, Paul Newman . . . Everybody who was anybody stayed at the Cannes Carlton.

I still remember my amazement at the sudden sight of Gregory Peck, who'd played Atticus Finch in *To Kill a Mockingbird* fifteen years earlier. How tall he was! I recognized so many well-known actors walking through the hotel corridors, crossing the foyer, eating in the dining room, just like me. 'There's Roger Moore!' I said to myself, longing to tell Keith, who'd had to stay in London to look after the shop. At the airport I'd passed Ringo Starr, and as I turned to look back at him, disbelievingly, I saw that he'd turned too, to look back at me.

What am I doing here? The little girl who'd arrived shivering at Southampton, whose mother had kept her warm with a flowery Marks and Spencer cardigan, was now mingling with international stars. And one of them had clearly recognized me.

I had a kitty for tips and other expenses.

'If a maid comes to your room, give them ten francs,' our producer told me. But although I had more money to spend promoting the film in Cannes than I'd received as my performance fee, I found I was soon running out of cash. The maids were completely fascinated by me, and a rumour had clearly gone round the hotel about the woman in room whatever-it-was with the exotic beads and plaits. So, every five minutes I'd hear a knock on the door and another maid would be there with soap or a towel or some other little something for the room. Just for a chance to look at me. But, of course, I'd have to give each of them another ten francs.

I had a favourite oversized and well-worn white T-shirt with a pink and yellow clown on it which I'd brought for my nightie – it was a bit grey by then, but very comfortable. The very first night, I came back to my room to find my dingy T-shirt made into a beautiful arrangement on the bed – the maid had turned my bed down and transformed my 'nightie' into a flower, with a pink clown centre.

Agghhh! I thought. *How embarrassing.* So, the next morning, instead of tucking the shirt under my pillow, I hid it.

But once again, when I came back that evening, there it was back on the bedcover again, this time turned into a swan. The maid had been through my wardrobe! By day three, I decided I'd better spend some of my kitty on a new nightie. Of course, when I saw the prices in the shops I soon changed my mind, and admitted defeat.

After the premiere of Black Joy, we held a press conference and I sat at the table on stage with Anthony Simmons, Norman Beaton, Trevor Thomas and Paul J. Medford, the cute ten-year-old from Barbara Speake Stage School who played my son and went on to become Kelvin Carpenter in *EastEnders*. But none of the questions were coming my way.

'Well, don't you want to speak to Miriam?' Anthony asked the reporters.

'What? Is *she* Miriam?!' they said, in astonishment. And then the cameras started clicking and didn't stop. Nobody had recognized me with my hair in blue beads. They thought I was just somebody's girlfriend sitting on the platform. But after that they wouldn't leave me alone.

The hairstyle I'd created was already a sensation in the UK. I'd been quite taken aback when I started to go places and saw people looking like me. The BBC regularly sent out instructions to enthusiastic viewers showing them how to do the beads. They were synonymous with my name across the Channel, but a completely new thing in France, where Black women were still inclined to straighten their hair or wear wigs.

From that moment at the press conference, I was surrounded by photographers and TV cameras wherever I went. They snapped me in a bikini on the beach. As we drove very slowly down the Croisette Promenade in an open-top Cadillac to promote the film, past beaches and gardens and fancy hotels and casinos, people actually grabbed my plaits. It was like being in a human zoo.

On 17 May, I was walking down the red carpet wearing my favourite beautiful white muslin Biba dress for the premiere of *A Special Day*, an Italian film about Hitler's visit to Mussolini in Rome, when one photographer suddenly grabbed hold of my arm and shoved me between two people behind me. Of course, my first instinct was to push him off.

'Get off me! Get off me! What do you think you're doing?'

It was bad enough people touching my hair all the time, and I've always hated being manhandled.

'You take picture with Carlo Ponti, Sophia Loren.'

'I don't care who they are! Don't you pull me about like that!'

Everybody seemed to want a piece of me. I was offered lots and lots of acting parts, mainly in foreign productions, and a German director asked me to go and make a film in Germany – but I said no. I didn't like the sexual undertones in the script, and besides, I had my life in London. In fact, not long after getting back from Cannes, I was working in the shop when I got a message from my agent telling me the Royal Shakespeare Company wanted me to join them. So, I could have been the RSC's first Black actress, six years before Josette Simon joined the company in 1984. I was so flattered, and certainly tempted, but once again, I knew it would be giving up too much. For what? To be the third spear-carrier from the right? I was far too happy in *Play School*, and somehow already had a strong feeling that the programme would be part of my destiny.

In Cannes, Anthony told me that some important people from a magazine wanted to meet me. So off I went.

'We would like you to be in *Playboy* magazine,' the men announced, clearly expecting me to fall over with gratitude.

'Oh?' I said.

Playboy was famous for its raunchy centrefolds, featuring a Playmate of the Month, complete with a listing of each woman's birth date, body measurements, turn-ons and turn-offs. By the early seventies, these were full frontal nudes.

'We want you to be our centrefold wearing nothing except for your blue beads.'

'Sorry, but no thank you,' I told them immediately.

'But we're going to make you an international star!' they assured me.

'No, thank you.'

'We'll give you lots and lots of money,' they said hastily, amazed at my rejection of what they could only see as an unmissable opportunity. 'Thousands of dollars.'

'No, thank you,' I repeated. To appear nude in a magazine

was against all my principles. No amount of money or fame could tempt me.

In only half a year, I'd seen how much I was changing children's lives. I could picture my future ahead of me, working with children, making a difference in the world. Why would I want to ruin all that, give up everything I had achieved, for such a short-term gain? I always threw my mind beyond the horizon to look into the future, visualizing the consequences of any decision before committing myself.

They couldn't believe it. Floella Benjamin had said no? Nobody said no to *Playboy*.

Taking off your clothes was nothing unusual in the seventies. Most actresses did nude scenes at the drop of a hat. It was no big deal. Now actresses are demanding closed sets, making conditions. Then nearly all directors were male, and they just expected women to strip off. It was written into all the scripts. But I always questioned that.

'Why is this character nude here?' I'd ask. 'There's no need for her to be naked.' I'd already turned down lots of dramas when directors wanted me to appear topless or nude. 'No,' I'd been saying firmly, ever since *Hair*. Always. Why would I suddenly say yes to *Playboy*?

I believe that women should have a choice about these things. And we do have a choice. Whenever I said 'no', I always knew it was likely to mean I'd never get another job from that person, but that was my choice.

On the night of the premiere, the film's reception was so incredible that people applauded when we walked into the Carlton dining room – a fabulously grand room full of white pillars and gold leaf, gilded ceilings and glittering cut-glass chandeliers. I felt on top of the world. I was floating on air. I really did have to pinch myself to believe what was happening.

I'm in Cannes. With all these movie stars. I really wasn't prepared for all the attention and adulation. I'd seen how stars were treated on television and in magazines. To be part of it was unbelievable. It was great.

Norman Beaton was sitting next to me at the table. Suddenly, he turned to me and said, loudly:

'So, what's so special about your body that you don't want anybody to see it?'

What? I was completely taken aback, not just by the humiliating question, but Norman's aggressive tone.

'Why didn't you want to do a nude scene with me? It's in the script. What's so special about you, eh? Who do you think you are?' he continued, refusing to let it drop.

It was terribly embarrassing for everyone present. There we were, out in public, celebrating our success in a posh hotel restaurant, and I was under attack with everybody listening. I managed to keep my dignity, and kept smiling. Completely ignoring Norman, who was then forced to shut up, I turned to Trevor instead.

'Trevor, what's our call for tomorrow? Do you remember?'

Still smiling sweetly. I refused to get into an argument. Why should I have to justify my decisions to another actor? Or to anyone? This was between me and the director.

The following day, I saw Norman walking towards me down the corridor. To his great surprise, when he reached me, I confronted him.

'Don't you EVER talk to me like that again,' I hissed, furiously. My karate classes had taught me the value of the unexpected attack. 'Or I'll have your guts for garters. Do you understand me?'

He was speechless. He couldn't believe the force of my fury.

'Don't you dare EVER, EVER, EVER talk to me like that again,' I repeated.

And he never did. After that he could not have been more respectful and gentlemanly towards me. We smiled at each other knowingly when we met. He knew he didn't mess with me, and I hope it meant he never treated another woman in this way again. And nobody ever knew what had actually happened between us that day. I'm proud to say that at the Festival *Black Joy* was nominated for the Golden Palm Best Picture Award. Nevertheless, I am still waiting to be cast in my next leading film role!

I continued to push for casting diversity at every opportunity, and as a result the range of parts I was offered slowly began to expand. London Weekend Television was becoming more open-minded, and so I was cast as just an ordinary woman in a Friday-night police crime drama called *The Gentle Touch*, and although I played a nurse in one early episode of *Angels*, in another I played an unpleasantly feisty patient who threw a plate of food over her nurse. But without my blue beads, people often didn't recognize me in such dramas. A woman came into the shop the morning after that programme was screened and started asking me whether I'd seen that scene in *Angels* the night before with that horrible, rude woman.

When I was asked to audition for a new series called *Maybury*, starring Patrick Stewart as the psychiatric consultant in Maybury General Hospital, the director Richard Stroud and producer Ruth Boswell once again wanted me to play the usual part of a nurse. As always, I looked through the script to see what other opportunities there might be. One role grabbed my attention right away: Kayreen, a person diagnosed with schizophrenia who had killed her own children.

That's who I want to play, I decided. The part was so complex, and well developed. I felt very deeply about it and believed strongly that I could do it. Of course, it had been written for a White person, because that was always the assumption. If the writer didn't specify 'Black' in brackets in their cast list, the directors thought it meant the actor had to be White. And if they weren't nurses or prostitutes or bus conductors, Black characters always had to be making a statement or having some kind of problem.

Although they'd called me in for the nurse role, which was a character in the whole series, Richard and Ruth agreed to let me read Kayreen, a character in just one episode. I played her as a lost soul who wanted to protect her children, and I put my whole being into that audition.

By the end, Richard and Ruth were both in tears.

'The part is yours,' they said. They loved the human touch I gave the character. To get more experience and understanding of my character's situation, they sent me to spend a day in a mental hospital in East London.

I wore my bubbly wig so that nobody would recognize me, took a deep breath, and was admitted into the secure unit. It was eye-opening. Life-changing. I met all kinds of different people with different problems. I remember a Black man who had poured tar over his entire body and believed he was Jesus. There was an Asian woman who had been driven mad by domestic violence. One man kept stroking my hair, and trying to get me to come into his room, pursuing me wherever I went.

Uh-oh. My hair was moving. A moment later, before I had time to move away, he grabbed my wig and threw it across the room. I was completely exposed. Of course, the television was on all the time in the hospital and everyone knew exactly who I was. The Lady from *Play School*. They were very excited.

I stayed all day and wanted to stay for longer. It was a place I felt people could relax and be themselves, a kind of haven where you could shed all responsibilities and escape from violence. The experience gave me enormous insight into the character of Kayreen, and I felt an even deeper affinity with her as I laid my face against Patrick Stewart's smooth head during filming, showing that I trusted him completely.

During this time, many producers and directors tried to get me to compromise myself. One very powerful director cast me, unbeknownst to me, because he fancied me, not because he thought I was talented. We were filming on location and he invited me to meet his family and to his children's school. I thought he was kind and thoughtful.

Week three arrived and we were on set. He came up as close to me as he could with his light meter.

'I've waited three weeks for you,' he muttered in my ear. 'I'm not waiting any longer.'

I feigned laughter.

'Don't be silly!' I giggled, anxious, shocked, determined. 'What about your wife? Your children? Is that really what you think of me?'

He didn't take it well. The next time I turned up for filming, I discovered my scene had been cut. And for the rest of the job, the same thing happened.

Cut. Cut. Cut.

If he'd found a chance to try it on with me and been rejected a few weeks earlier, he'd have cut me out completely. Meanwhile, another actress I knew responded to that same director's come-ons, and her career soared for a while.

Yet when I see him I keep on smiling. He didn't stop me

developing my career. And I kept my sense of dignity. Sure enough, I didn't work for his company again.

This kind of thing happened all the time. I'd gone for a BBC job in the early 1970s and another powerful producer auditioned me alone in his office.

'Can you move, Floella?' he asked, and I began to dance. He threw himself on top of me. I was horrified but my fighting instincts hadn't died. I kicked him as hard as I could and ran away from the building, devastated. Why did it always have to be so difficult? I cried to my mother, but who could I report him to? Who would have listened? It was always the same in those days, whether in a garage in Gypsy Hill or an office at White City. His word against mine. I'd only be accused of stirring up trouble, or ridiculed. 'Never get jealous of what other people have,' Marmie used to say to me. 'You don't know what they had to do to get it.'

I know it still happens now but things are beginning to change.

We have to teach girls that they have the right to say no, and give them the confidence to do so. Women and men must be unafraid to speak out. It's not easy to call someone out on the tube when they're groping you in a crowded carriage. But that's always been my approach.

'This man is touching me,' I say very loudly.

Never give them the benefit of the doubt. Never imagine that unwanted pressure is accidental.

Chapter Twenty

I never thought I'd have children. Babies of my own were simply not part of my vision during my twenties. I had so many other people's children in my life, and no burning desire to be pregnant myself. I'd spent my twenties enjoying life to the full. I loved exploring the exciting and creative world into which I'd hurtled since leaving the bank and meeting Keith. Having discovered how to deal with adversity and setbacks with confidence and a smile on my face, I was ready to put even more energy into trying to make the world a fairer place.

And then we moved house. We sold our little flat in Herne Hill and had the incredible luck to find a huge double-fronted house within our budget in another part of South London. The owners were Hugh Barclay, a clerk in parliament, and his wife Hilda, and at that time it was the local Liberal Party headquarters. We were the first people to view it and couldn't believe how undervalued it was. We made an offer straight away. It was at a time when gazumping was rife but Hugh promised to honour the agreed price. 'A gentleman's word is his bond,' he said. It had a huge back garden, and plenty of space for all our different ventures. Of course, Marmie came round to see it as soon as we'd moved in. She brought my four-year-old nephew

Steven with her, Sandra's second son. Marmie loved boasting about her grandchildren and they adored her. 'The more, the merrier' was her approach.

It was a beautiful summer's day, and Steven was playing happily in the garden.

'Isn't that lovely? Look at him playing there!' I said to Marmie.

'Well, you should have your own children, and then *they'd* be playing in your garden. Why don't you have kids now?'

'Do you think I should?' I said, a little startled. I was thirty years old, yet the idea had simply never occurred to either me or Keith, even though all my brothers and sisters except Junior had children by then.

'Yes!' said Marmie.

'Why?' I asked.

'Because when you bring children into the world, you live in hope that your child will make a difference, and change the world. Who knows what their destiny might be?'

I'd never thought of it in that way before.

'Shall we have a baby?' I said to Keith.

'Well, let's get married first,' he replied. 'We can go down the road next week.'

So, there was no romantic proposal, no getting down on one knee. We never really had a honeymoon. We just wanted to get on with having children.

Family and friends went crazy when we told them.

'About time!' they all said. We'd lived together for seven years by then.

We were pretty naive about the whole thing, and Marmie quickly pointed out that organizing a wedding wasn't quite as quick and simple as we'd imagined. So, we ended up tying the knot six weeks later on 27 September 1980 at Brixton registry office, four days after my thirty-first birthday and two days after Keith's. But it wasn't a conventional affair. I wore an art deco dress I'd bought ten years before for five shillings in a charity shop in Glasgow, and Marmie helped me get ready. I tell children that, in our commercially led world, it's not what you wear, it's how you wear it that matters. A friend who bred orchids helped us decorate the house with them, and also lent us three Rolls-Royces from his collection, which made heads turn in Brixton. The reception was at our new house with two hundred invited guests from all walks of life; directors and producers, celebrities, TV and theatre stars all mingled happily. Millionaires danced with BBC cleaners in our front room disco. In the back ground-floor room, we laid out the food: Caribbean roti, curry and four-tiered rich West Indian cake made by Marmie, and Italian food brought by one of our restaurant-owner friends in Monmouth Street. The garden looked beautiful, with lights festooning the apple trees, put up by Keith that morning, and, like every room in the house, it was packed. We were so lucky that year to have an Indian summer, and the day was glorious in every way.

January was always quiet in the shop, so we usually went on holiday then. In 1981, with Arrow in the back of the car, we set off for a converted mill in Cornwall that turned out to be damp, cold and so unromantic I didn't think I could possibly have conceived. So, I went back to work feeling quite glum. I wasn't used to things not going to plan. Filming the first of several appearances on *Bergerac* was a good distraction. Acting Juniper in the first episode, I enjoyed driving a Lamborghini, singing my favourite Sarah Vaughan song, 'Lover Man', and discovering the beautiful island of Jersey.

Not long after our return from Cornwall, I complained to Marmie that my boobs were itching.

'You're pregnant!' she told me. And of course, she was right.

I hadn't thought much about the consequences of having children for my work, but I soon realized how rarely I'd spotted a visibly pregnant presenter on television. Would this be the end of my career? Would I just disappear from the screen? I went to see Cynthia Felgate. She didn't have children herself. Neither did Anne Gobey. In fact, it was unusual in the 1960s and 70s for a woman in senior management at the BBC to have a family. The first Sex Discrimination Act had become law only five years earlier; maternity leave and pay were patchy to non-existent in the UK. I really didn't know what her reaction would be.

'Listen, Cynthia. I'm pregnant.'

It can hardly have been a shock to her. She knew why we'd decided to get married.

'Wonderful! Wonderful!' she said. 'We'll make a feature of it in the programme.'

That took *me* by surprise. I didn't have to leave? Fantastic.

I told my *Play School* children the news on air one Friday.

'Now, listen everyone. I . . . am . . . pregnant. That means I've got a baby growing inside me. So, if you see me getting bigger and bigger, it's not because I'm eating too much, but because my baby is growing. Isn't that wonderful?'

All hell broke loose. The week the programme was broadcast, we were leaving to go on holiday to Greece. At Heathrow airport, I was mobbed.

'Is it true you're pregnant?'

Parents rushed up to me, delighted by the news. Their children were excited. Everyone seemed to be thrilled about the

'*Play School* baby'. My baby belonged to the nation's children. Children used to send me pictures they'd drawn of me with my blue-beaded plaits and inside my tummy there would be my baby, also with blue beads. Viewers sent me gifts of all kinds, handmade toys, clothes, books, teddy bears for the baby, paintings, cards. One of the tabloids came to do a fashion shoot, and I wore a yellow outfit with blue piping I often wore on the show. The story even hit America. 'There is a pregnant presenter on television,' CBS News announced. It really was that unusual to see a woman visibly with child on screen, other than in a drama. Tina Heath, who replaced Lesley Judd on *Blue Peter* in 1979, had made history the previous year by demonstrating an ultrasound scan of her baby live on the show, and also climbing to the top of Westminster Abbey while heavily pregnant, but for some reason this had attracted less attention, perhaps because I worked until nearly eight months and was so visibly pregnant.

I started getting letters from other presenters, thanking me for helping to break that barrier so publicly.

'Now I can get pregnant too,' they told me. There was life after birth.

We prepared a beautiful room for the baby, all in yellow and blue. Johnny Ball gave us his daughter Zoe's old cot, a lovely rocking crib, and Keith painted a mural to go with the fantastical nursery rhyme wallpaper he'd put up. I went to antenatal classes and learned how to breathe and bear down. My *Play School* children watched me grow and grow, and I made my last appearance on the week beginning 24 August 1981, by which time I was eight months pregnant.

A week before my due date, I woke up in the middle of the night with my first contractions.

Huff. Huff. Huff.

I tried to follow those breathing instructions, but it just wasn't helping me get through the pain. So, I leaned against the wall, and instinctively began to wriggle my hips. Ahhh! That was better. Round and round I went, until the movement turned into a belly dance. It felt great, and I wriggled through the night, with everything apparently under control until, at about five in the morning, I was surprised by a gush of liquid.

Of course, I was straight on the phone to my mum.

'Marmie! What's happening? I can't stop weeing!'

'That means your waters have broken, Flo. You need to get to hospital.'

Keith sprang into action. He'd read the manual. The frying pan went onto the stove and the house filled with the nauseating smell of sizzling eggs and bacon – the last thing I wanted at five o'clock in the morning.

'Nearly ready, love!'

'I don't want to eat,' I moaned.

'The book says you have to. "Give your wife a proper breakfast. She's got a long day ahead."'

It was hard to get down, but I obediently swallowed the food, and we jumped into the car. The sun was just coming up and the streets were empty. Keith's long-held fantasy of speeding over Battersea Bridge was finally fulfilled, and I began to spew up my breakfast all over the back of our white Golf GTI.

'Find a four-hour parking meter!' I commanded as we arrived at Hammersmith Hospital, where my sister's midwife friend, Jenny, worked. Unfortunately, Jenny was off-duty that morning, so we were greeted in the maternity ward by a midwife we'd never met. I was still belly dancing.

Keith was keen to demonstrate his credentials as an involved father.

'Up till now it's all been textbook!' he told her proudly. It had indeed been a perfect pregnancy.

The midwife clicked her tongue and rolled her eyes impatiently, and threw a green gown at me. I was immediately enraged.

'Listen, you,' I said, looking her straight in the eye. 'This might be your hundredth baby but it's my first. If you don't like that fact, go and get me someone who does.'

These were the days when the medical profession often treated patients, especially mothers, like objects on a conveyor belt. When I'd first met my doctor, he hadn't bothered to look up from the notes he was scribbling until I crawled on the floor and called, 'Coooeee! I'm here! This is what I look like.'

This midwife was similarly taken aback, but once we had formed a relationship in this way, we became great friends. When the moment came, she grabbed my hand and said, 'Push! Push! Push!' Keith was the other side of me and I grabbed hold of his favourite shirt and ripped the sleeve off!

They gave me the power and strength to keep going when it felt impossible. But even with them beside me, and later Jenny too, eventually I got to a point when everything seemed stuck and I felt quite defeated. *I can't do it*, I thought. *I just can't push any more.* At that moment the memory came to me of a documentary I'd once seen showing a South American mother giving birth in a field, labouring in the middle of nowhere, with none of the facilities I had around me. A strong image of Sebastian Coe winning the 1,500 metres also flashed into my head. All the inspiring force and energy of this unknown mother and a world-beating athlete suddenly flooded through me, and I was overwhelmed with a *Chariots of Fire* sensation. With a huge almighty push, the baby was born. It had taken less than four hours.

'Is it a girl?' I asked eagerly.

All through my pregnancy I'd longed for a girl. I couldn't forget Marmie's words. 'Have a girl, you have a daughter for life. Have a boy, he's your son till he finds a wife.'

Jenny knew this. She turned to Keith.

'You'd better tell her.'

'It's a boy,' he said.

Oh no, I remember thinking as they handed him to me. I put the tiny baby to my breast, and he immediately latched on and began to suckle. I looked down at him adoringly, unable to take in the miracle in my arms. Within a few minutes, the paediatrician walked into the room to check the baby. To my astonishment, at the sound of his footsteps, my newborn baby instantly stopped feeding, and his eyes actually seemed to follow the movement of the man as he walked behind my bed and round to the other side. The baby was clearly aware of this new presence in the room. When the footsteps stopped, he went back to his feed.

Incredible. I didn't care now if I had a girl or a boy. I had a wonderful baby, so sharp and alert, so handsome and perfect. *Aren't I a lucky girl?* I told myself.

Aston was born on Tuesday 29 September 1981. Keith put up a sign in the window of our shop: 'It's a boy!' Before long we had press photographers snapping away in our hospital room. It was national news. Even *The Times* ran a 'news in brief' headline announcing the *Play School* baby: Floella Benjamin, presenter of BBC television's *Play School*, has given birth to a 7lb boy. The baby, who was born at the West London Hospital, Hammersmith, on Tuesday, will be called Aston, her husband, Mr Keith Taylor, a fashion shop owner, said yesterday.

Flo plans a TV debut for her baby boy, announced one tabloid. Flo has received hundreds of cards from her army of fans – all under five years of age – and she wants to introduce Aston to them on her TV show.

175

The BBC had already sent us a huge bouquet, and hundreds more bunches of flowers and cards and congratulation messages from friends and strangers all over the country soon started to arrive. I must have been the happiest woman on the planet at that moment. There was just so much love coming our way. Everything in the world seemed rosy.

And then, still in hospital, I eagerly opened another envelope and I found a piece of soiled toilet paper.

What are you doing here? We don't want you. Get that Black . . . You can imagine the rest of that hate-filled message. It hadn't crossed my mind there could be anyone in the country who actually hated me and my baby. Yet someone out there was feeling so much anger and disgust about my good news that they had gone to the trouble of doing the most disgusting thing imaginable.

This was an important lesson for me. I couldn't let all the flowers and presents and admiration mislead me. I couldn't afford to have a false sense of security, because there was adversity still out there, and it could hit any time, with no warning. I had to remain on patrol. I couldn't let my guard down under any circumstances.

It was brought home when Keith reluctantly rang to tell his mother she had a grandchild. Marmie was so proud of all her children's children, so we could only imagine his mum would be equally delighted.

'I haven't got any grandchildren,' his mum said to him. She refused to acknowledge Aston because he was Black. We planted a red rose bush in the garden to celebrate Aston's birth.

Within a few months, I was back at work, first as a guest live on *Crackerjack*, famous for its pencil prizes, and recording my first *Play School* programmes for transmission on the week of

7 December. We realized we wouldn't be able to keep working without a nanny, and of course, wanted the very best. So, we had gone to the agency and taken on a highly trained, very proper Norland Nanny. Sure enough, Bridget was super-duper efficient and well-meaning. But she tidied and reorganized our whole house. Suddenly we couldn't even find our own cutlery. She always thought she knew best, and tried to take charge of everything.

'You're too tired to be looking after Baby,' she used to tell me. 'Sit down. I'll make you a cup of tea.'

The first day I came back from rehearsals, I immediately rushed to Aston's gorgeous room, dying to pick him up.

'Mummy's home!' I wanted to say. I felt quite desperate to smell him and cuddle him again.

Bridget stopped me on the stairs.

'I'm sorry, you can't go in there. Baby's sleeping.'

And then *she* went into the nursery and I could hear her cooing over him.

I rushed downstairs.

'That woman will have to go,' I told Keith. 'I can't have her taking over my life like this.'

So, I took Aston with me to the BBC. Since he was such a quiet, well-behaved baby and slept all night and I had no problems breastfeeding, I innocently imagined that was what all babies were like. I'd pictured him sleeping peacefully in his pram as usual while I rehearsed.

There was uproar. He was not welcome.

'You can't bring a baby here!' they told me, outraged.

I called Marmie, and a friend of hers kindly came up to White City on the tube to sit in the car with Aston while I worked.

I had seen workplace nurseries in operation at a Norwegian TV station the previous year when I went over to appear on their version of *Play School*. Why shouldn't the BBC do the same? A child-friendly set-up like that would benefit everyone. But in 1981 the BBC still thought if you wanted to have a baby, and wanted to be near it and breastfeed for any length of time, you'd just have to leave. Soon after that, Esther Rantzen also got pregnant, and she too demanded that the BBC had a creche. But the first only opened in 1990, after a fifteen-year campaign. There were never enough places for everyone who needed one, and twenty years later all the BBC's nurseries were closed down.

We found a lovely new nanny with a very different style. She lived on the top floor of the house, and always handed Aston over to me when I got back from work.

This was a very joyful time in my life. I had fulfilling work on *Play School* and *Play Away*, much loved by children and parents alike. Aston made his first television appearance when the BBC sent a huge Outside Broadcast truck to film us together for one of the *Play School* 'through the window' sequences. His nursery filled with lights, camera operators, continuity, directors . . . Aston seemed to enjoy the excitement.

I was invited to talk in public about my belly dancing experiences during labour by Sheila Kitzinger, the great pioneer of woman-centred birth. She campaigned passionately for decades to help mothers enjoy the process of labour using natural techniques and was particularly outspoken about the importance of pelvic floor exercises before and after birth, a lesson I've never forgotten. She taught me that women ought to be able to pick something up with the strength of those most important muscles. I happily spread the word myself.

I'd never had so much attention in my life before. Suddenly I had a voice, and this meant I could help other women, and children too.

Chapter Twenty-one

By the time Aston started nursery school, we'd closed the shop and arranged our lives so that Keith, now my full-time agent as well as my manager, could work much more from home, and one or other of us could pick him up at the end of the day. Six o'clock became our family magic hour, when we all sat round the table together. I was always home to tell Aston a bedtime story, read a poem or sing a song before he went to sleep, just as my parents used to do for me and my brothers and sisters.

'*Rock gently, sailboat, rock us all to sleep . . .*'

I managed to spend more time with Aston by involving him in my work. So, we did regular photographic shoots for parenting magazines, making things together as if we were on *Play School*, with Keith behind the camera.

In fact, I thought I was quite the expert in having babies. I used to show people how to belly dance when you're in labour, and often demonstrated on television. Miriam Stoppard came to our home and we did a programme together about natural birth. I boasted about my four-hour labour. Wasn't I clever? Wasn't I marvellous?

When I started doing Christmas pantos, I agreed to a job only if it was a short run and not too far from home, and if they could find a part for Aston too. Our first panto together was *Puss in Boots* at Camberley Theatre in Surrey. I played Puss and Aston was Baby Puss, a mini version of me. Keith and I would hold his hand in the wings until his cue, and then an actor would take over and they'd walk on stage together. Aston always did his little piece with such confidence. He was a born actor.

Life was good. I felt on top of the world. Miss Wonderful. Everything seemed within my power. I honestly thought I was invincible.

And so, we decided to have another baby.

'Come on, Keith!' I said. 'Let's get pregnant.'

He always complains this was so unromantic! But sure enough, I got pregnant again. *Great*, I thought. *Here we go*. Everything was going to plan.

Long before I was showing in any way, I was about to make a speech in a big hall in a city hotel in Sheffield for the launch of a new children's publishing imprint, called Century Hutchinson, which went on to produce some fantastic giant activity books for pre-schoolers with me.

I went to the ladies' to get myself ready and quickly realized something was wrong. I was bleeding. I was eight or nine weeks pregnant, and nobody knew, and I was losing my baby. What could I do? I finished putting my make-up on and went to the podium and gave my speech. I kept smiling. I went home and cried.

We tried again.

It happened again.

This time I was at the Headland Hotel in Cornwall, in 1986, and again I couldn't go to hospital. I had to rush back to London, because the next day I was filming very early in Columbia Road flower market for a Channel 4 series I was presenting called *A Houseful of Plants*. Again, I had to keep smiling. That morning I put on a face that I thought would hide everything. But I'll never forget the taxi driver who picked me up.

'Hello, Floella!' he said cheerfully. 'How's it going, luv? Now, when are you going to have another baby for that little nipper of yours?'

Poor man. I went mad at him.

'Sorry! Sorry! I should have thought,' he said hastily. 'My sister-in-law's just had a miscarriage too. I know what you're going through.'

Those years were the unhappiest and toughest of my life. I cried a lot. Whenever I saw a pram, I'd look inside at the baby lying there and feel miserable.

But I couldn't give up.

'Come on, Keith,' I said for the third time. He was really suffering too, as would-be dads often do, although they're frequently forgotten. Eventually we managed to get pregnant again. And then he had to go to America for work. My mum and sister Cynthia were away on a weekend trip and Sandra lived in Cornwall. So, I was on my own with Aston when, once again, I began to miscarry.

By this time, I had been to see a wonderful gynaecologist at King's College Hospital called Kypros Nicolaides, who would soon become Professor in Foetal Medicine. He always made me laugh with his outrageous comments.

'How do you expect to get pregnant wearing those?' he said to me at one appointment, looking at the big knickers I had to wear in the studio to keep the radio mic in place.

Kypros told me that I had to have a scan next time it happened. So as soon as I saw blood, I left Aston with a friend and rushed to King's A & E.

The ultrasound operator stared at the screen.

'Are you quite sure about your dates?' he asked.

'Yes, absolutely,' I replied.

181

'There's only a sac here. The embryo hasn't developed, I'm afraid. You're going to abort, so we need to do a D & C and take it all out.'

Heavy-hearted and feeling completely defeated, I nodded.

'Fine, fine,' I said. 'Do whatever you have to do.'

'You'll need to sign this to give your consent for the procedure.'

He gave me the form, which I dutifully signed. Then he slipped another piece of paper in front of me.

'And could you give me your autograph too, because I love you.'

I laughed and said, 'Of course!' And suddenly all the A & E nurses were asking for my autograph too. And then a porter came to take me up to theatre, and as he pushed me along the corridor, he began to sing one of my well-known *Play School* songs:

'*Head, shoulders, knees and toes . . .*'

Those words were the last I remembered before the anaesthetic took effect.

Even before I'd woken up in the ward after the operation, other patients and their visitors quickly recognized me.

'Is that Floella Benjamin over there?'

They came right up to my bed and began to ask for autographs too. I had to lock myself in the loo to escape. The nurses would only let me go home once I'd done a wee. But I could also see the funny side. It was almost like a black comedy, and without that laughter, I might have crumbled. But everything happens for a reason. I had nobody with me, and if I hadn't been laughing, I'd certainly have been crying. Because everyone wanted to see me and I didn't want to be unfair to anyone, I couldn't let myself go. I had to smile and sign away and be my usual warm and friendly self.

Back at home at last, I couldn't cry and upset Aston. So, it was only when Keith and Marmie and my sisters came back that I could finally let it all out and tell them the awful news.

Three miscarriages. Would I ever have another baby? It felt an impossible task, and I found it harder and harder to keep smiling. Except when I went to see Professor Nicolaides.

'Don't wear the big knickers!' Kypros kept telling me. 'Try and get pregnant again.'

Despite how common they were, miscarriages were a completely taboo subject in those days. I proposed making a television programme about pregnancy loss and nobody wanted to know. Even though it affected so many, you simply couldn't talk about it. I found this sad and frustrating.

My miscarriages also made me realize something terribly important about myself, and this was a revelation. I wasn't considering other people's feelings enough. I was caught up in a whirlwind of euphoria. I had become too wrapped up in myself, when I should have understood that, unbeknown to me, my joyful way of expressing myself about motherhood must have unintentionally become a cause of terrible pain to others. All that talk about how easy it was to have a baby must have seemed like bragging. I realized I had to shut up about what a marvellous mother I was. I wanted to apologize to the whole world for my Miss Invincible act, for being overenthusiastic about my pregnancy and Aston's birth. How could I have done that, never thinking about what other women might be going through at the same time? My experience made me conscious that you should never, ever ask a woman when she's going to have a baby. Feel yourself blessed, but never boast about having your children.

I had treated having a baby like making a TV programme or opening a shop – as another challenge to which I could

183

easily rise. How wrong I was. I thought I was a natural winner in all circumstances. It was a painful journey, learning exactly why, for the first time in the life, I hadn't achieved something I'd set my heart on. I had to learn to make a lot of adjustments. I began to fully understand that everything happens for a reason, even if at the time you can't be sure why.

It was like a slap in the face.

Come on, Floella! I told myself. *Who the hell do you think you are?*

Chapter Twenty-two

Every morning I wake up and think, *What can I do to change the world today?* I live and breathe to make a difference.

Being on *Play School* brought home to me the fundamental importance of childhood. I started doing a lot of work for different children's charities, taking part in all kinds of celebrity events to raise money, from running my own junior golf tournament supported by top showbiz golfers to competing in motor races, including around Brands Hatch – although I confess, I hadn't expected to be driving our battered old orange Fiat, complete with roof rack, when I agreed to take part in my very first motor rally. We had just sold our sporty Triumph Dolomite Sprint to help with the down payment on our house, which Keith was doing up. Others were driving Bentleys, Rolls-Royces and gorgeous classic cars. The crowds pointed in amazement at my rusty wreck.

As my profile grew and grew, I got more letters than ever. Many of these contained terrible, heartbreaking stories of suffering and abuse, and it was clear to me that children were always at the bottom of the heap. Nobody was looking out for children, especially during their early foundation years. Nobody was speaking up for them. How could I change that?

I was convinced that one thing that would make all the

difference in the world would be to have someone in government whose specific job it was to look out for and speak out for children. Their needs were consistently being overlooked, along with the needs of parents and carers looking after them, which in the 1980s was mostly mothers. This seemed to me to be the sign of a country that wasn't taking care of its future, and a system of government with very short-term ambitions and priorities.

All government policy should have in mind both children and their parents, whether they work inside or outside the home, and childminders, teachers and teaching assistants in schools and nurseries all need to be considered too. Teaching and childcare should be regarded as vocations of dedication and value, and paid a proper wage. Educating and caring for children is the most important job in the world, and needs respect and reward. A nursery school teacher is just as important as a university lecturer. Equally, parents who stay at home should never be dismissed as 'just housewives'. I strongly believed that a cabinet-level Minister for Children could ensure not just that children were taken into consideration during the development of policy, but that their needs would also be properly funded.

Of course, by then I was a mother myself, so I had an even better understanding of the whole picture, but this wasn't my main motivation. I was very lucky to have a supportive husband and an infrastructure in place that allowed me both to work and to spend time caring for Aston. My ambition has always been to change the world to help other people. Since I had a platform and opportunity to speak out, I felt I had a duty and responsibility to use my new-found power.

The first time I wrote to the government requesting a cabinet-level Minister for Children was in 1983. There was no interest, but I managed to have a conversation with Virginia Bottomley about it when she was Secretary of State for

National Heritage under John Major from 1995 to 1997, and after that Joan Ruddock took up the baton, and fought hard to make it happen. Change starts with conversations. I knew Virginia Bottomley was receptive to thinking about children and their well-being because of her work on after-school classes in Brixton. In fact, in the late eighties, when I was campaigning to get seat belts on school buses, her husband Peter Bottomley, then Minister for Transport, was helpful too. I've always found it useful to have supportive people in government to write to so that we can discuss the issues I care about. With every change of government and every change of cabinet, I kept on writing about a Minister for Children. For years I was fobbed off. It was always the same: a brilliant idea, yes, but unfortunately there just wasn't the money to create a whole new government department. But I didn't give up.

When you put children first, you're thinking about making things better in the long term, not the short term. I was going into a lot of different state schools during this time, and I could see how badly things were falling apart. The whole education system seemed to be caving in, and the status of teachers was changing dramatically. So, I was extremely concerned in the early 1980s that, as a country, we were getting our priorities wrong.

Change takes time. The important thing is never to let your determination waver. If you stay resilient and don't abandon hope, it will happen in the end. I learned that when I was young, when Marmie insisted I face every adversity. Whether campaigning for seat belts or diversity in books, on screen, on stamps or art for children, or Windrush Day, or a Minister for Children, my childhood habits have kept me steadfast. By habit and training, I'm a long-term thinker.

Stay there. Dig deep. Never give up.

*

But, just occasionally, you have to admit defeat, and move on. Then you simply have to believe, as Marmie did, that everything happens for a reason.

When Cynthia Felgate told me that the powers-that-be had decided to axe *Play School*, I was completely stunned. I simply couldn't believe it. I had worked on the programme for over eleven years by then. There would be a new programme for pre-schoolers, I learned. Something fresh and different with new presenters. But to me, it was like taking away the ABC. How can you redesign the alphabet? I felt that *Play School* was a programme so perfectly fit for purpose that it couldn't be improved. Over the years, it had evolved, with new graphics and theme songs, and by 1987 the clock had gone digital. At the same time, *Play School* was embracing a much more diverse range of presenters and directors who had a variety of approaches. Of course, the programme could keep changing. It could be fit for the twenty-first century. Why throw the baby out with the bathwater? Why reinvent the wheel?

Naturally, I spoke out. Since I was already campaigning for a Minister for Children, I started using every interview I did to make my case about *Play School* too. I talked about how sad I was, how well loved the programme was, what a treasure we had in it. I'd been doing lots of other programmes and actually appeared very little on *Play School* that year, so I certainly wasn't concerned about my own income, but I worried that the BBC bosses weren't putting children first. Thousands stood to lose that safe, familiar space which had made them happy for so long. I was anxious the disruption would be detrimental to the viewers' well-being. *Play School* was a haven, even for older children, who were comforted by it after a hard day at school. It was a constant in their lives that allowed them to embrace their emotions.

The newspapers quickly picked up on my campaign. Soon the whole nation began to ask the same question:

'Why are you taking off *Play School*?'

Letters from the public began to pour into the BBC.

'Oh Floella! Our room is full to the ceiling,' one of the young women in the *Play School* office told me. Big, grey mail sacks were piled up high. The country simply couldn't understand the BBC's decision. So many millions of children had already learned the fundamental elements of education thanks to *Play School*, in a way which would last a lifetime. It seemed almost a crime to take away a programme which had revolutionized children's television. So, I took every chance I could to raise the issue, and gather support from the public, in the hope the BBC would change its policy. I soon discovered, though indirectly, that the BBC didn't like this at all.

I had always had a fantastic relationship with Cynthia Felgate. I trusted her completely because I knew she believed in me. She was the kind of person who was always looking out for opportunities for all her junior colleagues to stretch themselves, and had a truly wonderful way of building people's confidence. She had already encouraged me to spread my wings in other ways and try things I'd never done before, or even dreamed of doing. So, it was thanks to Cynthia that I'd begun to write children's books. As I said, since I couldn't find enough published material with diverse characters, we'd decided to create our own. The first such stories I wrote to tell on *Play School* were about the little boy called Jason who lived in Trinidad. Soon some of these were published by BBC Books, and before long I was writing all kinds of books for children: stories like the ones Dardie used to tell us, folk tales from around the world, animal stories, a book about a boy in a children's home, a joke book, a book about making things from old stuff people usually throw away. Cynthia also got me to write songs and sketches for my new BBC programme called *Lay on Five*, which started in 1985. As its star, I was the first Black person to feature in the animated opening titles of a children's show.

There had been a significant moment in 1984 when I'd been so upset about being cut out of the opening title sequence for *Play Away* that I nearly walked out of children's television altogether. But when I threatened to quit, Cynthia came to my dressing room and told me in no uncertain terms to stop crying, put on my make-up and get on with it. I'll always be grateful for that piece of advice.

'How dare you be so selfish?' she said to me then. 'You're doing this for the nation, for millions of children, not for yourself.'

There are times to speak out and times when you have to swallow your pride, and live to fight another day. I often wonder what my life would be like today if I'd quit children's programmes then. I didn't seek fame; it found me!

I imagined Cynthia would support my efforts to save the programme we both loved. But I was wrong. Cynthia warned me that higher powers in the BBC wanted me to shut up. My campaign to stop *Play School* from being axed was making me very unpopular with the bosses.

'They'd rather you didn't keep standing up for *Play School*,' she told me. 'It's not going to help your career.' We were very close and she was trying to look after my back. She tried to reassure me that they would do their very best to make sure children's needs were properly met by whatever programme replaced *Play School*. I had to trust her.

After twenty-four glorious years, *Play School* went off the air in 1988. I recorded my last ever week's programmes for broadcast on New Year's Day with Nick Mercer. The programme's successor was called *Playbus*, and then renamed

Playdays after about a year, and it ran until 1997. But it never achieved the same iconic status, or is remembered today as fondly as *Play School*.

Little did I guess what was going on behind the scenes at the BBC.

Chapter Twenty-three

'I'd love to become a television producer,' I'd said one day to one of the BBC producers, some time before *Play School* was axed. Her response was crushing.

'Oh Floella, you've got to be terribly, terribly clever to be a producer.'

So, she clearly thought *I* wasn't clever enough.

I could have been completely deflated. But Cynthia's great faith in me ensured that I didn't give up my producing ambitions.

In the autumn of 1987, when *Play School*'s fate was clear, I met a woman called Rosemary Shepherd one evening at a party and realized she was the commissioning editor of children's programmes at Channel 4. So, I said the same thing to her:

'I'd love to become a television producer.'

'Well, why don't you come and show me your ideas,' she said warmly.

Channel 4 was then the baby of the media world, launched in November 1982 with commercial funding, but effectively publicly owned. The first 'publisher-broadcaster' with all content made by independent producers, it was set up specifically to provide programming for minority interest groups. So, diversity was part of its remit, and they were always looking for different ways of doing things.

This is easy, I thought. In the car on the way home, Keith and I discussed what we might do.

'How about a programme centred round a tree?' he said. 'A talking tree, who interacts with real children?'

'And a treehouse?'

'Yes, good idea, and in the root of the tree there's a gnome.'

'Great. Let's call him Tommy.' We began bouncing ideas, and the next day Aston joined in.

'Tommy can make things, like the *Elves and the Shoemaker*.'

'And Floella invites children into the treehouse, and with the talking tree you do songs and stories.'

'And we can get guest storytellers who come in and tell a story or sing a song or play some music. We can have a piano and a guitar.'

We went to see Rosemary a few days later and talked her though our proposal, which we called *Treehouse*.

'Sensational!' she said. 'I'll have thirteen episodes.'

What? Keith and I had to stop ourselves from laughing out loud. We didn't even have a production company, yet Channel 4 wanted us to make their flagship pre-school programme.

'Go and see Godfrey, and he'll get the contracts done and tell you what you have to do next.'

Rosemary sent us off to another department. And that was it. We were given a total budget of about a quarter of a million pounds. We rushed off to Companies House that very afternoon and bought an off-the-shelf limited company for a hundred pounds. It was called Crystalrowe. As we were so new to the game, Channel 4 gave us a production manager, called Sally, who drew up the budgets and payment schedules, and sensibly included a huge contingency. I watched over her shoulder, getting her to explain every column and category, how everything worked and was cross-referenced, so that I could learn all about every detail and completely understand the infrastructure of programme-making. Although I was completely confident about the content of our series, at this point I had no experience of what needed to be done behind the scenes, and Sally really taught me the ropes on the business side of things: cashflows, logs, who had to pay what. It reminded me of my banking days from twenty years before. I also learned an enormous amount from the people at Hillside Studios in Bushey, where we filmed and edited *Treehouse*. Sally seemed to be spending money like water on production. I couldn't help feeling I'd be able to keep costs much lower if I were in charge.

At last we were ready to go into the studio. The multi-talented puppeteer Nigel Plaskitt was our 'Mr Tree'. I had a whole string of famous guest artists lined up, including Rudi Walker, Linda Bellingham, Rick Wakeman and Smiley Culture (David Emmanuel). We were really happy with the scripts and the set.

And then I discovered I was pregnant again.

We had just been in Hong Kong to see my sister Cynthia and her family, who lived there, and I told Keith I was feeling a bit sick. I couldn't stomach the delicious Chinese food at all. As soon as we were back in London, I went to see Kypros and he scanned me.

'Look! There it is. The foetus in the sac.'

For the next six months I'd go to see Kypros every single Friday without fail on my way back from Birmingham, where I recorded *Daytime Live*. He got me through that pregnancy in every way – mentally, emotionally, medically – and I owe him the world. I was thirty-eight by then, so even without the previous miscarriages, my age meant that this was officially a high-risk pregnancy. I had to have special blood tests to check for abnormalities, and, at my request, Kypros sang a particular song down the phone to give me my result so that I'd know everything was fine: '*Congratulations . . . and jubilations!*'

It could not have been a busier time. We had two offices in upstairs rooms in our house, which we'd started to call The Factory, since every room was always such a hive of activity. Everything seemed to be going swimmingly.

Then out of the blue, in April 1988, the phone rang. It was Rosemary Shepherd and she wasn't happy. Michael Grade had controversially taken over as chief executive of Channel 4 earlier that year. He was a well-known axeman, and as BBC 1 Controller, he'd postponed *Dr Who* before its ultimate cancellation and threatened to take off *Dallas*. Rosemary was calling with news of Grade's plans for his new broadcasting empire.

'Michael Grade wants to cut all children's programmes, including yours. There's a meeting this morning. I'll call you at three.'

'Tell Michael from me he can't do this!' I wailed. 'Tell him I've got all these top stars ready to start filming. Tell him everything's lined up.'

I knew Michael was a man who listened to reason.

'Don't worry, Floella,' said Rosemary. 'You won't be out of pocket. We'll reimburse all the money you've spent so far.'

'That's not the point! I want to make these programmes!'

Already desperately nervous about my fragile pregnancy, I lay on the floor of our small office, praying. *Please don't do this to me. Please don't let this happen.* With *Play School* coming to an end when I'd felt at the height of my career, I was desperate to make my mark elsewhere and establish myself as central to children's programming. I couldn't go back to the BBC, where *Playdays* was already running. ITV's regional channels made all their programmes in-house. As an independent producer, where else could I go? But I had to stay calm. I couldn't let myself get upset as I was afraid the stress would bring on another miscarriage. *Breathe, Floella*, I told myself firmly. I lay there quietly, anxiously waiting, until Rosemary finally called me back.

'It's OK. Michael says you can go on making this show. But this will be the very last children's programme for Channel 4.'

I'll never forget the relief I felt at that moment. Thirty years would pass before I finally got Channel 4 producing kids' programmes again by persuading the government to change the legislation.

I put my heart and soul into *Treehouse*. The rules for child performers are very strict. We recorded two shows a day, using one set of children in the morning, and another in the afternoon, all with chaperones, from a well-known stage school in Acton called Barbara Speake. We had to keep their education going all the while. One morning we had a terribly pretty little girl to work with, with blonde Shirley-Temple-style curls, but she was being chaperoned by her mother, who kept giving her endless drinks of Coca-Cola, and nothing but chocolate to eat. I couldn't believe it, but it was hard to intervene when it was her own mum. The unions were also very strict, so it was impossible to overrun. We had until one p.m. on the dot, and it was five to as I said my final goodbyes, sitting with Mr Tree, surrounded by six small children.

'Hope you've enjoyed the show, everyone! See you next time!'

I was wearing a baggy pale-yellow jumpsuit, with zips all over it, nicely hiding my bump, since I didn't want anyone to know I was pregnant until I was safely past six months. The sweet-toothed little blonde girl was sitting right beside me, and though I couldn't see how green she'd gone, I felt her trembling on my leg, and immediately guessed what was about to happen. I had no choice. There was no time for another take, and I had to preserve my outfit at all costs. We had another programme to record that afternoon. Still talking, still smiling, I stuck out my cupped hands.

'Bye-bye!' I said to the camera calmly.

Just out of shot, my hand filled up with revolting, warm, dark vomit, brown with chocolate. Your own child's sick is bad enough, and any sick at all can be a challenge when you're pregnant. But I'm a professional. The programme was in the bag, and that was all that mattered.

Chapter Twenty-four

Everything in our family seems to happen in September.

My pregnancy anxiety was never-ending. For months I nervously counted the days, crossing everything I could, longing to get to the time when I knew that even if premature, my baby could still survive. Visibly pregnant, I was presenting a second series of A Houseful of Plants, with Plant Doctor Chris Fairweather. When August arrived, I tried even harder to hang on, worried about having a child who might be the youngest in the class.

By then, an ultrasound had revealed I was having a girl. Six-and-a-half-year-old Aston chose the name Alvina for our baby, but he called her Vinny, and he used to rub my tummy and chat to her. When 1 September dawned, Aston and I danced together wildly.

'Any day now, Aston!' I told him. 'Any day now, she'll be here.'

We had planned everything. It was still the summer holidays, so he was going to go to Marmie's as soon as my contractions started.

At 1.30, Sesame Street was on, and I went upstairs with a lunch tray, so I could eat while resting in bed. Halfway up the stairs I stopped, and called out to Keith.

'The baby's coming!'

My waters had broken.

Keith quickly rang my mum to tell her he was on his way to Beckenham with Aston.

'No, you don't! You get her straight to hospital! Call for an ambulance right away!' she told him.

So, Keith did just that and our neighbours looked after Aston instead. We had a hole in the fence at the end of our garden which led to theirs, and their two daughters, Spud and Sprout, were as excited about my baby as Aston was. Six-year-old Sprout burst into the room and gasped at the size of my belly when she caught me in bra and knickers as I was changing in our bedroom. I was dancing and singing around the room. I hoped the sight of me hadn't put her off for life.

Then the doorbell rang and a paramedic stood on the doorstep in surgical gloves.

'I'm going to deliver your baby, Floella Benjamin!' he announced triumphantly.

'No! Get off me!' I said, horrified. 'Take me to the hospital.'

I spent that ambulance journey screaming for gas and air.

'If my children could see you now . . .' joked the paramedic.

They took me to A & E in King's, and examined me.

'Crumbs!' I heard. 'The baby's nearly here.' Once again, they wanted to deliver me then and there.

'No! Take me upstairs. Please take me to the maternity ward. I don't want to have my baby here!'

Another mad journey, with me lying on the trolley while we went crashing at top speed through all the swinging doors, while Keith tried to video the scene, and keep hold of my bag, and not get knocked over. One of my jelly shoes flew off my feet, and I yelled at him to grab it. Into the big lift we went, and still I was calling out for gas and air.

Too late for that. I just registered the number of the door they wheeled me into.

'Number five! My lucky number!' I cried out.

All the advice I'd given in the past on the BBC, advising others how to deliver their babies with dignity, breathing calmly, belly dancing, how to take control and enjoy your labour . . . every single one of those wise words went right out of the window.

I remember the voice of an Irish midwife in my ear urging me to push. And my own pathetic voice feebly responding:

'How do you push?'

'Down. Think down.'

I pushed with all my might and out my baby suddenly popped. I waited for that first cry and all I heard was silence. Little Alvina was covered with meconium and couldn't breathe.

'Get me a suction machine!'

The first wasn't working. They tried another, but that failed too.

'Get me an effing machine that works!' yelled the paediatrician.

Everyone was rushing around, so it was Keith who ended up plugging the third machine into the wall. I could just see a tiny leg moving. 'Kicker' had been our daughter's name in the womb. *Keep kicking*, I thought. It meant she was alive.

I heard the shlooshing suck of the machine clearing my baby's airways, and then at last, at last, a thin cry.

'Waaehhhhhh! Waaaeehhhhh!'

It was going to be all right. It was exactly one hour and twenty minutes since my waters had broken on the staircase. I was a wreck.

Two days later, Alvina was diagnosed with newborn jaundice and had to go into a big plastic incubator, with special blue lights, and they monitored her bilirubin levels. The streams of family visitors had left, and I was lying in my bed exhausted, trying to get some rest, when I was woken around midnight by a repetitive thudding sound coming from the other side of our small side room. Thunk. Thunk. Thunk. Alvina was kicking as usual. Except this time, I saw she was hanging half out of the incubator, on the point of falling to the hard lino floor. A rather grumpy nurse, who seemed to have taken a dislike to me, had somehow failed to close the side panel properly.

I don't know how my treasured baby got there and I don't know where I got the power, but I was across the room in a flash.

Whoosh! She was in my outstretched hands, and I put her safely back and locked the panel.

I'll never forget standing there beside that incubator while a pure, cool sensation flowed through my body. It was a spiritual feeling of enormous strength.

'Thank you, thank you,' I whispered.

For the second time in my life, I felt something I could hardly describe had rescued me, in the nick of time. A sixth sense. An extraordinary power. A moment of epiphany. I can only describe it as an out-of-body experience, which I recognized purely because the same thing had saved me when I was about to choke that boy with his lollipop, long ago. How different everything could have been if my precious newborn had fallen.

I went calmly back to bed, knowing Alvina was safe, knowing that I was blessed.

We planted a pink rose bush to celebrate her birth.

Not long before Alvina's birth, Aston went through a very difficult phase of refusing to eat. Coming from a food-centred family, I found this extremely stressful. We then discovered that his little sister didn't want to sleep. We were expecting to have another baby as easy as Aston, but Alvina would wake up and demand attention every two hours. So those early months weren't always easy. Granada had just launched *This Morning*, with Richard Madeley and Judy Finnigan, and I was employed as a roving reporter interviewing writers, illustrators and other important people in the book trade about children's literature. There were times when I was so exhausted that I almost fell asleep on the job; I actually drifted off on camera in a warm conservatory in the middle of one interview with a publisher who had a particularly monotonous voice.

There was no danger of that happening when I went to Great Missenden to interview Roald Dahl for the same programme. I knew from his daughter Tessa, a fellow actress, how impatient the great writer could be, so when it came to filming the 'noddy shots' after I'd finished my interview with him, showing his reactions, I decided there was one sure-fire way to keep his attention.

'You know, Mr Dahl, you can always spot those people who don't do a big job in the morning when they get up,' I began. Maybe I'd been changing too many nappies recently. And then I was off. 'You go into a lift, and you see them with their shoulders all hunched, looking so uncomfortable. But I find when you flush it all out first thing in the morning, you feel you can cope with anything, don't you? You feel good for the rest of the day. But you do need the right throne to sit on. Without the right seat, you can't give a good performance. Isn't it awful how filthy some public toilets are? At least in America, you get those paper covers now. But I must say, Mr Dahl, your toilet seat is wonderful. So comfortable, and the mahogany so regal. You can really settle down. How I wish more people would do that! The world would be a much better place—'

'I think we've got enough!' The producer broke my flow, but Roald Dahl just leaned forward and said:

'My dear, you're a woman after my own heart. I take linseed every morning to make sure I can go properly. Why don't you come into the kitchen and we can have some linseed together? I could talk to you all day!'

Sadly I couldn't stay as I had to move on to my next interview.

Another memorable interview assignment I had was when in 1988 the producer of *BBC Daytime Live,* Steve Weddle, asked me to go to Belfast to present an item for the show in the height of the Troubles, when bombs went off daily. While I was there I was taken down the dangerous Falls Road. I interviewed Catholics, Protestants and the peace women, who all said, 'You understand, don't you, Floella?' I found the people warm and receptive and they thanked me for coming to their country when others stayed away. I wished I could truly bring them together. But one thing they all told me was that their children loved watching me on *Play School*. In those times of terrible anxiety and fear, the programme was a point of light for children.

Before long Keith and I were working on a new children's series called *Playabout*, for British Satellite Broadcasting, known as BSB. Until satellite channels shook up broadcasting in the late 1980s, viewers had had a choice of only four channels: BBC1, BBC2, ITV and Channel 4. As BSB and Rupert Murdoch's Sky competed for pay-television supremacy, square and round dishes sprang up like mushrooms on individual properties and housing estates alike. Sky's multichannel service was unashamedly populist, while BSB aimed for higher-quality programming and picture quality.

After the success of *Treehouse*, a Channel 4 children's producer who'd moved to BSB in 1989 declared that our production company, which we later renamed Floella Benjamin Productions, was the only one they'd use for pre-school programmes, and commissioned sixty-five episodes of *Playabout* from us. At that time, a number of producers who'd previously worked for the BBC moved across to the new satellite station, and I began to hear the same story from them: at the Beeb they had tried to put me forward as a presenter of a new programme, and even if the proposal went through, my name was always rejected. My popular programme *Lay on Five* was not re-commissioned.

The worst moment came in 1989 after I had been working for some time on an idea for a drama called *The Golden Thread*, which told the story of *Windrush* through several generations of one family. The characters in this family saga arrived in Britain as children and then went into politics and property development and theatre. Dardie had helped me map out the whole story, in conversations which went on for hours. We were very excited, and the head of BBC Drama was very excited too. There had been nothing like it on television before, and the *Windrush* experience had never been explored in fiction from the perspective of a single family either. The treatment was finished, and six episodes were mapped out and we were just waiting for the green light for the actual commission. We knew the series would need an experienced and knowledgeable writer, and so we had lined up Mike Phillips, who, with his brother Trevor Phillips, went on to write the 1998 book *Windrush: The Irresistible Rise of Multi-Racial Britain*, to go with the thirtieth anniversary BBC TV documentary series.

I was at Hillside Studios working on *Playabout* when a call came from the drama producer we were working with.

'What is it?' I asked, anxiously. She was in tears, and could hardly speak.

'I'm really sorry, Floella, but I've got bad news. The BBC don't want to do this drama. The powers-that-be have changed their minds, it seems.'

I was devastated by this latest turnaround. I'd invested so much emotionally in the project, and I just couldn't understand what was going on. I was at the pinnacle of my TV career, yet I kept being invited and then immediately rejected for work by the BBC. Luckily, our production company had built up a good reputation by then and we were never without new commissions from other channels, and I was also constantly busy with charity and other work, even releasing a pop single in 1989, called 'Don't Touch Me'. Keith took the photo for the record cover at midnight as I sat with Alvina on my lap.

Years later I discovered the truth. I'd been presenting the ITV travel show *Wish You Were Here*, enjoying visiting Spain and Vienna and cruising from Florida to the Caribbean. Soon afterwards, one of the producers went freelance, and then asked me if I'd like to present a new series she was proposing to the BBC, but was told by the commissioners that she couldn't use me. This time, I decided I had to find out why the same thing kept happening, and asked her if she could help. She enquired, discreetly, and I was shocked but in some ways unsurprised by what she reported back. On my BBC file, there was a note saying I could no longer be used as a presenter. Without knowing, without any right of reply, I had been accused of promoting commercial products on a BBC programme. Of course, this was just an excuse, and certainly wasn't true. I believe that this was actually a punishment for speaking my mind about the axing of *Play School*.

Completely ignorant of any of this in the late 1980s, my many setbacks had made me wonder if I'd ever work for the BBC again. I was also shocked to learn that the BBC was apparently trying to sell the new satellite company the entire *Play School* archive for rebroadcasting, along with all their other pre-school programmes.

'They want BSB to buy their back catalogue, you know,' I

was told in confidence. And then they jumped to a conclusion I hadn't considered. 'I think the BBC might be trying to put us off employing you. Maybe they don't want you to provide our children's programmes?'

I had no proof but, rightly or wrongly, I began to think that there were certain individuals at the BBC who were trying to stop me from working *anywhere* ever again. But, of course, this only made me more determined, and fortunately my reputation and track record spoke for me. *Playabout* went into production in 1990.

I am an avid supporter of the BBC, always promoting the corporation on many levels to help make change, and I will be for ever grateful to the BBC, as it gave me a platform to reach the world. But large institutions are often infiltrated by unethical individuals who use their power to harm others and influence the corporate culture in a counterproductive way, which seeps into the core of the organization.

In the end I think Marmie was more outraged and upset about the rumours of unfair treatment I might be receiving from those within the BBC than I was. She never stopped fighting to protect her children. So after nearly twenty years of constant rejections, she convinced me to challenge this injustice and bring it to an end. In 2007, I contacted Mark Thompson, the Director General at the time, and we met at a secret rendezvous, the Royal Commonwealth Club, Northumberland Avenue, where we sat in one of the alcoves, and I felt as if I were in a spy movie. He was appalled when I told him what had been rumoured to be happening and vowed to get his lawyers to uncover the truth and any evidence to support my concerns. They didn't ever find any, but soon afterwards the Controller of BBC Children's offered me a huge job: narrating the animated wildlife series *Mama Mirabelle's Home Movies* and then several episodes on the *Doctor Who* spin-off, *The Sarah Jane*

Adventures, as Professor Rivers. To this day I have no idea whether the rumours were true but in any event hold no resentment or hatred. Instead I smile, especially when I was selected as one of the BBC's 100 faces celebrating their centenary.

By prioritizing speed over quality, Sky won the race to be the first satellite broadcaster on air in the UK, launching, as Murdoch himself put it, on 'a wing and a prayer' in February 1989, in time to run rolling live coverage of both the release of Nelson Mandela and the fall of the Berlin Wall. BSB finally made its broadcasting debut in April 1990, after many delays, and having failed to attract nearly enough subscribers for its infamous 'squarial' dishes.

For BSB, we created a sensational new programme, once again very loosely based on the best aspects of *Play School,* trying to echo that sense of continuity, security and fun for young viewers, with stories, music, movement and 'makes' alongside essential educational elements such as time, numbers, letters, colours and shapes.

Our children continued to be involved in our work as much as possible, so we were never away from them for long. Aston did the voiceover for the titles, and helped me write stories and act them out. We were both encouraged in this by Aston's teacher Pat McLean, who became a lifelong friend. She knew I always dreamed of being a bridesmaid, so asked me to be maid of honour at her wedding to her soulmate Nick Tumber. Aston appeared in the programmes we recorded during his school holidays. Alvina, who was called Kitty by all the family because she still kicked and scratched like a little kitten whenever you tried to change her nappy, came to the studio in Bushey with our live-in nanny when she was tiny. Like me, she was an early talker and walker, and also joined in with the filming herself as soon as she could – not always happily, because she was so protective of me. When we were recording one show, one of the stage school children had to slap a cream pie into my face as the finale to a story called *The Queen Who Lost Her Laugh*. Alvina instantly burst into tears.

'Leave my mummy alone!' she cried.

In *Playabout*, ten or so different presenters, including me, Bobby Gee from Buck's Fizz and Don Gilet, appeared with two puppets called Grandma and Grandad who lived in a grandfather clock. We wanted to encourage children to look up to their grandparents and see older people in a respectful way, so the presenters were always asking questions and seeking help from the puppets. Luckily, Grandad knew everything, and enjoyed meeting the guests!

Having learned the ropes so carefully while we were making *Treehouse*, including the importance of a contingency budget, I was able to take on the role of production manager myself on *Playabout*. The first sixty-five episodes of *Playabout* went down a storm, and when I delivered the paperwork to Louise Chick, the BSB cost controller at Marco Polo House, the company's glamorous post-modern headquarters beside Battersea Power Station, she was amazed and impressed by the fact that we'd come in ten thousand pounds under the production budget.

'Absolutely incredible!' Louise told me. 'This has never happened before. You keep half, and we'll keep the other half.'

We were away. BSB immediately commissioned another sixty-five programmes, and from that day on, Louise paid any bill I sent in right away, including the production fee, so we were never out of pocket for long. There was even talk of a five-year *Playabout* contract.

Life was good. As a mother, as a presenter, as a producer and as a campaigner, I felt the new decade was getting off to a very good start.

PART 3

WHEN ONE
DOOR CLOSES
ANOTHER OPENS

Chapter Twenty-five

Unbeknown to me, one of my most important guardian angels watched over me for some time before entering my life and changing it for ever. This was someone who would one day become almost as important to me as my own mother; a true role model and mentor.

Thanks to *Play School*, I used to get sackfuls of correspondence sent on from the BBC every week, messages of admiration and requests for support for all kinds of different causes, mostly connected with children. Piles of letters continued to drop through the letter box each morning. Replying carefully to every single one, I gave everything I could, appearing at events, endorsing campaigns, agreeing to be patron or president of the charities dearest to my heart, giving out prizes and awards, drawing raffle tickets, making speeches and visiting playgroups, nurseries, schools, children's centres and prisons.

But one regular correspondent stood out. Handwritten with a fountain pen and slightly hard to decipher, these letters took a surprisingly familiar and affectionate tone:

My dear Flo . . . they usually began. And they always ended very simply: *love Tony.*

I was constantly intrigued. The writer let me know how much they liked me on *Play School* and what a difference I was making to children's lives and thanked me for whatever I had just done, whether it was demanding a Minister for Children, calling for higher pay for teachers, publishing a book or making a programme.

Keith and I used to joke about an SAS man who'd once written to tell me how much he loved me, saying he wanted to take me away, and we always half wondered if he might one day descend from a helicopter, come flying through the window and whisk me off. But this 'Tony' struck me as a different kind of admirer altogether. Who could he be?

Meanwhile, I had developed a way to sum up my approach to life: I called this 'my three Cs', which I practise every day.

The trauma of multiple miscarriages had helped me focus on the first of these: Consideration. Nothing is more important than having empathy for other people. And putting yourself in another person's shoes. It's so important not to be judgemental, especially when you don't know anything about the person.

The second 'C' that guides my life is Contentment. To be happy with what you have at that given time and not to do anything to get what you want. What's right for you will come in time, so be satisfied. That's a really hard 'C' to practise.

Finally, 'Confidence' to look in the mirror every day and to like the person looking back at you. To live your life as a decent human being because if you are happy with yourself it's easy to have high self-esteem. So give and love unconditionally: the more you give, the more comes back to you when you least expect it.

Of course, all three of these Cs take courage: the moral courage to stand up for truth, equality and for justice. Never be afraid of the future or let the past hold you back.

The three Cs and a big smile had helped me so much all through life, and I wanted to share my philosophy with others, using all the expanding opportunities that were coming my way.

As I took on more and more voluntary and public sector work, my reputation as a person who got things done grew and grew, and my public profile steadily rose. I found it hard to say 'no' to any charity, and I always like a challenge, so I was extremely busy – and all the while continuing to make children's programmes, and be a good mother to Aston and Alvina. At that time I was working particularly closely with the National Children's Home, a charity created to help vulnerable children and young people and their families, now called Action for Children, the Showbiz Car Club (fundraising for Mencap), Sparks, the children's medical research charity which has now merged with the Great Ormond Street Hospital, and also the Sickle Cell Society, which raises awareness of an inherited blood disorder, mainly affecting Afro-Caribbean people.

Then one day in 1984, the mysterious Tony wrote to invite me to the prestigious Women of the Year Lunch, an annual charity event to recognize and celebrate women's achievements. In those days, it was always shown live on television.

I turned up at The Savoy Hotel, full of curiosity. What would this Tony be like? A vision in black and white greeted me enthusiastically:

'Darling Flo!'

At last the penny dropped. My Tony wasn't a man, but a woman: Antonella Kerr, Lady Lothian, a rebellious marchioness. Her jet-black hair, white blouse, black waistcoat and a piratical black eyepatch were her uniform.

'Darling Flo! The Pied Piper of the nation! That's how I think of you because I know children would follow you anywhere you went.' And she turned to the other guests nearby. 'Look, everyone! Flo has arrived!'

Tony made me feel as if I could fly. She greeted me so warmly, and made me feel so comfortable that it gave me the sense that I had earned my place there. Yet, to be thrown into this world was one of the biggest excitements of my career. I felt an instant connection with Tony. She loved children too, and wanted to make the world a better place for them, and she had seen how much her own six children and her many grand-children loved watching me on television. Although she moved in the highest echelons of society, and her husband was one of the most titled men in the British aristocracy, Tony herself had no airs or graces at all. Always a champion of the underdog, she used her establishment contacts to promote equality and justice wherever she could. Tony embraced me into her fold with such unconditional love that I identified her immediately as a guiding and protective spirit. It was as if we were long-lost friends; true soulmates.

'Every woman who is here is a Woman of the Year,' she used to say. We weren't competing against each other for the title; we were working together to make sure all women were valued, up and down the land. Tony had decided to create the WOTY Lunch after realizing how much the achievements of powerful men depended on informal networking opportunities from which women were largely excluded. She wanted to support those 'special' women who she believed 'made the world go round'. She defied naysayers who told her she'd never find five hundred extraordinary women who met her criteria of success. The organization she founded in 1955, before life peer-ages could be conferred on women and when female hereditary peers were not allowed to sit in the House of Lords, is still going from strength to strength.

Five hundred women talking and laughing excitedly, getting to know one another in the dining room of The Savoy: we made a deafening sound. I felt honoured and awed to be among so many familiar faces I recognized from television and news-papers, many wearing elaborate hats. You never knew who you might sit next to or rub shoulders with at these gatherings. The room was like a 'who's who' from every corner of society. That day I lunched with Olympic gold medallist Tessa Sanderson, the artist Bridget Riley, the astronomer Heather Couper and my own cousin, Joan Armatrading. The Duchess of Kent was the royal guest of honour. I met people I'd never heard of, women from all walks of life and from across the political spectrum whose passion and determination were bringing great changes to the world.

The theme of the day was 'How to be First' and our panel of guest speakers was equally eclectic: the Right Honourable Dame Mary Donaldson, the first female Lord Mayor of London in eight hundred years; Brenda Dean, the first woman ever elected to head a major industrial trade union in the UK; the bestselling author Lady Antonia Fraser; and, most memorably, Valentina Tereshkova, the Russian cosmonaut who became the first woman in space in June 1963, in *Vostok 6*, and remains the only woman in the world who's ever flown a solo mission. I later discovered it had been Mikki Doyle, the Women's Editor of the *Morning Star*, and a founder of Women in Media, who introduced Tony to Valentina. The daughter of a tractor driver, she was a machinist in a textile factory and an amateur sky-diver in her mid-twenties when she offered her services in the space race to the Supreme Soviet. Eleven years after being selected for this groundbreaking mission, she became a politician, a member of the Presidium.

Her call sign on that mission was 'Seagull' – *Chaika*. Through her interpreter, she told the women gathered at The Savoy of the wonder of seeing Earth from space, 'like a beautiful jewel', and how this had made her determined to protect it from destruction. Valentina made herself an expert on ecological problems, and began to put all her energies into her work as an ambassador for world peace. When you look down on our fragile planet from such a distance, it gives you perspective, she explained. You can see that as human beings, and particularly as women, we are as one. We need to unite to preserve in peace the miracle that is our planet. I wonder how she's feeling in 2022 as Russia invades Ukraine.

That first lunch with Tony set the pattern for the future. Time and again, she introduced me to people – the good and the great – in a way which made me feel very special, and set the tone for how I would be received by others. Often, I could hardly believe she was talking about me.

'Now you must meet this very important person, Floella Benjamin . . .' she'd begin.

I felt quite humble. Nobody had ever spoken about me like this. She offered me a seat at the table, and I sat down with her gladly.

Liking my spirit, she soon took me under her wing. Tony had a strong relationship and religious bond with the widow of Martin Luther King Jr, Coretta King, who was a speaker at the lunch in 1986. She was a softly spoken, beautiful woman who continued to spread the message of peaceful change. When Tony absorbed me into their circle of friendship, I told Coretta what a great influence her husband had been on my family's life, and that this would stay with me for ever.

Tony was one of the few people in the world who completely understood Keith, and could see his brilliance and magnificence. I introduced her to Marmie and they loved each other too. Before long, I was happily describing Tony as my second mum, and we spoke on the phone almost daily for decades. Tony encouraged me to join the organizing committee of the Women of the Year Lunch. Then she put me in charge of arranging the speakers at the annual lunch. Within five years, she'd decided I'd make a good deputy chair.

Suddenly, thanks to Tony, I'd been thrown into an exciting

new world of eminent and influential people. Other people may have been secretly looking at me and thinking, *What's she doing here?* but Tony didn't care. Like Cynthia Felgate, she believed in me, through and through. As a result, she too got me doing things I'd have never dreamed of attempting before. She knew I'd never be afraid to speak my mind or be cowed by critics. Tony gave me the opportunity to discover a whole new side of myself. This would shape the rest of my working life.

One of her big concerns was the effect of artificial additives in food – then usually called 'E numbers' – on children's health. In 1986 Tony launched an event at The Savoy called the Health Festival, which she asked me to help her run. She was way ahead of her time and realized decades ago that what children ate affected their mood, brains and emotions. I also became involved in another organization she'd founded: Valiant for Truth, which celebrated heroes in society who weren't afraid to speak out. Through this, I got to know Marmaduke Hussey, then chair of the BBC. I nominated Roger Cook, one of the earliest investigative journalists, who won the award in 1990.

From my earliest years, my parents had made me see that in order to achieve as a Black person, I'd always have to put 100 per cent effort into everything I did. I don't know what brakes mean. *Vrroooom.* I charge through life with my foot on the accelerator.

Tony loved this quality, and saw immediately that whatever new position or responsibility she might give me, I'd go for it with all my energy. We worked together on many campaigns, and our 'animated discussions' on how best to organize these often went on for so long and could be so heated that Keith sometimes thought we were having a terrible row. But she was so clever and wise that I now sometimes wonder if she didn't deliberately use our battles as a kind of training ground for me, so that I'd have to really think about any decision I ever made, and be completely ready to fight for it and justify it. She taught me to both 'talk the talk' and 'walk the walk'.

So, we'd argue for hours, thrashing out our latest problem, and then at the end of a phone call, I'd always sing to her.

'*Pack up all my cares and woe,*
Here I go, singing low . . .'

'Bye Bye Blackbird' was 'our' song.

Chapter Twenty-six

And that's how I found myself in June 1990 sitting on an Aero-flot plane heading for Russia.

This was the era of Glasnost and Perestroika, and the tide was turning fast. It hadn't been a year since the fall of the Berlin Wall, and it was clear that the Cold War was coming to an end, but nobody knew exactly how this would happen. As the USSR teetered on the brink of break-up, those in the know worried about civil war. Tony was completely convinced that whatever transpired would affect the whole world, and she thought the best way to promote democracy was to reach out the hand of friendship. Tony's old friend Valentina had invited her to bring a select group of influential family and friends to Moscow. In this way, Valentina and Tony hoped to build bridges and demonstrate what cultural riches Moscow had to offer. They called our group 'The Moscow Fellowship'. Two fluent Russian-speakers, Elizabeth Smith of the GB–USSR Association and Sir Fitzroy Maclean, one of the West's top experts on Eastern European politics and culture – and allegedly an inspiration for James Bond – acted as our co-ordinators. Soft diplomacy, at a crucial moment in history. Elizabeth was married to John Smith, then the Shadow Chancellor of the Exchequer, soon to become the leader of the Labour Party.

Keith stayed in London to look after Aston and Alvina as well as oversee our latest production. He was a perfect dad, but it was a shame he couldn't share the Russian experience with me.

As soon as I sat down on the plane, a very fierce flight attendant appeared. She seemed more like a prison guard than an air hostess.

'Miss Benjamin, you come with me,' she ordered.

The other delegates whispered and wondered why I'd been singled out like this. They were a very distinguished bunch: Tony's husband, Peter Kerr, the Twelfth Marquess of Lothian, was a former government minister who'd had significant positions in the Foreign Office and was a delegate to the UN during the Suez Crisis; Barbara Hosking, Director of Yorkshire Television, had been secretary to two prime ministers; Jane Scott, Duchess of Buccleuch, had art conservation expertise and was a former fashion model, and her politician husband then owned the largest private estate in the UK. Their son Richard, then Earl of Dalkeith, was married to Tony's daughter, Elizabeth, known as Bizza. Bizza and Richard were both on the trip, along with Bizza's siblings, Cecil and Ralph and Ralph's spouse Mary Claire. So our number also included a historian, a radio presenter and chair of Scottish ballet, an art dealer and an artist. And then there was me, the 'Pied Piper for Britain's children'.

The air hostess took me to the front of the plane, where about six bigger seats were separated off by a limp grey curtain which didn't even close properly, and she announced:

'I'm told you're an important person so you must sit here.'

'Oh. But what about the rest of my party? Can they come too?'

'No. *You* are important. You sit *here*.'

I realized that my old friend Francis de Souza, who was in charge of VIP customer services at Heathrow, and always took the stress out of flying for me by giving me a special room where I wouldn't be mobbed by fans, must have had a word with Aeroflot. Of course, I refused to leave the others, and went back to sit with them.

When we arrived in Moscow, we were taken to our accommodation at the Academy of Science, a bleak place where the KGB could easily keep tabs on us. Tony said it reminded her of an Edinburgh University hall of residence without the students. But in every other way, our welcome was lavish beyond belief, and what we saw was spectacular.

President Gorbachev was still hanging on to power, trying to keep the Soviet Union together while introducing freedom by degrees. Still from the sidelines at this stage, although within a year he'd be president himself, Boris Yeltsin meanwhile called loudly for a race towards capitalism. There were terrible food shortages, and we saw people queueing for hours in the hope of getting hold of what little there was to buy. There was a dark joke going round about a woman standing in Red Square with an empty shopping bag who couldn't remember if she was going to the shops or coming home again. You could only be sure of buying food in special dollar shops, which ordinary people couldn't use.

Yet we were served caviar from gold platters. We were taken to museums with extraordinary collections of paintings, which, of course, had never been on loan to the West. We were awed by gold coaches encrusted with rubies and emeralds. I remember a room in the Kremlin Armoury full of Fabergé eggs, jewelled imperial gifts. We watched Tchaikovsky's *The Queen of Spades* at the Bolshoi and went backstage after the opera, and we attended the midnight changing of the guard in Red Square under a rippling red flag. Tony was a devout Catholic, and we lit candles in dark incense-filled shrines beneath the blue onion-shaped domes of the Holy Trinity St Sergius

Monastery and Trinity Cathedral at Sergiev Posad (Zagorsk in Soviet times), the spiritual centre of the Russian Orthodox Church. The chanting was hypnotic.

At a cultural festival, I danced on stage with a troupe of fiery dancers in glorious costumes with lambswool hats, shiny black boots and flying red coat tails.

'Oh, you Russians are so talented!' I said, as they taught me the moves.

'We're Georgian!' they said angrily, and my eyes were opened to the range of different cultures within the USSR, and the ferocity with which national identities had been preserved, despite the best efforts of the Communist system. Two years later, one of the bloodiest and least resolved of the many conflicts triggered by the break-up of the Soviet Union erupted: the Georgia–Abkhazia War.

And then our guides – or minders – took us to Star City. In those days, this was like a hidden inner metropolis, unmarked on any maps, a secure zone where the Soviet cosmonauts received their training secretly, under military jurisdiction. We drove through a forest up to the highest gates and fences I'd ever seen in my life, which towered like skyscrapers above our coach. Admitted into another world, as luxurious as Beverly Hills, we were welcomed by Alexei Leonov, the first person in the world ever to walk in space. On 18th March 1965, he beat the US effort by two and a half months, but almost died several times during the mission.

A short bald man with sticking-out ears and an impish smile, Leonov took one look at me and opened his arms for a big hug.

'Blondie!' he said, delightedly, with a misplaced sense of humour. 'Welcome to Moscow!'

Tony gave me her customary build-up whenever she introduced me in Russia. Telling people I'd been a BBC presenter went down well because so many behind the Iron Curtain had learned English from the BBC World Service, listening secretly on shortwave transistor sets.

Tony wanted me to visit a school, of course, where we met seven-year-olds who could quote Shakespeare. They were fascinated by me because they hadn't met any Black people. They had probably never seen anyone before who smiled as much as me.

Smiling wasn't a big thing in Russia. I saw a great deal of pain on my visit.

At one function, I couldn't stop myself from going up to a cloakroom attendant wearing khaki-coloured overalls and a very glum expression so that I could push up the corners of his mouth.

'Come on!' I said. 'Smile! Smile at me.'

His smile was like sunshine. Most of the Russians I met could speak English. They were intrigued that I had no inhibitions about marching up to anyone and asking:

'What's making you unhappy?'

We were never left on our own. It was clear from the clicks on the line that every telephone call had other listeners. I became very disillusioned. My father had talked so often and so positively about the meaning of Communism, and the possibilities of an egalitarian society. But the reality we encountered in Russia was so different, so much less romantic. The difference between the empty shop shelves and potholed roads and the glamour and wealth we were treated to behind closed doors showed me how unfair the system was. I saw the world so differently after that.

On one of our last days, we were walking across Red Square when Tony took my hand, and held it very tightly.

'Floella, I've brought you here for a reason. You've witnessed a part of the world that not many have seen. People will listen to you and they'll follow you. I know you can lead the future for the children. So, remember, don't ever be afraid to speak out if you think things aren't right. You must always speak up for justice and equality.'

And I suddenly realized my true destiny. I was now in a political environment of the kind I'd never imagined being exposed to, even though politics was in my bloodstream. I had to use the power and influence I'd gained to bring progress to the world. I had to live up to Tony's expectations of me.

Back home, I was soon in full swing with our production, and our house, The Factory, was frantically busy. One day the phone rang and our PA, Nadia, picked it up.

'It's the Russian embassy for you, Floella,' she said, with eyebrows raised, cupping her hand over the receiver.

A man who introduced himself as Vladimir told me they had some pictures of me. They wanted me to come to collect them. It was urgent. Keith and I jumped in the car and set off for Kensington Gardens right away.

Security at the Russian embassy was very high. When the gates opened to let out a car, Keith, in his innocence, drove in. All hell broke loose. Alarm bells rang. Forbidding-looking men in uniforms shouted at us furiously:

'What are you doing? Get out! Get out!'

'But we're here to see Vladimir,' I explained. 'He's expecting us.'

Keith was made to wait in the car in the car park, while I went through security. Then they took me inside, and left me in a grand room with green flock wallpaper and huge draped green curtains, with a table by the window. In the middle of the carpet was a chaise longue and a chair. I sat there in silence, alone, for what seemed like for ever, with that strange feeling that I was being watched. Eventually I heard heavy footsteps approaching across a wooden floor, and in came Vladimir. A stern man of about forty-five or fifty, he wore a brown suit and had slicked-back hair over a pear-shaped face with narrow piercing eyes that immediately made me uneasy. In his hands, he carried a set of photographs, but he kept the images out of my sight. What could he possibly know? What on earth could I have done?

'So. Floella Benjamin.' Ominous pause. 'I hear you're an actress.'

The way he said 'actress' didn't sound approving, but I nodded.

'Yes, that's right.'

Where was this going?

'Hmmmm. We know about you "actresses",' he said accusingly.

'Do you?'

I was feeling very uncomfortable by then. What exactly was he insinuating? Later, when I started doing regular prison visits, I'd get a similar feeling on being searched by security – that fear that somehow you'd done something wrong without realizing it, and they'd catch you out.

'Yes, we do. And we have pictures. From Moscow.'

He looked at his hands, and shook the photographs disapprovingly, still keeping them away from my view. My mind was whirring frantically. What incriminating photos could anyone have possibly taken?

'You actresses. We know about you,' he repeated.

Of course, I was dying to see the pictures. I couldn't imagine what they could possibly reveal, but I kept my cool and continued to smile. This was a man who knew how to make his

225

victims sweat. He had the advantage of surprise, but I held my nerve. The last thing I'd expected when summoned to the embassy was to be interrogated.

A final pause, as he eyed me up. And something must have satisfied him, because suddenly he said:

'Here are your pictures!'

I took them politely and made a hasty exit.

Obviously all the photographs he gave me were perfectly innocuous: shots of me dancing, shots of me at Star City, shots of us together in museums. It was all most mysterious, and to this day, I don't know what the whole incident was really about. Maybe the Soviet government simply wanted me to know they were keeping tabs on me. Or did they think they could recruit me as a spy because Tony had told them I had great influence over children? Perhaps I'd been watching too many Bond movies?

A few months later we had a visitor from Russia. On the coach trips, we'd been entertained by a wonderful balalaika group, led by a musician called Sergey. He and his family impressed the Duchess of Buccleuch so much that she invited them to perform at the Edinburgh Festival that August. On the way back from Scotland, Sergey stayed with us in London. I'll never forget his words when we took him to a supermarket in Brixton, a perfectly ordinary one, not especially big. To him, it was like Aladdin's cave. It might have been another planet.

'I wish my mother could be here,' he said, with tears running down his face. 'Look at the food! Everywhere! In Russia we have nothing.'

Sergey joined me on the set of *Playabout*. He took part in one of the very last episodes we ever recorded and played his balalaika.

*

But all was not well in the brave new world of satellite pay-television, where two rival companies, Sky TV and BSB, were still battling it out, struggling with technical problems and massive financial losses while potential customers held back for fear of spending money on equipment that would soon be obsolete. On Friday 2 November 1990, we were in the editing suite at Hillside Studios working on *Playabout* when the *Nine O'Clock News* came on. The newsreader announced the birth of BSkyB, which was billed as a 'merger' between Sky and BSB. In practice, this was a forced takeover by Rupert Murdoch's News Corporation. The new MD was the ruthless Australian TV executive Sam Chisholm.

By Monday morning, there were new security guards outside BSB's headquarters, Marco Polo House, refusing to let BSB's old staff into their offices when they turned up for work. Out of a combined staff of 1,400, more than a third lost their jobs. The treatment of the old BSB team was brutal.

Louise Chick called me right away. There was panic in her voice.

'Floella! Have you got your money?'

'Yes,' I reassured her.

'All of it? All of your production fee?'

'Yes.'

'And have you paid it in yet?'

'Yes, yes, I have.'

'Fantastic,' she said, with relief.

From that moment on, nobody got paid. Relatively speaking, we were the lucky ones. At least we'd finished filming the latest batch of programmes, and we weren't out of pocket like some other production companies. But that was the end of our hopes of a five-year contract, since Murdoch didn't want any children's programmes at all. They weren't profitable enough.

What had Marmie always taught me to do in the face of

disappointment? I could hear her voice, even before I rang to tell her the news.

'You pick yourself up, Floella, and you start again. Remember, every disappointment is an appointment with something better.'

Chapter Twenty-seven

Aston adored Alvina. He treated her like his own perfect treasure and loved to kiss and caress her. A perfect brother, he
cuddled her and sang her songs whenever he could when she
was a baby, and enjoyed teaching her the ropes throughout
their early life together. Their special bond made me think of
the children as my two little musketeers – one for all, and all
for one.

By the early nineties, both of them had become quite fed up
with all the attention we attracted whenever we were out
together as a family. It felt impossible to go anywhere in public
without someone rushing up for an autograph. Although he
was a brilliant actor and liked acting and starred in many
school productions, his own TV appearances as well as mine
were bringing the wrong kind of attention to Aston at school,
from teachers as well as other pupils. He made it clear that he
wanted to step back from the limelight himself, and I was sympathetic. Alvina had also had her share of the spotlight, with
appearances in our Channel 4 schools production *Hullaballoo*,
in which she shone like a star in every programme. 'She's happy
now' was her tagline to the lovely sequences she starred in with
the mime artist Les, played by Jason Webb.

Of course, as they got older, they were also getting more and more homework from school and I was very strict about our after-school routines. If my children sat in front of the television, it was always only to watch a particular programme, one which I felt was trustworthy. They knew exactly when they'd have to switch off the set, and go and do some other activity, whether this was school work or music, hockey, cricket, running or some other sport. They both excelled in sports. Aston loved hockey and cricket and played for his county. Alvina captained her house sports teams too. I believe children need a disciplined structure around them in order to learn the most important values in life. How else can they know what's good and what's bad, how to resist temptation, when to say no, when enough is enough, or what kinds of behaviour are acceptable? Mulling over these thoughts as I developed my three Cs philosophy, I eventually published my advice to the young as a light-touched but serious book called *For Goodness Sake! A Guide to Choosing Right from Wrong*.

All the new possibilities in broadcasting were exciting developments in many ways, but I felt that they weren't necessarily good for children. Quality was deteriorating as everyone tried to get in on the act. Many parents were beginning to use televisions like babysitters, so I tried to use my influence when speaking in public to persuade mothers, fathers and carers not to let their children gawp unsupervised, hour after hour. As I pointed out, it was the television equivalent of eating an endless diet of burgers, Coke and chips, and just as bad for children's bodies and minds. I made it my mission to discourage televisions in children's bedrooms, as well as violent video games, which were prevalent at the time, and I always stressed the importance of the 'off' button. Now, we've got the internet.

My work was taking the whole family to all kinds of interesting places, so our kids met fascinating and famous people around the world, as well as some of the most deprived children in the UK. I wanted them to experience as much of life as possible, but I was also careful to keep them grounded – so second-hand blazers and charity shop and jumble sale finds were the norm. Although, according to a double-page spread in the *TV Times*, I had broken a record in the late eighties for making the biggest number of television appearances in one day, I decided in the early nineties that it was time to cut down my own visibility on screen for the sake of my children's well-being. I even turned down an offer from Disney to work in the US, because I didn't want to leave them for a long period.

In 1990 we finished renovating a house we'd bought near Le Touquet in northern France, a private escape for the school holidays where we could enjoy family life in peace. Across the Channel, nobody knew who I was. In fact, it wasn't me but our R Type Bentley, a classic car from the early 1950s, that drew admiring crowds wherever we parked it. Keith had had a lifetime dream to own a Bentley and had found this one in a local garage in South London, partly restored and covered by a dustsheet. When it was revealed, he bought it spontaneously without any discussion. I was none too pleased when he told me but Aston pleaded for him.

'Let him have his dream, Mum.'

I relented and I have to admit that I grew to love the car's beautiful lines and luxurious interior.

The kids loved the freedom of my anonymity in France and we spent most of our summer holidays there for eleven years. We had lots of fun driving over to the house, playing guessing games and singing together as we headed for our secluded little single-storey villa in the pine forest, surrounded by sand dunes. The house had two bedrooms, a conservatory, a patio and a huge garden, and when I saw the white-painted walls gleaming through the trees, I felt it was a home from home. There was even a large annexe where family and friends stayed when they visited.

There was so much for the children to do there, with stables and tennis courts nearby, as well as the beach. They loved going cycling, swimming and skateboarding, and as well as riding real horses, they'd often have a spin on the merry-go-rounds on the seafront. At night, we'd sit on the patio playing our favourite Bob Marley album and look up at the stars.

We had a very enjoyable routine. I'd take the children to the bakery twice a day, to get croissants in the morning, and bread for lunch.

'*Deux baguettes, s'il vous plaît*,' I started confidently one day. To my annoyance, the shopkeeper reached for some older, staler loaves, rather than the ones I could see being wheeled out at that very moment, warm and fresh from the oven.

'*Non, non, non!*' I insisted, pointing to the trolley. I wanted the hot ones. '*Il fait chaud!*'

The shopkeeper knew exactly what I meant and handed me some fresh baguettes.

Aston burst out laughing. His French was much better than mine.

'The weather's hot!' I'd declared emphatically.

He and Alvina still tease me about that day.

'What was it like when you were little?' Aston and Alvina often asked me. And like Dardie, I told them little stories and tried to paint pictures in their heads. But there were no children's books around that could help them imagine what it felt like for a little girl to be uprooted from the Caribbean and start a new life in England.

At a book awards ceremony in 1993 I met a publisher called

Colin Webb, co-founder of Pavilion Books, and we got chatting about this.

'I would love to write a book about my childhood,' I told him. A few years earlier I'd returned to Trinidad with the children for a *TV Times* feature, and it had brought back many memories, especially when we visited the docks, which I'd last seen as twinkling lights from the deck of the *Marqués de Comillas*.

'You should,' he said enthusiastically. 'You write it, and I'll publish it.'

'Really?' I said. It all seemed a bit too easy.

But it really wasn't. For some reason, I couldn't get into the right zone. For ages I thought about this book, but I just couldn't get started. Hoping to be inspired by a trip to the Caribbean, we spent a whole summer holiday in Jamaica, but ended up having too much fun together in the sun. The words just refused to come.

Every so often Colin would say:

'So, where's that book?'

And all I could do was make excuses.

Until finally, late one summer night in France, when we'd had a busy day of sea and sun, and everyone else had gone to bed exhausted, I found myself sitting up in a chair in the living room and thinking about the past. Something clicked into place. I got out my pen and found some paper, and I started to write.

My first memory was when I was three years old . . .

Everything that had happened to me came pouring out, all the good things and all the bad things, and I just wrote and I wrote and I wrote. I kept going until four o'clock the following morning, and the paper became wet from my tears. I relived many different emotions and experiences and at times found the process completely overwhelming. I realized how important my sister Sandra had been for me in my early years, and of course, I also saw clearly how the bedrock of my parents' love had kept me feeling worthy and loved even through those terrible fifteen months of abandonment when they had both gone to England.

I couldn't stop until I'd finished. Each night, at eleven o'clock, I'd sit in my chair again, with the sleeping house settling around me. There was nothing to distract me. When I needed to think, I could step outside into the pine-scented air of the forest, and gaze up at the night stars through the trees, hearing nothing but the hum of insects.

In my mind I turned four years old, five, six, seven . . . All the memories of the first ten years of my life came back to me in minute detail and I set them down on paper, as evocatively as I knew how.

Each morning, I'd show Keith and the children what I'd written during the night.

'Mum, this is wonderful!' Aston told me.

After we came home from France, when I'd finished, my parents and brothers and sisters read the whole manuscript too.

'How did you remember that?' asked Marmie in amazement, when she reached my description of the tree outside our little white house in Marabella, and the way we used to lean out of the window to pick its leaves.

'Oh yes, I remember that too!' said my brothers and sisters, exclaiming over one detail after another.

Somewhere deep, deep inside me, the knowledge of what had happened to us all had been waiting to be unlocked. I'd put a lid on the bad things for so long that they were vibrating like the contents of a pressure cooker, ready to explode. When my lid flew off, I remembered everything. Through *Play School*, I had learned to see through the eyes of a child again. I had written my story through the eyes of a child too, in a way that

With newborn Aston, my bundle of joy, surrounded
by flowers sent by well-wishers, 1981.

With Mr Tree, created by Keith for our
first independent television production,
Tree House, for Channel 4 in 1988.

With my beautiful miraculous
newborn baby Alvina, 1988.

Aston meeting and presenting a drawing he'd done to Princess Diana at the Pre-School Playgroups Association in 1986.

Aston and me dressed as big and little Puss in *Puss in Boots* in 1984 – our first panto together.

Our first family Christmas, 1988.

With my devoted
guardian angel,
Tony Lothian OBE,
and Valentina
Tereshkova, 1990.

Left With Sir Sydney
Samuelson, another
guardian angel.

Below With Colin Webb,
another guardian angel
who originally published
Coming to England, with
his wife Pam and their
daughter Victoria Walters.

Aston aged ten and Alvina aged three. They adored each other and still look out for one another.

Alvina, aged thirteen, meeting Nelson Mandela at a reception for him at South Africa House in London.

Left Taking on the challenge of walking 100 miles along the Great Wall of China for the charity Action for Children.

Celebrating my ninth consecutive London Marathon in 1998.

Marmie and Dardie celebrating their seventieth birthday with all their children. (*Back row*) Roy Junior, Ellington and Lester. (*Front row*) me, Sandra and Cynthia.

Me with my statue by sculptor Luke Shephard at Exeter University, with my sisters Sandra and Cynthia, 2017.

With my family in the Robing Room at the House of Lords preparing for my introduction, one of the most important days of my life. (*From left to right*) Sir Thomas Woodcock, Baroness Ros Scott, Sandra, Ros Edwards, Alvina, Keith, Aston, Tim Snowball, Lord Navnit Dholakia and Lester.

Me and Keith with Alvina at her PGCE for Geography graduation from the University of Brighton, 2014.

Above At Buckingham Palace after receiving my damehood medal in 2020 with Alvina, Keith and Sandra. Sandra and I both wore something that belonged to Marmie.

Left Me and Keith with our son Aston, an international hospitality lawyer, at the Ritz, celebrating after the Covid lockdown 2021.

Me and Dardie enjoying a rare occasion out on the town, celebrating his seventy-fifth birthday, 2001.

Marmie and me at the Chelsea Flower Show in 2005.
She loved attending and was an amazing gardener.

Me and my RHS Chelsea Flower Show *Windrush* garden,
which won a Gold medal in 2018.

a child could understand, and adults too, because we've all been children.

I tried to convey the way that we were all indoctrinated into believing that we were coming to somewhere we belonged, and that we'd be welcomed. And the terrible shock of discovering that this was far from true. Parents and children alike had kept that pain and trauma buried deep inside. At the time, we all just had to prioritize getting on with life, and we'd never sat down and compared our experiences of racism. It was something you just didn't talk about in those days. People could rarely bring themselves to share hurt so profound that you felt it was ripping you apart inside, that feeling like a knife stabbing you in the heart, over and over again, or of being repeatedly punched in the belly, or the anxiety of never knowing where the next attack might come from.

Colin was delighted with the manuscript. Although many people weren't ready to hear it, he and his wife Pam really understood how important it was to be telling this story. He gave me lots of freedom, and I ended up writing three times more than he needed, but he was a brilliant editor, and knew exactly what to do with the material to make it appeal to readers aged eight to twelve, our target audience.

'This book is going to become a classic,' he said to me. 'It will be on the shelves long after you've died. This is really going to inspire other people.'

Coming to England was published in 1995. Little by little, I realized how many other people had been through similar experiences, and how important it is for you to come to terms with your childhood sufferings. So many people of all ages in different circumstances all over the world can identify with the emotions and trauma in my story, and relate to my feelings about being left behind, about starting again, and the struggle of having to make new friends in a new place. It's a story about being different, facing adversity as a child and dealing with it. Adversity can break you or make you stronger – I believe in the latter.

The obvious next step for us was to try to get a commission for a TV drama based on the book. There was only one place to go. The BBC alone had the budgets for historical dramas of this kind.

'Children don't want this kind of story,' the head of Children's Drama told us. 'We don't want to be looking back.'

Her priority for children was to reflect contemporary life, she explained.

So that was that, we thought, disappointed.

Chapter Twenty-eight

'You're just the sort of person we're looking for.'

How many times have I heard that in my life? I had become ever more prominent through my charity work and my association with the Women of the Year Lunch. The more often I spoke in public about the issues that mattered to me, the more often the phone would ring with other invitations. My parents have always encouraged us to take up opportunities, so whenever I see the chance to make a difference, I jump at it.

Ever since I'd first got to know Virginia Bottomley, she'd encouraged me to put myself forward for public roles, such as hospital trusts, but I never felt that medical boards would use my skills best. One day in 1995 she told me she'd found the perfect role for me: the National Film and Television School was looking for a new governor.

'David Puttnam is the NFTS chairman and he wants to meet you,' she said.

He was the famous producer of hits such as *Chariots of Fire*, *The Killing Fields* and *Midnight Express*. We arranged to meet for lunch at Claridge's, the luxury hotel in Mayfair. His very first question still makes me laugh.

'Are you a Tory?' he asked. The fact that it was Virginia

Bottomley who introduced us and the way she talked about me had clearly set up a certain expectation in his mind.

'I'm just somebody who wants to make a difference,' I explained.

We immediately got on like a house on fire, and I stayed on that board for seventeen years. We certainly made a difference during that time, because when I first became involved with the famous international film school in Beaconsfield, there were next to no Black students. It seemed like a closed world to most young people of colour, and since the fees were so expensive, the film school was an impossible dream for anyone who couldn't afford to pay. I wanted to change that.

It was the same old story: if you don't see yourself on the screen, then you don't feel included. If the NFTS could become more diverse, it would not only mean opportunities for film-makers from different backgrounds in all fields – directors, writers, sound and lighting technicians, cinematographers, producers – but it would have a huge impact on the creative output of the whole country. More and more people of colour would be drawn into the industry by seeing people like them appearing in film and television programmes, and also making them. But you have to start somewhere.

I knew the only way for the NFTS to progress in this area was by seeking out talent in the right places, instead of waiting for it to come knocking on the door. Dedicated scholarships and bursaries were the most important first step, and this meant raising funds from donations, the government and broadcasters. Producer Nik Powell, co-founder of Virgin Records and the NFTS director from 2003 to 2017, took the issue very seriously, and we worked closely together. We had to be proactive to make a real change. The NFTS began sending out scouts to colleges and universities to encourage people from a broader range of backgrounds to apply for our courses, which were all postgraduate degrees. Over the years, I sat on many scholarship selection panels. We also started entrepreneurial courses for budding producers.

At my suggestion, the NFTS began to issue press releases highlighting recent films and programmes made by or with the involvement of NFTS alumni. Many of today's successful Black and Asian filmmakers got a kickstart to their careers thanks to the NFTS's commitment to diversity. It makes me very proud. For years, I was a real pain, constantly asking questions and making demands, pushing and pushing for answers. Where were the Black cast members in the graduation films? In the credits? Where were stories of people of colour being told?

Some people didn't get it at first.

'Come on, Floella!' they'd say. 'What are you talking about?' There was no such thing as unconscious bias training then. One person once said to me, 'I don't know why you're always going on about the media. We've got Black footballers! We've got Black singers, haven't we?' Where was the problem? They just couldn't see what I was seeing. They couldn't see what was missing.

Eventually, it became embedded in the entire educational process at the NFTS, so that everyone trained there now learns the importance of diversity awareness as a matter of course. You might feel you're saying the same thing over and over again, and that nobody is listening, but if you have the courage of your convictions, and keep smiling, eventually you'll be heard. Mind you, in 2014 Nik asked me to chair the NFTS annual fundraising dinner committee and I decided to call it 'The Diversity Nirvana Gala'. But when I asked some Black and Asian actors to support me on the evening many declined because they still feared that speaking out would harm their careers.

*

When Wayne Drew, producer of the BFI Awards, invited me to join the judging panel for the 1990 Short Animation Award, I had little idea where this would lead. I'd never been on a jury before, and I was quite naive perhaps. I was very struck by Nick Park's first film *Creature Comforts*, so when all nine jurors sat down together to discuss the contenders, I launched straight in with my praise.

'Isn't it a wonderful film? *Creature Comforts* is surely the winner!'

And another jury member turned to me and said dismissively:

'You would say that, wouldn't you, being a children's person.'

As if 'children' was a dirty word.

I'm a bit like a car. I'd been happily in cruise control, but at that I let out my throttle and moved up several gears. 'Listen,' I said to him firmly. 'Just because I'm a "children's" person, it doesn't mean I can't have an opinion. *Creature Comforts* puts bums on seats. The film industry is dying on its feet because people aren't thinking about audience appeal. *Creature Comforts* is for grannies, for parents and for children. Everybody can get something out of this film. And it's a great piece of artwork.'

Legendary director and cinematographer Sydney Samuelson CBE, the first British Film Commissioner ever appointed, was also on the jury, sitting at the other end of the table. At this point he leaned forward.

'Do you know, *I* like *Creature Comforts* too, so I'm with you, Floella.'

For about two hours, the two of us argued the merits of *Creature Comforts*, persuading the other jury members one by one. It was hard work talking everyone round, but eventually Nick Park's animation, now so famous, won by a majority.

That one jury member whom we'd failed to convince wrote

to Wilf Stevenson, then Director of the BFI, to complain about me being on the jury.

Lo and behold, *Creature Comforts* went on to win an Oscar in America, and also won awards and nominations at seven other major international film festivals. Nick Park also won countless other awards for his films, and in 2000 he released the highest-grossing stop-motion animation ever created, *Chicken Run*. And Wilf – now Lord Stevenson of Balmacara – has been one of my greatest supporters ever since, telling me he sees me as the voice of common sense in the Lords.

Meanwhile, Sydney Samuelson – who would soon be knighted – was quickly becoming a new guardian angel for me, pushing and promoting me wherever he could.

'You're just the sort of person we need at BAFTA,' he said, one day. 'Will you join?'

I was thrilled to be nominated for membership, and within a year or so, at his urging, I found myself on the council of the British Academy of Film and Television Arts. I'll never forget turning up for my very first meeting in 1993.

'What are you doing here?' A man I'd never met before was eyeing me up and down with that disdainful look. It didn't even occur to him I could be on his level. I looked him in the eye and replied:

'I've come for the council meeting. What about you?'

Of course, I was the only Black person in the room. But I made my contribution and spoke my mind whenever I needed to, especially around diversity. Fortunately, Sydney and the chief executive, Harry Manley, were very supportive.

Around this time, I was approached by the Royal Mail to join the Stamp Advisory Committee who scrutinize and select the designs of Royal Mail stamps. I found the decision-making process fascinating, but at one of my early meetings we were looking at the designs for Christmas stamps for 1994.

The decisions were made months before the new designs were released in the autumn. We sat around the committee table, taking it in turns to voice opinions on the artwork. Each stamp showed an image of children dressed up to take part in a nativity play: Mary, Joseph and baby Jesus, a pair of angels dressed in white, the three kings with their gold, frankincense and myrrh. Nearly everyone else there, whether they were designers or union officials, such as Brenda Dean, commented on the colours and style of the designs. I was the last person to speak.

'My heart is broken,' I said. 'I'm bleeding inside. Because you're telling me that for my own children and for the millions of the children that I represent, Christmas does not involve them. They do not matter. Every one of the images of children on these stamps is White. Can't we have some Black faces, Asian faces, Chinese faces? At nativity plays in any inner-city primary school you'll find that kind of diversity. Stamps are one of the first pieces of artwork many children will see. They need to see themselves. They need to know they belong. Can't you see that?'

I remember another committee member saying to me afterwards: 'I'm terribly sorry. I just didn't see it.' It was such a common response. So it was my duty to open people's eyes.

To give them their due, Royal Mail then rewrote their criteria, and changed the 1994 stamp design right away. I remained on the Royal Mail Stamp Advisory Committee for eight years and loved every moment. I was part of history as stamps are collectors' items and with us forever.

In 1995 BAFTA set up the Elizabeth R Commonwealth Broadcasting Fund, funded by the royalties donated by the Queen from the 1992 BBC documentary marking the fortieth anniversary of her reign. This fund supported the development of broadcasting skills in the Commonwealth with travel bursaries and training opportunities.

'You're the obvious person to chair this, with your Commonwealth background,' said the Academy chair Ted Childs, producer of *The Sweeney*, *Morse*, *Peak Practice*, *Sharpe* and many other trail-blazing series.

I must also have seemed an obvious person to chair BAFTA's Children's Committee, and I took on this role in 1997. Ted encouraged me also to put myself forward for election as chair of the Television Committee. And then I received an unbelievable phone call.

'How dare you rise above your station?' You might imagine this was an anonymous call, but no, the speaker was another man with connections to BAFTA. 'Take your name off that ballot paper. We don't want your kind as chair of this committee.'

I couldn't believe what he was saying. Yet again, I was under attack. Was it because he thought I was incompetent or was it because of the colour of my skin? This man quickly began talking to various BAFTA members behind the scenes, persuading them that they should not vote for me. So, Karen Brown won, which of course may have happened anyway, and I became her deputy. She was unaware of these undercurrents and we worked really well together, but after only about three months she resigned for personal reasons. Eventually the efforts of this person to prevent me from being chair (which started again after Karen Brown resigned) were foiled by Doreen Dean, Assistant Director of Film and Archive, who knew everything about BAFTA's constitution and made it quite clear that the rules stated that as deputy, I had to step into the role. So that's how I became chair of the Television Committee too in 1997, much to Sydney Samuelson's delight. I told nobody what had happened, not even revealing the truth to Sydney until a few years ago. As always, in public, I kept on smiling and working hard, and honing my skills in persuasion and debate in the battlegrounds that mattered most. I'm not a victim, I'm a winner.

In 1999 I was elected outright chair of the Television Committee, which gave me new opportunities to argue for change and campaign for greater diversity at BAFTA. I always tried to look at the problem of exclusion from all angles. At that time, Black people only ever won Special Awards – a gift from BAFTA, rather than a competitive award. During my time on the council I fought long and hard for both Oprah Winfrey and Trevor McDonald to receive Special Awards, confident that I'd get there in the end with Ted and Sydney's backing. But I also fought for diversity on juries. Each BAFTA council member chaired a jury for the awards, and I insisted that everybody tried to find at least one person of colour on their particular jury. This move drew many more Black film and television makers into BAFTA. Yet still there simply weren't enough programmes being made which accurately reflected our country's diversity. Surely the best way was to make that a criterion of entry for the awards? But I hit a brick wall on that particular battle, because it was felt that would be a form of censorship and, as one committee member said, 'Over my dead body.' This was tough to come to terms with. But then again, think how long it's taken for the Academy of Motion Picture Arts and Sciences to acknowledge that the Oscars had a diversity problem: new standards for best-picture nominations will only come into effect in 2024.

Still, I truly changed the culture at BAFTA and I'm so proud of that. And twenty years later, they asked me to help shape their diversity policies. 'Of course!' I said, and explained the value of taking care in not only selecting presenters who were

White, even if the nominations for best actors and actresses and directors still weren't coming in. I don't care who gets the credit or how long it takes, as long as change happens in the end.

But what about children? Their programmes rarely won when pitted against the whole range of genres, yet the work of children's practitioners was so important for the whole nation.

'Wouldn't it be wonderful if we had a separate Children's BAFTA Award ceremony?' I suggested to Ted Childs. 'We can have different categories and also an overall winner which can be awarded in the main BAFTAs.'

'Set it up,' he said right away, and allocated me a budget. So, I went to see all the broadcasters, to get them on board. I approached the BBC last, knowing that their previous dominance in the award field would make the corporation reluctant to admit more competition. But the commitment already confirmed by the other broadcasters meant the BBC also embraced the new award scheme. I saw it as essential for people to understand that the Children's BAFTAs made perfect sense, and would ultimately ensure that practitioners for children were properly valued. I presented the first Children's Awards ceremony at BAFTA in 1996, and although Tony Robinson was giving out an award, he protested loudly on stage because many, like him, were concerned it would mean children's programmes would be sidelined. But in fact, the Children's Awards have gone from strength to strength, and I'm delighted we can now celebrate all the different categories of children's films and programming, from current affairs to animation.

As the chair of the Television Committee I was actually due to become overall chair in 2000, but Tim Angel CBE of Angels Costumes was making such important changes as chair of BAFTA at the time, and really changing the profile of the organization, and needed another year to finish the work he and his team had started, so I agreed to let him stay on for an unprecedented extra year. But, just as Ted Childs had predicted, I was then passed over the following year as a result, which left me broken-hearted. Ted still jokes that I was the best chair that BAFTA never had. In 2004, I was honoured with a BAFTA Special Lifetime Achievement Award, a glorious surprise. At the awards night, watching the way I was introduced and the show-reel they'd put together, I nearly cried. I'm now listed as one of the BAFTA greats on their website, and my portrait hangs on their boardroom wall. I didn't see that one coming.

Chapter Twenty-nine

A decade after my first introduction to Tony and the Women of the Year Lunch, once I'd gained experience initially as a committee member and then as deputy-chair, Tony decided it was time I became chair. This was in 1995. Having a Black woman at the very top meant a great deal to her, and she always used to say Black people should take their rightful place in society. When Nelson Mandela was released in 1990, Tony called me to rejoice, and we both danced in our bedrooms. However, there was considerable whispering behind my back and even some disapproval from certain members of the WOTY committee, who for some reason seemed convinced I was going to turn it into a Black, left-wing pressure group. I laughed when Tony told me about one woman who came to express her doubts about my suitability.

'Well, you know what you have to do, don't you? Go and tell Floella!' Tony had told her.

'Oh, I couldn't do that. She's my friend.'

'With friends like that, who needs enemies?' Tony joked when she reported the conversation to me.

Of course, I was very keen to increase diversity at the lunch, and I invited more guest speakers of colour than had ever appeared before. I also decided to include the stories of different Women of the Year in the luncheon brochure, so that it wasn't just full of glossy advertisements. And I wanted to make sure the menu itself showed how much we valued other cultures, and reflected my own. It was time for a Caribbean lunch.

The chef at The Savoy was Anton Edelmann. Having eaten his lunches since his arrival at the hotel, I knew he was a fantastic cook, specializing in cuisine that was modern and international, but rooted in classic French and Italian techniques. When I discussed my plan with the maître d' he was enthusiastic.

'I'm sure Anton would be thrilled. Let me have a menu and we'll arrange a tasting.'

A few weeks later, full of anticipation, I sat down alone in front of a crisp white tablecloth, prepared to be amazed.

The first course was out of this world. Anton had transformed Jamaica's famous national dish, ackee and saltfish, into a stunning soufflé. The dessert was divine: an exotic tropical mousse, whose flavours instantly transported me back to my island in the sun. But the main course that I'd requested, Caribbean chicken with rice and peas, was completely inedible: a bland and undistinguished stew more like a school dinner than a Trinidadian treat.

I called over the maître d'.

'Could I please see the chef?'

I waited half an hour. No Anton. An hour went by. Still no Anton. I waited for nearly two hours before calling the maître d' once again.

'Could you please tell the chef that I'm not going until I've seen him, and I'll sit here all day if I have to.'

By then he was looking a bit battered, but he was very polite.

'Certainly, madame.'

At last, Anton Edelmann appeared – thin blond moustache, face red from the hot kitchen, tall white hat – wiping his hands on his white apron as he emerged. He bustled towards me in his clogs in what I soon recognized as a characteristic cross between a shuffle and a strut.

'So, what is it? Why do you want to see me?'

Not in a good mood. I smiled, of course.

'Darling! Here you are! You are the man who's going to save me from having my head on a platter. You're going to make me the most incredible Caribbean menu, and you'll get the chicken just right, as perfect as the starter and the dessert I've just eaten. Now, I know you can deliver. Let's sit down and discuss how to go about it.'

And that's how we became friends. I told him where to get the right spices, exactly how to season the meat properly, how you have to marinate it for a good long time so that all the flavours penetrate right to the bone, how to turn the juices into a gravy. He took everything on board and the result was a triumph, because Anton is a genius. He's never afraid to explore. It was only months later that he told me that he'd come out of the kitchen expecting to meet some bossy pompous lady with a blue rinse, but that I'd charmed him instead.

By this time, Keith and I were well established as producers of lifestyle programmes.

'Anton, I love how you interpret Caribbean flavours and ingredients. You really are a genius. I'd love to take you to Jamaica and Trinidad so you can see for yourself where the food comes from and cook it in your own unique way. Will you make a television programme with me?'

This series was called *Caribbean Light*, and it went out on Carlton Food Network in 1998. Anton was a hit because he's so flamboyant and has such a great screen personality. On one programme I taught him how to make a dish with duck, sweet potato and mango. He recreated it for the menu at The Savoy, and called it 'Floella's Duck'. On Christmas mornings he'd invite us to bring the kids to the hotel kitchen for a scrumptious champagne brunch. A second cookery series accompanied by a book of the same name soon followed: *Caribbean Kitchen*. Then Keith and I made *Africa on a Plate*, discovering the little-known cuisines and culinary delights of thirteen different countries from the Ivory Coast to Tanzania. We wove culture, history and politics into all our cookery programmes. Food was proving a wonderful window onto the world.

When we were in Trinidad with Anton, we had a cameraman who was not enjoying the night shifts and challenging locations, so Keith and I decided it was time to take an important step towards independence. We realized that with Keith shooting footage himself, we could save both time and money. So, we bought our first expensive professional camera, along with lighting and sound equipment. The next big step was to invest in our own editing suite. Non-linear editing was just taking off in 1998, and it made less and less sense to head off to a post-production house in Soho with our tapes to do something we could do more quickly and cheaply ourselves.

We were hesitant at first, but finally convinced by a young man called Sumit, a Dulwich College boy who'd come to us for work experience, and proved to be a computer wizard. He ended up teaching us the secrets of digital editing. A whole new world was opened for us when we bought Apple computers, huge screens and a new editing software package, all of which was installed in our dining room by a technical genius called Steve Hills with whom we'd worked for a long time at Hillside Studios. It felt a ludicrous amount of money when we shelled it out, but in fact, it all paid for itself within eighteen months, thanks to a brand-new pre-school children's series we were making for CITV (Children's ITV) called *Jamboree*: 'Lots of fun for you and me!'

Jamboree ran for four seasons, until 2001, and starred a colourful cast of fleecy puppet-like characters called the Bopkins. Billy, Betty, Bizza and Baby. Baby, who always carried a teddy bear, was played by Warwick Davis, and his wife Sammy played Betty. The Bopkins were modern children, and after they'd made their beds each morning, they ran to a desktop computer and put a silver disc into the drive. They took it in turns to choose the icon on the screen which would lead to the next segment. Every episode began and ended with me playing games and singing songs with children in my garden, at Floella's House. It was very contemporary, and also fun and educational.

Perhaps the best thing for me and Keith about *Jamboree* is that it brought Ros into our lives. We needed a new researcher/ production assistant, and after doing the initial interviews, Keith had been particularly impressed by a young woman called Ros Edwards, who'd just graduated from university.

'I think you need to meet her,' he told me.

She nearly didn't get the job. At that stage our company was still officially called Crystalrowe, so when Ros walked into the room she wasn't expecting to see Floella Benjamin, the presenter she'd grown up watching on telly. She was totally thrown, and the shock made her go completely to pieces. Collapsing into uncontrollable giggles, for some minutes Ros simply couldn't string two words together. The sight of me in the flesh has this strange effect on some people: I've seen so many morph like magic into their childhood selves, simply not knowing how to react in the presence of someone they feel they already know so intimately.

So that wasn't a very auspicious start. Once Ros started

work for us, however, it was our turn to be blown away by her calm efficiency and honest-to-goodness integrity. Marmie once came round in our absence and saw her at work and she reported back in glowing terms:

'That girl would die for you, Flo. She treats the company as she would her own. You'll never find a more faithful soul.'

Born the year I started presenting, Ros is truly my *Play School* baby, and I think of her now as another daughter.

Chapter Thirty

Visiting so many different parts of the country and so many schools during the 1980s and 90s, and working closely with all the main children's charities, it had often seemed that as a nation we were on our knees. I had never seen so much poverty and inequality, and of course, it was children who suffered worst.

I'd had great hopes for Tony Blair from the first time I heard him speak, and as soon as he came into power after the Labour landslide of May 1997, I wrote to congratulate him. Of course, I also wanted to raise the possibility of a cabinet level Minister for Children. He replied immediately.

'Brilliant idea!' he said.

Soon afterwards we met in person at a function where he told me he had always admired me, and suggested I become involved in the Labour Party. I'd already been wooed by Glenys Kinnock, who was a vice-president of the Women of the Year Lunch, and Theresa May once suggested I became a Conservative MP after hearing me speak at a breakfast event for women at the Café Royal. Members of the Green Party and the Liberal Democrats had also sought my support at various times. But at that point I still felt that I could be more effective if I weren't attached to any one party.

253

Gordon Brown and David Blunkett were equally supportive of the idea of a new high-profile Minister for Children. Within a year, a new office had been set up in Westminster, and lots of people from different charities were working together to make my idea a reality. On 22 June 2003, the Labour MP for Barking, Margaret Hodge, was sworn into the Privy Council as the inaugural Minister for Children and Families. I felt great that twenty years of lobbying had paid off. For the first time ever, children's services would come under the Department of Education and Skills, and this role had responsibility for all policy affecting children's welfare, from early years and childcare, to special education needs, teenage pregnancy strategy and support for family courts. I felt triumphant. The letter-writing and telephone conversations and meetings I'd had over all those years had been something of a marathon, but we were over the finishing line at last.

And all the while I kept on writing to Tony Blair, whenever I could see something that needed fixing, or that I wanted to congratulate him about. 'Why don't you do this?' I'd say. Or, 'Don't do that!' And he'd always write back.

Britain had begun to change fast. New and progressive opportunities were opening up everywhere, including at the Palace of Westminster, where Labour's election promise to reform the House of Lords – a tough battle – would soon be implemented. Hereditary peerages were abolished, and the number of life peerages created was vastly increased. Meanwhile, jobs traditionally only given to insiders, or ex-army types, were recruited publicly and fairly for the first time. My brother Lester, who had a first-class degree in Electrical and Electronic Engineering by then as well as lots of experience working for Greenwich Council, successfully applied for the role of Head of Maintenance and Operations. But when he started work, and went to pick up his access-all-areas security pass, he got a shock.

'No, there must be a mistake,' he was told. 'This is the kind of pass you need.'

The staff who issued ID had assumed that just because Lester was Black, he could only have come to work at Westminster as a cleaner or security guard. So, they'd refused to give him the access he needed to go anywhere on the estate. Lester was not one to make a fuss, but when his boss realized what had happened he was furious, and marched Lester straight back to the office.

'This man is now in charge of all of you,' he told them, making sure Lester had the appropriate pass.

'Thank you very much,' said my brother, very politely.

He wasn't angry. Marmie had taught us all that confrontation doesn't work when you have battles to fight. Charm and a lovely smile are far more persuasive, far more likely to diffuse a difficult situation. It was yet another example of that question that any Black person in Britain faces when they're rising in status: *What are you doing here?* Sometimes it's implicit. Sometimes it's said out loud. But it's no use letting yourself be riled by it. Step by step, Lester got his entire workforce on his side by being kind but determined, giving everyone the chance to shine, never alienating a single person, always demonstrating through words and deeds exactly what he was doing there: taking care of everything and everyone, including his staff. Soon it was obvious to everyone.

How proud we were the first time we saw him on television at the State Opening of Parliament. Having heard all about the complex practicalities from Lester, we knew he'd be following the Yeomen of the Guard through the lavishly decorated chamber of the House of Lords after their ceremonial search of the cellars where Guy Fawkes hid his gunpowder in 1605. Passing the famous red benches, each carrying a lantern in a white-gloved hand, the Yeomen looked resplendent in their archaic red and gold uniforms. But our eyes were on Lester, looking so handsome in his morning coat, holding himself so proudly, exuding duty and responsibility. (Almost two decades later he retired and received an OBE for services to parliament.)

In 1998, Keith's mother died. His half-brother rang, asking him to collect her belongings. She had left behind a couple of suit-cases full of photos, mementos, papers, letters and diaries. It took nearly a year before I could start sorting out her stuff – Keith had no interest in it – but at that point, I became a bit of a detective.

It turned out she had loved writing things down. But the diaries were very sad. She must have been suffering from mental problems, and she obviously loved Keith, although she never showed him any appreciation while she was alive. As I read, I felt I understood more and more about her and their difficult relationship, and then in the address section of a diary from 1976, I suddenly chanced on the name Kenneth Taylor, with a Blackpool phone number.

'Isn't that your dad?' I said to Keith.

'Yes, but that's years old. It won't still be the same.'

'You might as well call it. Let's look up the new code.'

I listened to Keith dialling. Someone at the other end picked up the phone.

'Hello. Can I please speak to Kenneth Taylor?'

'Just a moment. I'll go and get him.'

Keith sat down very suddenly.

'I think I'm going to need a whisky,' he joked, trembling with shock.

And then I heard him say:

'I'm Keith Taylor. I think I'm your son.'

Silence.

But then, when it had sunk in, Keith was overjoyed. It turned out that Keith's mother had told Kenneth that his son didn't want anything to do with him. So, she had told the same lie to both to keep them apart. We arranged to go and visit him as soon as we could. After so many years of searching for his father, at the age of fifty, Keith's emotions about actually seeing him again were very mixed: he was anxious and excited, happy and nervous at once. I decided it might be better if Kenneth didn't know in advance that I was Black, so we sent him a recent photograph just of Keith, and set off for Blackpool with the children. Aston was seventeen. Alvina was ten. We all knew there was a possibility the children could be rejected by their own grandfather but we wanted to take that chance. To us it was an adventure, and we wanted to find out for ourselves what Keith's dad was like. We were all so intrigued.

On the car journey there in our Volvo V50 we played Cher's 'Believe' on repeat.

The first shock when we drove up to the address Kenneth had given us was that I recognized it. I'd already seen a photo of the house in Keith's mum's suitcase. So, she must have been there at some point herself, and spied on Kenneth. I had decided a reunion this momentous should be recorded, so I got the camera out ready, and as soon as Keith rang the doorbell, I began to film the scene.

Keith's dad, a man in his early seventies, came rushing out and immediately hugged his long-lost son. Aston and Alvina ran to hug Kenneth.

'Grandad! Grandad!' they said, quite unselfconsciously. It was harder for Keith to call him 'Dad', a word he'd never used in that way before.

Keith introduced me too and I looked for that tell-tale sign in his eyes but just saw happiness. We all went inside to meet Kenneth's new wife, a very small and friendly seaside landlady. They'd run a little guesthouse together, but for Blackpool's holidaymakers rather than touring actors. Once we'd sat down, she leaned forward and said to me in a friendly way:

'Your face looks very familiar. Don't I know you?'

She recognized me from television. Neither of them batted an eyelid about the colour of my skin or that of the kids – golden, as we used to say, if ever they were bullied at school. 'You're Black and White mixed together, which makes you golden, and everyone loves gold.'

We all got on very well and hoped Kenneth would be in our lives for years to come. But within a few years of us meeting him, Keith's dad suddenly died. It was a horrible shock. They had had so little time together.

In 2000, we were away filming another Caribbean cookery series for Carlton Food Network called *A Taste of Barbados* when a tourist guide on a boat trip reeled off all the famous people who had visited Barbados, and then commented that the only person who never came to the island was the British Prime Minister Tony Blair. He'd even been offered an honorary degree by the University of the West Indies, and hadn't bothered to go and collect it. That made me prick up my ears. I wrote to him right away, telling him what I'd heard.

Listen, Tony . . . You've got to get yourself down to the Caribbean! Everyone's saying terrible things about you. It's not good enough.

I felt he was pushing for Europe, but neglecting the Caribbean and the Commonwealth.

And he listened. Anji Hunter, Director of Government Relations and Tony's right-hand woman, wrote to say that he was planning to go. Cherie Blair and I share the same birthday, five years apart, and as soon as we met we'd had an immediate bond. Each year, we exchange birthday messages and Christmas cards. When she knew they were going to Barbados – which turned out to be the first of many visits – Cherie wrote to me saying that she knew we'd made programmes about Barbados, and could she see them so that she'd know what to expect, and learn about the place in advance. So, expecting to have to deal with all sorts of security checks, I went along to Downing Street myself, a VHS copy of the series in my hand. But when I arrived, I breezed through the gates because all the policemen recognized me from their *Play School* days. Cherie told me later how much the programme had helped her understand the island.

I was also learning about parts of the Caribbean I'd never visited before. I'd heard a great deal about Cuba from my father, who was a big admirer of Fidel Castro, who claimed to have launched the revolution that ended racism. I wanted to see Cuba for myself too, so when we were commissioned to make *A Taste of Cuba* in 2001 I leapt at the chance.

I wasn't disappointed by the sheer beauty of Cuba, which is nearly as big as England. The varied and diverse landscape, with its palm-fringed beaches, rainforests and sweeping mountainside pine forests, was breathtaking. One thing that did surprise me, though, was that being a Black person in Cuba wasn't quite what I'd expected. Castro's efforts to make Cuba a race-blind nation had ended the blatant discrimination of the previous regime, but it had also made it hard to discuss race at all. Naturally, the impact of hundreds of years of slavery doesn't vanish overnight.

Wherever we went, people seemed amazed to find a Black woman in charge of a film and TV production company. The first official to greet me made his excuses and rushed from the room, unable to cope with his shock of finding I was in charge.

We talked to one Black woman who was head of the national theatre, but otherwise everyone we met in power was light-skinned, of Hispanic rather than African origins. We saw Black entertainers singing and dancing in Santiago de Cuba, but it was noticeable how few there were in any position of authority.

Ros had arranged all the accreditation for every interview in advance, which was essential. We were told by the government fixers that we'd be able to see and film everything we wanted, so we got to see the entire island, which is more than many Cubans. Unfortunately we didn't put Guantanamo Bay on the list, which at that time was just a US naval base and had the only McDonald's on the island. The notorious military prison was opened inside the base in 2002 after 9/11.

From the start of our visit, there was talk that we might even be able to interview Fidel Castro himself. Of course, we were naturally full of anticipation about this, and waited hourly for the call to action. One location was a small island in an archipelago just off the north Cuban coast. A former buccaneer hideout, Cayo Coco had become the site of several very fancy all-inclusive resorts in the previous decade. As our crew bus headed down the twenty-seven-kilometre-long causeway which joined it to the main island, we were flagged down by the army.

'Everyone out!' ordered the soldiers.

Our government guide Jorge was clearly anxious.

'But these people have permission. They can go everywhere.'

'The Comandante is here.' That was Fidel's official title. Would we finally get our interview? The soldiers told us where to go, and our bus headed off to a huge luxury hotel, a newly opened venture that was part-Canadian and part-Cuban.

Once again, we were ordered off the bus. We all stood there anxiously, waiting for the next instruction. I was thrilled to think that at any moment I'd actually be in the presence of Fidel Castro. I imagined telling Dardie. But no . . .

'Get back on the bus!' We were commanded. Our adventure was over before it had begun. There would be no interview with the Comandante. Clearly, we had been inspected from afar and found wanting in some way.

The following day we were awarded a kind of second prize: an interview with a man called Eusebio Leal, known as *el historiador*. The official historian of Havana and a close friend of Fidel and Raoul Castro, Leal had been single-handedly responsible for saving Old Havana from dereliction and ruin, restoring this extraordinary city and enabling its UNESCO World Heritage List status in 1982. He became a Goodwill Ambassador for the United Nations in 1996.

'Bring an interpreter,' they told us. 'He doesn't speak English. You've got half an hour and you must be there fifteen minutes beforehand to set up.'

Everything went according to plan. As soon as Eusebio Leal entered, it was immediately clear that this was a man of great intelligence and authority. He was a writer and presenter, with his own radio and TV programmes, and a brilliant communicator, recognized internationally. We talked animatedly about Havana, his beloved homeland, and the history and people of Cuba. Leal told me the streets of Old Havana were awash with African blood, because in years gone by African slaves were made to fight there like gladiators, and slaughtered for the amusement and entertainment of audiences of elegant Hispanic ladies.

We finished filming after precisely thirty minutes, and then he turned to me and said in perfect English:

'You are the best foreign television team that has ever interviewed me!'

I was delighted, and wondered why.

261

'You want to talk about *my* Cuba,' he said. 'Most people just want to hear about American cars, broken-down buildings, assassination attempts on Castro, exploding cigars . . . but nothing about the spirit of Cuban people, or Cuban life.'

And he then told us we were honorary Cubans.

'The poor deserve beauty too,' he said, which struck a chord with me. 'I'm going to make the Cuban nation proud of Havana, and ensure that our city is a force for unity.'

Chapter Thirty-one

I also turned out to be just the sort of person Peter Mandelson wanted on board the final team working on the Millennium Commission. This was a public body, set up by John Major, which used funding raised through the National Lottery to help different communities mark the transition from the second to the third millennium. Between 1993 and 2006, over two billion pounds were invested across the land in buildings, bridges, cultural centres, celebrations and environmental projects like the Eden Project in Cornwall, giving a major injection to places and groups that risked being left behind. Working with Mo Mowlam, Michael Heseltine, Heather Couper, Tessa Jowell, Chris Smith, Richard the Earl of Dalkeith and others, I could be in no doubt that I'd joined 'the great and the good' of our land. I felt honoured and empowered. I'd been sitting on the Millennium Dome Advisory Litmus Group since 1998, but this was a much bigger thing. This was about legacy, and serious change.

During the previous decade, I'd gained more and more experience of getting things done, putting in hours of unpaid work on boards and committees for voluntary sector organizations. Once you've started the ball rolling, there's a ripple effect. One thing always leads to another. All my charity work had prepared me well for public life. I'd learned what makes a good chair. I'd learned how a committee operates. I knew just how important it is to have a seat at the table if you want to get something done.

At the very first meeting of the Millennium Commission, I looked down the list of proposals. There wasn't a single Black-led project among them. Once again, I had to be true to myself, and I immediately spoke out.

'I'm sorry, but I cannot sit on a committee which isn't supporting any Black projects,' I said.

Nobody else had noticed. So Blair and Brown agreed to add extra funds – around £90 million – specifically for what were then known as 'BME' projects. One flagship initiative that came out of this was the Stephen Lawrence Project (now renamed Blueprint for All), set up by his mother Doreen Lawrence to ensure that future generations of young people could enjoy career opportunities denied to Stephen by his senseless murder in 1993. The Bernie Grant Arts Centre in Tottenham was another significant step forward. It opened in 2007 with a brief to support the development of culturally diverse artists, and the building was designed by the Ghanaian-British architect David Adjaye. The centre was named in honour of one of Britain's first Black MPs, who came to the UK in 1963 from British Guiana when the government was inviting citizens in crown colonies to settle in the 'Motherland'. In fact, Bernie was one of the very first people ever to tell me I was the sort of person they needed in the House of Lords.

On *Spitting Image*, the 1980s BAFTA-winning satirical puppet show, the figure of Conservative politician Michael Heseltine was iconic. He'd been depicted as a manic and narcissistic Tarzan figure, his floppy blond hair getting longer and messier and his promises to the voters more absurd with each episode. I wondered at first how I'd be able to work with this overpowering action man. But of course, preconceptions are always dangerous. He was nothing like that at all, and was himself very amused by his puppet. I found him reliably kind and generous: if you came up with a good argument, he'd give you his full support.

'If Floella's in favour, that's what we should do,' he'd often say in meetings.

My greatest ally of all on the Millennium Commission was the charismatic yet down-to-earth Labour MP Mo Mowlam, the Northern Ireland Secretary who'd negotiated the 1998 Good Friday Agreement. Like me, she was a big hugger, and she was always spurring me on with her no-nonsense enthusiasm for getting things done. In 1997 she'd been diagnosed with a brain tumour which eventually killed her, but while she was alive, she told everyone that it was benign. We both went up and down the country in those years, opening Sure Start centres, meeting people face to face and really getting a feel for those who could make a success of a project. We got behind the building of museums, libraries and other public facilities, and the work made me feel part of something historic. The only misunderstanding I ever had with Mo was when she invited me to her fiftieth birthday party, in September 1999, before the Dome had officially opened.

'We'll meet at the Wheel at one p.m.!' she said.

One of the attractions at the Millennium Experience housed by the Dome, now called the O2 building, was some kind of wheel, so, without thinking, Keith, Alvina, Aston and I excitedly got the tube to Greenwich. No Mo. And no sign of other guests either, which seemed strange. We waited around for a while, worrying I'd got the time wrong, and when nobody turned up, we came back home.

'Where were you?' asked Mo the next morning. Her birthday celebrations had been a great success . . . But they took place at the Millennium Wheel on the South Bank – now called the London Eye – not at the Dome. Aston and Alvina were bitterly disappointed. We could have been among the first to party in a pod, and seen London from a whole new perspective. But I'd blown it. I don't think the children have ever quite forgiven me.

'You're just the sort of person we need as a parent governor,' the master of Dulwich College, Graham Able, said to me in 2001, after Aston had spent ten very happy years there and started his degree in Sociology at the University of Exeter. I spent ten years myself on that governing body, working hard to support the school's needs-blind admission policy, so that any boy with the right abilities could end up at the school, rich or poor. The first chair I worked with, Sir Eddie George, Governor of the Bank of England, was the son of a post office clerk. He also had a big commitment to social mobility.

As I mentioned earlier, one of my mother's three jobs when I was a little girl was to do the laundry for the college's boarders at this school. Then her own grandson had gone to Dulwich College. And finally, there was I, her daughter, on the governing body. The same year, 2001, I was awarded an OBE for my contribution to television, so when I opened a new wing of Dulwich College, the inscription on the wall recorded that award.

Tony Lothian was delighted by the news of my OBE.

'Now you have bottom, Floella,' she told me proudly. It was her way of saying I had gravitas. 'When you have bottom, people listen to you.'

I'm convinced that if you're doing good, good will come to you.

A headhunter – one of the founders of the recruitment company Saxton Bampfylde – once noticed me addressing a charity event at the Royal Albert Hall. Of course, I had no idea of this at the time. But our paths must have crossed for a purpose: ten years later, in 2003, he decided I was just the sort of person Ofcom needed for their Content Board, which was responsible for promoting quality and safeguarding the standards of radio and television in the UK.

'They're looking for diverse people from all walks of life,' he told me. 'I think you'd be perfect. Are you interested?'

I went to the interview, not sure at all what to expect. I'd never met Richard Hooper, deputy chair of the regulating body and also chair of Ofcom's Content Board, but he greeted me with open arms.

'Floella!' he said warmly, reminding me instantly of Tony Lothian.

'Richard!' I responded with an equally theatrical kiss. I had met another of my guardian angels.

He introduced me to the interview panel, and we had a wide-ranging discussion, but I particularly remember talking about the need to put measures in place to protect the mental health of people taking part in reality television shows, which were becoming ever more popular – *Big Brother* was followed by *Wife Swap*, *Pop Idol*, *The Salon* and *Swag*. These kinds of programmes could propel unprepared participants into national celebrity status overnight. I said I thought the programme-makers ought to consider what happened to people after they'd been on the shows, and to think about the psychological impact of taking part. Little did I know that one of the men on the interview panel owned the company that produced one of the programmes I'd named.

Richard turned to him, and said:

'Well, Floella needs an answer. What are you going to do about it?'

I was mortified. I went home and told Keith:

'You told me not to tell everyone what they should do, and I didn't listen to you. Now I've really blown it.'

But I'd hardly had time to despair, when the phone rang. They wanted me after all. Richard Hooper was the best chair I'd ever worked under. He was like a conductor, managing all the contributors in a discussion to perfection, knowing exactly who to turn to, and when. I learned a huge amount from him. It was the most diverse board I'd ever been part of, with six women and five men.

Yet I soon realized that many people thought it was the colour of my skin, not my skills and experience, that had got me the post. A woman I met at an Ofcom function actually said to me:

'You only got the job because you're Black. They wanted to be politically correct.'

'Well,' I said, 'it's only because you're White that you've got to where *you* are. Now it's my turn. Anyway, read my CV.'

My impression once again was that some of my fellow committee members maybe didn't think I was of their calibre. One particular person seemed to criticize me persistently, all through our meetings. So one coffee break I went right up to them.

'You fascinate me. I'm intrigued by your thinking. Tell me, how do you do it, what makes you tick?'

They drew back, surprised. It was a subtle kind of confrontation, but it did the trick, and after that they gave me space, and showed me respect, and we ended up having a genuinely productive relationship. Even when you think others may doubt you, never doubt yourself. When I felt I was doubted, usually I was furious inside, but I knew I couldn't show anger. Black women were always being stereotyped as angry, or carrying a chip on their shoulder. If people think you're angry, they won't listen to you. So, I smiled, and I proved I could get on and do the job.

*

Meanwhile, my charity work, as patron, trustee and hands-on supporter, continued to multiply and take new forms. As well as supporting me, Keith also volunteered his time, becoming a magistrate at West London Court. He became a chair and was instrumental in setting up a dedicated domestic violence court and making changes to diversity on the bench. The need for this was highlighted one day when a Black lawyer came in and was immediately shown to the dock.

Charities often asked me to run marathons to support them, and although for years I refused, I did love watching the London Marathon on television, and I'd sometimes greet charity runners at the end of a race. They'd often fall into my arms, exhausted, sweaty, dejected . . .

'Oh. I didn't make my time. I'm a failure,' they'd pant, tearfully.

You're crazy, I thought. *You've just run a marathon. How can that be a failure? It looked like torture.*

Then, in 1999, Barnardo's wrote me one of the nicest letters I'd ever read, begging me to consider running in support of the charity. I was coming up for my fiftieth birthday. I was looking for a new challenge in life. I'd never run further than 400 metres before, and hadn't done that for years. So, this time I rashly said yes. And promptly failed to do anything about it.

Shortly afterwards, I was at the Millennium Dome, all dressed up in my yellow hard hat and high-vis jacket, thinking I was going to be recording a piece for the BBC National Lottery programme. Who should appear but Michael Aspel and his camera crew? What was he doing there?

'This is your life, Floella Benjamin!' he announced. I was completely taken aback, and all I could do was giggle helplessly. Keith revealed later how much he and the children had hated having to lie to me to keep that secret, but it was a rule of the show that it came as a complete surprise to its 'victims'.

In the famous *This Is Your Life* studio, my past flashed before me as he went through my red book. My brother Junior and his family made an appearance from America, and everyone told little stories about me, and it was all wonderful – except for the moment when Michael announced that I was going to be running my first marathon in three months' time. I'd not done any training. I hadn't had time to prepare in any way. The donations started flooding in, and the pressure was on.

The big day arrived and I did everything wrong. I wore far too many clothes. I ran in a cheap pair of trainers. I didn't know you should put Vaseline on your feet to stop them rubbing. I didn't carry enough sweets and energy boosters with me. I ate far too much pasta for weeks beforehand, because I'd heard you had to load up on carbs. Some good friends, Pat and Larry Chrisfield, had a house in Greenwich and invited me to stay with them the night before. Keith dropped me off.

'See you tomorrow at the finishing line!' he said, and drove away.

I waited at the red start line, baseball cap, T-shirt and running vest on, and fleece zipped up. Immediately I realized I was going to be too hot. First the hat went. Then the jacket. Then the next top. I just had to throw them all away, till I was stripped down to a vest. Used to sprinting, I was quickly exhausted. No way could I keep running for forty-two kilometres, so I tried to pace myself, running for a bit, then power walking, then running again. I eventually made it over the finishing line in six hours, by which time Keith had been wrapped in a blanket by a kindly volunteer who spotted him huffing and puffing as he ran along to The Mall to get from his distant parking spot, and mistook him for an exhausted competitor.

But I'd done it. And, being competitive, my immediate thought was, *Well, if I can do that in six hours without any training at all, with a bit of work, I can definitely improve.*

'I tell you what,' I said to the Barnardo's chief executive, before Keith could shut me up. 'I'll do ten consecutive marathons for you. Till I get to my sixtieth. How about that?'

I kept my promise, and in the end my best time was four and a half hours. I wished I had taken up marathon running at an earlier age. The joy of passing the six-mile point was like running on air.

One of the things I came to love about the London Marathon is its amazing atmosphere. You never know who'll be running alongside you. I nearly got myself in trouble in 2001 when, just before we reached the *Cutty Sark*, a drunken fan rushed towards me and clasped me in a smelly embrace, shouting, 'Floella, I love you! I *really* love you!'

'Help me! Somebody, please help me!' I screamed.

I managed to get away, but on Tower Bridge, I heard my name being called again, and once more felt a firm hand on my arm.

'Get *off* me,' I roared, shaking the man off, steeling myself for trouble.

'Floella! It's the BBC! We just want to interview you!'

Luckily the reporter saw the funny side when I explained my extreme reaction.

I began to understand the mentality of those collapsing runners I used to greet at the finishing line. I became determined to finish in under five hours. One year I was recovering from a torn ligament, while also suffering from that old *Black Mikado* foot injury, and then, quite early on in the race, I missed my step and stumbled in a gutter, which really made me see stars. After that, I struggled to move one leg after the other. Only the thought of my dear friend Ken Follett's substantial donation kept me going. Coming round the corner into the final stretch, I looked at the big clock at the end of The Mall and saw the number five. Oh no! I'd blown it. With two hundred metres to go! I collapsed on the spot. But before I knew what was happening, the arms of two supportive strangers had scooped me up, one on each side.

'Come on, Floella! You're nearly there! You can do it!'

They dragged me to the finishing line, and I crawled over it. I must have looked a wreck, but at least I finished. Usually, I'd still be running to the end, sprinting, still smiling, still waving. That year I looked absolutely terrible. Yet I've never raised so much money. After that exceptionally agonizing finale, donations just poured in.

That taught me a lot about the British public's instinct to support people in their hour of need. The more they see you struggle, but still keep on trying, the more they love you. Making everything look effortless is more likely to bring you criticism than praise.

Nothing has pleased me more than to hear from other Black runners that they'd entered their own first marathon after seeing me on television. Historically, not many Caribbean people run long distances, so it's great to change that image, and break the cycle. That's why I later became president of the Ramblers and then a vice-president of the Royal Horticultural Society. Running, hiking, walking, gardening . . . all these activities are so enjoyable and so good for your mental and physical health, yet there's a certain kind of exclusion which can make people feel they'll never 'fit in'. Everyone should feel welcome, and be encouraged to have a go at something new. That's how I ended up walking a hundred kilometres along the Great Wall of China to raise money for the National Children's Hospital, going into villages where they'd never seen a Black person before.

You never know where new experiences will lead you, and you never know what you might learn. In 2004 the Olympic Games were held in Athens, and to celebrate their return to Greece, where the Games began, there was a 'global' torch

relay, kicked off in Sydney by Australia's 400-metre gold medallist Cathy Freeman. Imagine how honoured I felt when I was
asked to carry the Olympic flame on one of the London legs.
Chariots of Fire music playing in my head, I pictured myself
running gracefully through Greenwich or Hyde Park.

'Where do you want me?' I asked eagerly.

'Peckham. The twenty-sixth of June.'

I confess I was disappointed. My problem with Peckham is
that I'm forever getting lost there. It's seen a lot of regeneration
in recent years, but in those days it was a still a deprived back-
water of South-East London which few people wanted to visit.

But when I arrived and saw the streets lined with excited
children of all races waving their St George's flags and cheering
as I passed, I had a rethink. *This is why I'm here*, I told myself.
*I'm running for the children. They know something great is on
their doorstep.* When I saw all those little faces and breathed
all their enthusiasm and joy into my lungs, I felt I was running
on air. It was so uplifting. Right away, I joined the campaign
for London to get the 2012 Olympics. I became a member of
the London Organizing Committee of the Olympic Games
(LOCOG) Diversity Board, and had the joy of handing out the
medals during the Paralympics. I will never forget the electric
atmosphere and roar of the crowd as I walked out into that
great stadium.

As I always say to people, it's not where you start, it's where
you end up that matters.

Chapter Thirty-two

In the spring of 2002, we were making a prime-time series for Carlton TV called *Statues and Monuments*, presented by Ray Gosling, which included a piece on the planned statue of Nelson Mandela now in Parliament Square which was created by the sculptor Ian Walters and finally unveiled in 2007. We interviewed Lord Richard Attenborough, who campaigned for this statue, and because I donated towards it, we were invited to South Africa House for a reception attended by Mandela. It was strange being inside that building after standing outside over the years protesting against apartheid. When Nelson Mandela came into the room he walked past all the dignitaries and straight up to our daughter Alvina, who was thirteen at the time, shook her hand and asked her why she wasn't home doing her homework. We were told 'no photographs' but I couldn't resist snapping that unforgettable moment.

The *Statues and Monuments* series involved a lot of location filming. One day, we drove up to Paddington Green to film a sequence about the great eighteenth-century actress Sarah Siddons, whose statue is still one of only a handful in London of named women celebrated for their achievements. It was mid-afternoon on a weekday, so we expected the area to be quiet.

From my seat on the crew bus, I noticed a group of boys on

the green who looked as if they were dancing. But when we got out, I realized they were fighting with knives. Instinctively, I leapt out of the bus and rushed into the fray.

'Stop it! Stop it! Stop it now!' I shouted urgently, while somebody called the police. They turned up very quickly, surrounded the boys, and identified the ringleader.

A tall and furious boy, he spat on the ground as the officer questioned him. His attitude was just terrible, and it incensed me so much that without a second thought, I positioned myself between him and the policeman – who was too surprised to stop me – and I started questioning the teenager myself.

'How dare you?' I said to him angrily. 'How dare you speak to a policeman like that? Don't you think they've got better things to do?'

He rolled his eyes at me dismissively.

'Look at me, look at me now now now now now!' I shouted, with a rat-a-tat-tat delivery as sharp as an army commander's. That got his attention. Then, locking my eyes with his, I began to address him, clearly and calmly:

'I am your guardian angel. I'm here to show you the power that you have. Look at all these boys here on the green. You're leading them. Just think what could happen if you used that power to lead for good. Just think what you could do with that. Now, I want you to start dreaming about me. These eyes of mine are the eyes of someone who loves you, and I want you to start loving yourself in the same way. I want you to start believing that you can make a difference for good. I know you can. Just show the world. Just do it. Now come. Come to me. Come and hug me.'

Falling into my arms like a little baby, he let out a whimpering sigh.

'There, there,' I whispered. 'It's all right. It's all right.'

Somebody loved him. Somebody cared about him and had

275

faith in him. That's what I had to convince him. Then I turned to the policemen.

'Just go easy on him,' I said.

The officers were obviously full of tension themselves.

'Can we have a hug as well, Floella?' one of them said.

'Of course!'

I often wish I knew what happened to that boy. How I'd love to find out what he went on to do. It wouldn't surprise me if one day I meet him again. Years after the event, I have met many of the people I had spiritual moments with and they have told me how much I changed their lives for the better, and that having someone show unconditional love made a difference.

The same month, a letter arrived from Frank Flynn, head of commissioning for BBC Schools Programmes, which had a separate budget from the main BBC. Researchers at Durham University investigating racism in primary schools had used my book *Coming to England* as a case study, and found it the perfect way to help children learn about modern British history. Frank asked us to come and see him as soon as possible to discuss dramatizing it.

We were still shooting *Statues and Monuments*, so we arranged to go to White City in our lunch break, and we took our own sandwiches along with us. The new Director General, Greg Dyke, had made such sweeping cuts in every department, including hospitality, that we thought we would be lucky to get a biscuit. Coming back to the White City building after all those years recording *Play School* and all the other programmes I used to do there made me feel quite emotional.

As we walked into the office, we saw that in fact Frank Flynn and his colleague Karen Johnson, commissioning editor in the Department for Drama and Documentaries, had laid on a proper spread with sandwiches and drinks. Well! Keith and I exchanged a glance. We could tell immediately that whatever their plans were, they were very serious about them.

Karen Johnson enthused about the research at Durham and the use it had made of my book.

'We really want to have *Coming to England* as part of our content. How do you feel about a dramatization?'

'That's fantastic!' I replied. Seven years on, and we were finally getting somewhere. 'So, who's going to make it?'

'You, of course! Who else could tell the story better? You wrote it. You've got your own production company and you're making great programmes. We want you to make it for us.'

I explained we were in the middle of a production at that moment, but we'd make it our next priority. Then we headed off to Greenwich, where we were filming that afternoon near the *Cutty Sark*. Within a few hours, we got a call from Karen. Her voice was urgent.

'Floella, we've had a meeting. We need costings from you by the end of the month to be sure of having the money in the budget for *Coming to England*. We've got eighty thousand pounds left to spend this year and we want to assign it to you. Can you do that?'

I got to work that night. On such a small budget, we realized we couldn't possibly shoot the programme fully acted out, with dialogue. We could bring down costs by using a voiceover with dramatized visuals-only sequences and tableaux. We'd done plenty of stories in our various children's shows that way, and we knew it could work.

'Make it look delicious!' I said to Keith, who was director and cameraman. I was sure he would – unlike many, he knew how to light the subtle shades of Black skin.

It's much harder to adapt your own work than other people's, so I got on with editing *Statues and Monuments*, while Keith went off to Barbados on an initial recce and to write the script. Smaller and less industrialized than Trinidad, Barbados actually looked and felt more like the island of my childhood than Trinidad itself in 2002. Thanks to having made our cookery programmes there, we had lots of friends and contacts on the island already, including our guardian angels, Jan and Ludo Marcello and the Deputy Prime Minister Billie Miller, Barbados's first woman barrister. Later, when we arrived for filming, she made a speech in parliament to welcome us, encouraging the whole island to help.

In London, we began to collect costumes, stopping the car outside every vintage and charity shop we passed to rummage through the racks for exactly the right 1950s and 60s clothing. Keith made a second trip to Barbados to scout for locations – he needed to find a church, a school, a fish market, and a house just like the one I lived in in Trinidad. The house was a nightmare to find, and he was feeling quite desperate until one day, quite by chance, he noticed that he'd parked the car right across the road from an estate agent. He explained what he was looking for to the receptionist. From the back room, out of sight, came a voice with a strong Bajan accent, sounding almost Cornish to Keith's English ear.

'Don't worry, Angela, I'll take care of that.'

An ageing White man emerged, introduced himself as Nick Paravacino, and drove Keith across to the ruggedly beautiful east coast of the island to a fishing village called Bathsheba. And there was the house: white, wooden and utterly perfect. Even the period furniture was just right. Nick had brought Keith to his very own beach house and he refused to charge us a penny for using it.

Back in England, Keith began the search for period cars to create the street scenes. We couldn't afford to hire these, so he used to drive around London leaving notes on suitable windscreens:

Floella from Play School *needs your help. Please come to Kingsmead street at nine o'clock in the morning on October 20th.*

Meanwhile, we began casting. The book starts with me aged three, and I'm thirteen by the time it ends, so we needed children to play me and my siblings at all stages of our childhood – six children, in three different age groups, who looked similar enough to be convincing. As usual, we went to Barbara Speake to find our child actors. Black complexions differ a great deal, and getting the skin tone right wasn't easy, but it was important to me to get that perfect. We were finally happy with our Lesters, our Ellingtons, our Juniors and our Cynthias, but we couldn't find an older 'Floella' or 'Sandra' anywhere.

Then we spotted ten-year-old Chloe Ketter-Thomas in a play at the Hackney Empire about the inquiry into the death of Victoria Climbié, *Those Who Trespass Against Us.* Chloe was a wonderful, vivacious actress, and perfect to play me. But we needed a quiet, timid girl for Sandra. So, I approached our local primary school, Rosemead, and explained to the head what we were looking for.

'Oh, we've got a whole row of children here for you to meet who all love acting!' she said, when I arrived. But, of course, nobody who put themselves forward was right for Sandra. I shook my head, and looked around the playground. At last I noticed a little girl playing on her own.

'She looks great,' I said.

'She's so shy,' the teacher said.

'That's the one I want.'

I'd found my Sandra. Kamaria George was absolutely perfect, and in the end, although they'd never acted before, her parents Rose and Len also played several roles in the film.

The next step was to find my own parents. Dardie was easy. Born in Balham to Jamaican parents, Nicholas Pinnock was a trained dancer as well as an actor, and as soon as we saw him walk we knew he was the one – Nicholas oozed Caribbean style and panache. He's since made a name for himself in Hollywood. My father always dressed very smartly, in a suit and tie with polished shoes. Funnily enough, although we thought we'd got Dardie down to a 'T', the first thing he said when he saw the film was 'I never wore a hat.'

But Marmie was mission impossible. We tried so many actresses, but nobody clicked. Either they had too strong a Jamaican accent, and couldn't adapt to the softer speech patterns of Trinidad. Or they had no charisma. Finally, we found someone whom I could maybe mould into Marmie with a bit of coaching. We offered her the job. Two days later her agent rang to say she couldn't do it as she didn't feel confident enough.

By this time, we had two weeks to go before filming started.

'What are we going to do? What are we going to do?' I kept asking Keith, ever more desperate.

Talking to people in despair, individuals who are at their wits' end, I've often tried to persuade them that when you reach rock bottom, this is the moment things will change. You just have to keep going and have faith and courage and refuse to give up. And sure enough, just as I'd almost given up hope, a brown A4 envelope popped through the door. Inside was a standard letter, and a CV, and some photos of a young woman who looked remarkably like my mother.

'My name is Davina Jackson,' the letter said. 'I've just left drama school. Please contact me if ever you're looking for somebody for your productions.'

Born in Trinidad. On the same day as my mum, so a Scorpio too. That was a good sign! She didn't even know I was making the film. She didn't have an agent. I called the number.

'Hello, is that Davina?'

'Yes.' The sweet, slow way she said that one word told me everything. Her accent was pure Trinidadian.

'This is Floella Benjamin Productions. Could you come and see us in the next few hours?'

'Yes, I'm living in Earl's Court. I'll come now, straight away.'

Sing-song, dreamy, lyrical . . . listening to her voice, I was sent straight to the Trinidad of my childhood. I just melted. I couldn't believe what I was hearing.

When she turned up, her hair was in plaits and she was slender and unassuming. Her skin was a little lighter than Marmie's. But as soon as she had put on a balloon-filled bra and the belted beige paisley-patterned dress we'd bought for Marmie's costume, and topped off the outfit with the right wig, it was as if the young Marmie I remembered was standing before us.

She read the part beautifully.

It was like a miracle.

Thank you. Thank you. Thank you.

Everything fell into place.

Chapter Thirty-three

So many different people pulled out the stops to help us make *Coming to England*. We couldn't have done it without them. The schedule was as tight as the budget, and we had little room for anything to go wrong. Thankfully, several miracles happened along the way.

At six o'clock one October Sunday morning, we took our crew and equipment to the nearby street of terraced fifties houses which looked very much like Mayfield Avenue and we began to wait. We'd already persuaded the residents to park their modern cars elsewhere for the day, so the sun rose over an empty road. As the appointed hour drew close, I began to feel more and more nervous. It was all very well to leave notes on windscreens, but would anyone actually take any notice?

At three minutes to nine there were still no cars to be seen.

Then suddenly, we heard the noise of an engine, and the first classic car drove round the corner. It was followed by another and then another, and another, and another: old Jaguars, a vintage Rover, some old bangers. All the drivers had turned up in appropriate period costume, and everything looked perfect.

At every stage, we found that as soon as my name was mentioned, doors magically opened, and our path was smoothed. A heritage railway called the Watercress Line in Hampshire did everything they could to help us film our authentic train scenes, letting us use their station, guard and steam engines for the day, for a tiny fee. For the carnival scene, we hired a ten-foot-high dancing dragon costume from Mahogany Carnival Arts, based in Harlesden and run by the amazing Trinidadian designer Clary Salandy, planning to film it in close-up, and crossing our fingers for a rain-free day. We set everything up in the nearby McDonald's car park, and I gazed upwards in despair. The sky looked so grey, and nothing like Trinidad. But once again, I was blessed: at exactly the right moment, and for just long enough for us to get our shot, the clouds briefly parted, the autumn sun shone crisply, and the skies turned bright blue.

Our biggest challenge was the arrival scene, the moment we docked in England after our long sea voyage. The real *Marqués de Comillas* was probably at the bottom of the sea, having been scrapped in 1962 after a terrible fire in a Spanish shipyard the year before. But we'd found an old steam dredger which conveniently didn't have the noisy vibrations of a diesel ship, and could look the part with some clever camera angles. I called Southampton Docks and explained what we were doing, and that we'd like to film our dredger docking, and the passengers disembarking.

'Is that really Floella Benjamin?' said an excited voice at the other end of the phone. 'Really? *Floella?* I'll do anything for you! We'll just need a hundred pounds to pay the guys who catch the rope, as they have to have overtime to work on a Sunday.'

This man, who was of course a *Play School* baby, literally moved the *QE2* for us so we could film our scene.

We put out the call for help from the local film school, and once again, the vintage cars turned up, and a local girl with great organization skills pitched in and sorted out our coach-load of extras to throng the wharf.

By then it was November, and a particularly cold and rainy

November too. Standing around for hours on the freezing dock-side, singing away at top volume so that the actors would move in time for the dancing scene, I came down with terrible bronchitis, despite having worn three coats. I went coughing to the doctor, who told me it was pneumonia and I had to go to bed.

'I can't! We're on a deadline.'

We ploughed on. The next challenge was to get the crew, actors, chaperones, continuity and make-up people to the Caribbean, together with the production team and all the costumes, props and equipment. All the children needed licences to leave the country. When we reached Barbados, our beloved friends Jan and Ludo Marcello, who had always generously come to our rescue when we filmed in the Caribbean, had arranged preferential rates at their all-inclusive hotel so everyone was having a great time! But they were behaving as if we'd arrived for a two-week party. I had to explain firmly that we were there to work, not holiday.

I got everyone settled and made sure they'd all learned their lines. Our first shooting day was still a few days away, on Sunday, and we were starting with the scene in church, because after that weekend, it would be decorated for Christmas. From the crew bus, Keith rang the bishop to confirm everything was OK for the shoot.

'You're not filming in my church,' the bishop said firmly.

I watched Keith's face fall.

'This one's for you,' he said, passing me the phone.

'Hello, Bishop! This is Floella Benjamin. We're just phoning to let you know we're all here. And we're so excited about coming on Sunday.'

'You're not filming in my church,' the bishop said again.

'What do you mean?' I said, trying to stay calm.

'Well, I haven't seen you personally since you've arrived,' he said.

'But I sent you an email,' I protested. 'We've already agreed everything. The flowers. The date. The vicar.'

'I haven't seen you *personally*.'

He kept repeating these words. My heart began to pump. Where the hell was I going to get a church in two days? I sat back in my seat, and took a deep breath. What was I going to do? Then it came to me.

'You know something, Bishop, I can feel the devil at work here,' I said, confidingly. 'The devil *knows* that I'm making *Coming to England* for good. The devil *knows* this is going to make a difference to children's lives. The devil *knows* how important this is. But the devil is trying to stop me every step of the way. We've already overcome so much adversity. Yet the devil keeps putting roadblocks in front of us. But I know that YOU, being a man of the Church, you won't let the devil win, will you?'

A short silence.

'You can film in my church.'

After that, Keith and I called it 'the Satan clause'. People in Barbados are generally very devout. So at the slightest sign of any further opposition, we only had to mention the devil for our obstacles to melt away.

In one scene in the book, young Floella witnesses a very dramatic full-immersion baptism in the sea. A wonderful pastor called Reverend Rock performed this for us. Never was anyone better named. Reverend Rock was our saviour and he supported us every inch of the way. He often came to see us at the hotel, to check everything was going to plan. And whenever we told him something had gone wrong he would tell us to stand up, and he'd give me and Keith a big bear hug. Then, at full volume, in a passionate voice that reverberated round the hotel lobby, completely unselfconscious about the holidaymakers in flip-flops and beachwear all around us, he'd begin to pray:

'Lord! These people are here for good, Lord. Give them all the strength that they need, Lord. Make sure they have what they want and that they get this film done.'

We got some pretty funny looks, but Reverend Rock's prayers seemed to be doing the trick.

The day came to film the scene when Marmie leaves us with foster parents. With all the technicians, and all the actors and extras, there were over fifty people on set. Keith was on camera and I wanted to make sure Chloe and Davina truly got the heart of this key scene, which is such a turning point in the story.

I looked up from the monitor at Chloe, our nine-year-old Floella, a great little actress. She was hesitant so I tried to paint a picture in her head. 'You don't know when you're going to see your mum again or when you'll be back with your own family. You don't know the people you're going to be living with. What if they're not nice to you? How are you going to feel in this situation? Now, show me some emotion.'

Tears welled in Chloe's eyes, and she began to cry:

'Oh Marmie, Marmie. Don't leave me, don't leave me.'

'Well done, Chloe! That's perfect. Well done,' I said.

And then the camera moved to Davina.

'Come on, Davina,' I said. 'You're leaving your children behind now. You don't want to but you know you have to. Your head tells you it's the best thing to do but your heart really, *really* doesn't want to. How do you think you're going to feel? You can do this, Davina. Show me your emotions.'

Chloe and Davina were some distance away, and I was looking at them on the monitor, so that I could see exactly what the camera was seeing.

'Come on, come on. Show me, show me,' I urged Davina.

And suddenly, on the screen, as I saw Davina's shaking hand, and the tears rolling down her cheeks, as I watched her anguish, I wasn't seeing the actress but my own mum – her figure, her dress, her pearl necklace. My whole life was concentrated onto that little TV screen, and I became that nine-year-old girl being left behind. But this time, instead of containing my distress, it burst from me. I started to shake, and then my knees gave way and I dropped to the ground, howling. I found myself crying uncontrollably, sobbing, gasping, panting. Weeping took over my whole body. I didn't recognize that animal sound emerging from me. I hardly recognized myself. What was happening to me? This wailing? This grieving? When my mum really left me I hadn't cried like that. But now, even surrounded by all these people, I couldn't stop myself. There was nothing I could do.

Big, strong Floella. Always in charge. Always giving the orders and getting things done. But now not even in charge of myself. I couldn't hear anything. I couldn't see anything. I had no choice but to give myself up to the emotion of that moment. The suppressed trauma had been released.

Twenty minutes passed. I was completely oblivious to Keith's efforts to comfort me. And then, as quickly as I'd been overwhelmed, I snapped out of it.

'Let's get cracking!' I said. 'Come on.'

I felt purged. I'd had no idea such a deep anguish was still sitting inside me, that I'd carried around the terrible pain of parting for so long. But every time I've seen that shot since, something flickers inside me. I feel I've come to terms with the leaving. I know my mum had no choice but to go without us. Yet I can't ever forget how I cried, watching that scene forty-three years later.

It was the time it took for a baby to grow: nine months from that conversation with Karen and Frank over sandwiches in White City, our film of *Coming to England* was first screened.

We edited it in our dining room, using our new edit suite. In fact, our editor Dan Mellow was still hard at work the day before transmission, with delivery due at six o'clock that evening.

That was the day the editing computer decided to crash in a big way. I called the BBC and promised to deliver it by eight o'clock. Then nine. Then ten. At midnight, we still weren't ready.

We edited all night. We knew it had to be on air in the schools' schedule at eleven a.m. And I was also due to address a Commonwealth event at Lancaster House. When we were nearly finished, I realized I had to revoice the final sequence, as I didn't feel the emotion was coming through in the right way. I sped down to our sound studio in the basement and recorded it again, until I was satisfied that the tone was perfect.

At six o'clock in the morning we were ready. Keith rushed the tape to White City to give it to the Compliance Department as they had to check colour, sound and grading before transmission, and I rushed to central London to deliver my big speech. Keith waited anxiously by the phone until eventually the BBC called to say the quality was OK.

After our film was broadcast, I started getting phone calls. A well-known Caribbean actor of around my age rang me in tears:

'Floella. That is my life. That is my dad, walking away with his suitcase. I never saw him again.'

Jane Scott, the Duchess of Buccleuch, also called to say:

'Floella, I can identify with this film so much. I was a little girl in Scotland and my parents sent me to boarding school in England and all the girls bullied me because of my Scottish accent. I know just how you felt.'

And I realized that the film wasn't just my story. Anyone who's ever been made to feel different or an outsider can connect with it. All our hard work had paid off. That film had come into being in that way for a purpose. We'd created something magical.

The response was unbelievable. Yet when we submitted it for a Children's BAFTA, it didn't even get nominated. It was a real mystery why the jury didn't select it. Perhaps they couldn't see the significance of the story. We were devastated. Our disappointment felt physical, like a series of punches. Keith had given the film all his creativity and he was just as shocked and heartbroken as I was.

Somehow, I had to pull myself together the same day to talk about *Coming to England* to an audience at Hammersmith College. I felt I had to explain why I wasn't my normal self. I felt like crying. At this a girl rose to her feet and began to clap.

'You don't need a BAFTA to know how much we appreciate your work and everything you do for us young people. We're your BAFTA,' she said.

I smiled and felt spiritually uplifted.

In fact, to my joy, *Coming to England* went on to win a Royal Television Society Award. Keith couldn't come to the ceremony as he was filming in Scotland, so I took my daughter Alvina. We sat at the back of the Savoy Ballroom where the awards were taking place, and suddenly I heard Alvina's voice: 'Mum, mum, they're calling your name! *Coming to England* has won!' Despite that initial rejection from the BBC Children's Department, they now show the film without fail every year.

The words of that young woman in Hammersmith, and the standing ovation that followed, meant more to me than any official acclaim. I learned then that you don't need prizes to be recognized and appreciated, and for the sake of people like this girl, I had to battle on. If you stay positive, and don't dwell on your disappointments, you can understand the true meaning of success.

Chapter Thirty-four

My son pretended to be outraged when I was awarded an honorary degree from his very own university. The letter arrived out of the blue in 2005, two years after Aston had graduated from Exeter University and when he'd nearly finished at BPP Law School. Alvina was about to do her GSCEs, and was also competing – and winning – in national athletics competitions, excelling in the high jump. She was a keen drummer too, and had recently proved herself a 'chip off the old block', according to her grandfather, who'd been very impressed by her performance in a school production of *Bugsy Malone*. She'd certainly achieved one thing I never had: she'd tempted Dardie to go and see her live on stage.

'How about this, Aston!' I said proudly, showing him my invitation to the degree ceremony.

'I spent three years working hard for my degree and you just waltz in . . . !' he said.

'Listen, son,' I replied, laughing. 'I may have left school at sixteen but I've been to the university of life and studied empathy and common sense.'

You could even say that I got my degree for my memoir for young readers, *Coming to England*. The book was already on the history reading list for trainee teachers at Exeter's outstanding Graduate School of Education, and Julie Dawick, the wife of Deputy Vice-Chancellor Paul Webley, was an enormous fan of all my work promoting diversity.

I felt so special and honoured to be sitting on stage in my academic gown at Exeter University that summer, with Keith and Sandra and my mum in the audience. The audience rose to applaud my speech, about the importance of childhood and the three Cs that guide my life, with warm enthusiasm. We were beautifully treated by the university and I went home very happy. That was the end of that . . . or so I thought.

Three months later I had a call from that same headhunter who'd introduced me to Ofcom. Was I interested in being the chancellor of a well-known university? He was a bit mysterious about which university was after me, and I wasn't entirely sure at first what a chancellor did – it soon transpired that there's no job description, and it's very much up to each individual to make the role their own – but naturally I said yes. I loved the challenge. Six weeks after that, another call confirmed that the university was Exeter and they wanted me to come and meet the senior team, and asked if Keith could come too.

We met at a hotel. Three men in suits were waiting for us in a low-lit room with a lamp on the table: Steve Smith, the vice-chancellor, David Allen, the registrar and secretary, and Russell Seal, chair of the council.

We got talking – about what I might bring to the university, how I saw the world, my views on the importance of education – and I began to visualize the role I could play.

'What you see is what you get with me,' I told them frankly. 'I like greeting people, I'm good at making people feel welcome, and special, whoever they are, and diversity is very important to me. But what I'd really like to bring to the chancellorship is heart.'

They thanked me, and said they'd like to speak to Keith

now, alone. I'll always remember going up the stairs and seeing them ushering my husband into the room, and the door closing behind him, and imagining a scene from *The Godfather* film. In fact, he told me later they must have just wanted to make sure he too was suitable to be associated with the university, and that he'd be completely behind me.

Within a few weeks, I'd got the job. Much later I discovered I'd been up against an ex-prime minister and a top City executive. So, in 2006 I became the fifth chancellor of the University of Exeter and the first Black woman chancellor in the country. For the ceremonies I wore a thick antique robe embroidered with gold thread which was given to the university by its first chancellor, Mary Cavendish, the Duchess of Devonshire, who had page boys to carry the heavy train. To their credit, I never felt the university used me as a trophy or token figurehead in any way. Steve came from a working-class family, and hadn't attended a particularly prestigious university himself, and he too had initially experienced that 'what are you doing here?' message certain people in the establishment can give off to those from atypical backgrounds. We worked together extremely well. He was an intrepid adventurer who boldly went where others feared to tread. He looked after the academic, business and financial side of things. My role was to help students understand emotionally why they were there, and how they could make a difference at Exeter and in the future by acting always with integrity, morality and honesty, and being people others can trust.

My appointment definitely raised a few eyebrows. What were my academic credentials? What was a *Play School* presenter doing at a university? Wasn't I just a TV personality, a worthless celebrity? Even the leadership of the City of Exeter apparently expressed their doubts about me. So, I knew I had to prove myself.

What Are You Doing Here?

I was over the moon to be invited by Universities UK to my first chancellors' event. I was one of only eleven female chancellors at the time, and went along with a spring in my step. *If they could see me now.* I collected my name badge and stepped into the room proudly. *If they could see me now.* Immediately a pompous-looking man bustled towards me and looked me up and down.

'What are you doing here?' he enquired.

I was astonished. Perhaps he thought I should be serving the drinks. 'What are *you* doing here?' I said with a smile. I wasn't going to let him dampen my spirits.

The following year, I was asked to give the keynote speech and sat on the platform with Princess Anne, chancellor of the University of London. I looked down and spotted my bustling friend. I think he definitely knew by then what I was doing there. The Princess Royal whispered to me with a smile:

'Do you realize that neither of us have been to university?'

Who would have thought?

When our son Aston had lined up for a brief handshake at his graduation in 2003, we'd loved sitting in the audience with all the other proud parents. But I couldn't help feeling the ceremony had lacked the personal touch. I wanted every student to leave university under my chancellorship feeling truly inspired and empowered by their special day, and to feel I cared personally about their success and their future. I had promised to bring heart to the graduations. My way of doing this started by instinct, and soon became my trademark. As each and every student stepped onto the platform in the Great Hall, I opened my arms to welcome them, and gave them an enormous and heart-felt hug. Before long, I was known as the Hugging Chancellor.

I also always said a few words to them, as I gave them their hugs, even though it meant each person stood on stage for a few seconds longer than previously, and timetables had to be adjusted accordingly. I was careful not to hug the young Muslim men, if they didn't want me to, and greeted them instead with a respectful *salaam*. For ten years, I presided over all the ceremonies. We would do three a day, for five days in a row, and then another four at the cathedral in Truro, where Exeter's Cornwall campus students had their graduation. And each year, the numbers attending the convocation ceremonies rose.

One year, the outrageous Rik Mayall, who had come to receive an honorary degree, told me he'd watched all the students come nervously onto the stage, and leave transformed, with a new spring in their step.

'How do you know what to say to them?'

'I don't know!' I replied. 'I never plan it, but when I see each individual, and read them as they approach – I read their body language and their faces and the way they walk – then somehow I always just know exactly what to say.'

When I started as chancellor I was warned that the engineers were very staid, and not to expect uproarious applause from them. They were indeed all very polite. The drama students, in contrast, were very boisterous. One year, one of these young men bounded onto the stage with a great flourish, and met me enthusiastically for his hug. I suddenly realized that my feet had left the ground. He'd picked me up and was whirling me around, declaring his love for me. My cloak was falling off my shoulders, my hat was over my eyes, and I was a mess, much to the amusement of the huge audience. When he finally put me down, and I got myself back in order, I said firmly:

'Let that be the last time this chancellor is swept off her feet!'

After that I was sure to adopt my karate stability stance, bending my knees just enough to be certain I couldn't be lifted without warning.

Around the same time, I'd joined a band called Damn Right, I Got the Blues, a rock'n'roll outfit formed by the bestselling writer Ken Follett CBE. He invited me to sing with them regularly after we'd performed together at the South Bank Centre, at the suggestion of Jude Kelly CBE. That very first time in London, we'd kicked off with a twelve-bar-blues version of the nursery rhyme 'Here we go Looby Loo'. Thanks to Ken, who became a dear friend, I finally learned all the rock'n'roll classics my jazz-loyal father wouldn't let us listen to when I was young, and we also rock'n'rolled the blues and soul standards, which I grew to love. We went all over the country and abroad with the band, and wherever we were, every time I sang with him, it took me to another world. I loved my new incarnation as a rock chick at the age of fifty-seven! Etta James, ZZ Top and Tina Turner had nothing on me!

'Wouldn't it be great if the band could play at the Exeter graduation ball?' I said to Ken soon after becoming chancellor.

Disappointingly, the ball at Powderham Castle was rained off by storms in 2007. The next year we launched our first set, this time at what is now called the Matford Centre, with the Rolling Stones' 'Start Me Up'. I wore stylish shades and plenty of gold chains around my neck, together with a red tutu dress and glittery red shoes. The students went wild. 'We love you, Chancellor!' they roared, throwing flowers at me and trying to touch my feet. That was a new experience. I was amazed to find myself singing on stage with thousands of people screaming my name and chanting, 'Change the world! Change the world!'

That love and affection from the crowds was electrifying and intoxicating. What a privilege it was to be able to touch so many young people's lives and souls in such a formative way. All over the world to this day, I come across Exeter graduates who say to me:

'Chancellor, your words are still ringing in my ears. I'm going to change the world for you.'

And so they do. William Graydon, aka 220 Kid, the musician and producer who graduated in 2013 in Biosciences and Sustainable Development, is a great example. He said my call to 'go out and change the world' stuck with him firmly, and now that he has a public platform and the ability to make a difference, he's funding a scholarship for disadvantaged students of colour. Another former student was involved with a hugely successful charity for transforming students' social mobility called UpReach. A new generation of world-changers is coming up behind me, and they mean business.

Chapter Thirty-five

'Your dad's not well. Come to the hospital, quick!'

Marmie's voice on the phone was so urgent that I shoved a hat on my head, and jumped into our new silver Mercedes CLS right away. I hadn't gone far when I was stopped by the police. I wound down the window. I knew I had committed no offence, but neither was I very recognizable in my hat.

'Is this your car?' the policeman said in an aggressive and sneering tone. I could see exactly what he was thinking: very smart car + Black woman = drug dealer/criminal. He radioed in to check if the Mercedes was registered in my name, and when this was confirmed, he waved me on with no apology and a most dismissive gesture.

Had nothing changed? It was 2007. Back in 1992, I had written to the Police Commissioner, Paul Condon, warning him of the dangerous attitudes too many police officers seemed to have, and offering to talk to the Met about awareness of racist behaviour and attitudes. Living in South London for most of my life, I had seen and heard of so many different incidents, and was familiar with the experiences of family and friends, including our Beckenham neighbour, who'd left the force in despair about the prevailing culture. Events such as the New Cross Fire and the Brixton Riots of 1981, when police prejudice led them to treat Black people as less than human, and certainly not equal members of society, had made a big impression on me. My own teenage nephew, Ellington's son, had recently been beaten up in the back of a police van and then charged with grievous bodily harm. Although he was a minor, they kept him in a cell overnight, and didn't even tell his parents. He was defended in court by Patricia Scotland QC, and the case was thrown out, after she ripped apart the fabricated evidence offered by the police. Nonetheless, as I said in my letter to Paul Condon, I had also worked a great deal with the Streatham community police, supporting their work with disadvantaged children as a special guest at disco dancing competitions, five-a-side football and on trips to amusement parks. So, I knew there were two sides to the police, and not every officer behaved the same way, I assured the Commissioner. But it was hard for lone voices within the force to achieve the change that was needed. Ironically, years later, a police guard at the House of Lords approached me and said that his granddaughter had brought home a copy of *Coming to England*, which had brought back some bad memories. He added, 'Please forgive me. I saw racism happen and stood by and said nothing.'

'Dear Ms Benjamin,' came the reply from Condon. 'There is no such thing as racism in the police force.'

That was the year before Stephen Lawrence was killed. Fourteen years later, it seemed as untrue as ever. Had I been harassed and insulted in that way for driving my car on any other day, I would have dealt with it very differently, but my mother's phone call had convinced me that delay was out of the question.

I found Marmie alone at the hospital, very distressed, as Dardie seemed almost near death. Aged seventy-nine, he was suffering from heart failure. He was far too ill for my mother

to take care of at home, and would spend four long and difficult months in hospital before he died. But before the end came
for my beloved father, I was called away to say my last farewell
to another person I loved more than I could say.

Until her husband Peter died in October 2004, I'm not sure if
Tony Lothian fully realized how much he was her backbone.
They had been together since she was eighteen, produced six
children together and had a huge clan of grandchildren. After
his death, she was furious that he had gone before her, and I
think it broke her. She wouldn't speak to anyone for months,
not even to her children.

Her worried daughter called me in early January 2007 to
say Tony was unwell and unresponsive, and please could I
come. At their family home in Ferniehirst Castle, an ancient
turreted border fortress overlooking the valley south of Jed-
burgh, I found Tony sitting in silence with her carer. She spent
all her days now in a carpeted downstairs room surrounded by
photographs of people from her past, her chair facing the
French windows which looked out over the garden towards the
tree of peace she and Valentina Tereshkova had planted
together in 1990. She wore a navy blue cardigan, and a tartan
blanket covered her knees.

It was the first time I'd ever seen her with her hair unstyled
and without her infamous eyepatch, which she'd worn since
losing her eye to cancer in 1970. Now her cancer had returned.
Before saying anything, I began to sing. '*Pack up all my cares
and woe, here I go, singing low . . . Bye, bye, blackbird . . .*'

A smile came over her face.

'Flo, darling.'

We had a big session reminiscing, about our trip to Russia,
about our shared excitement at the release of Nelson Mandela,

about all the things that really mattered to her. She talked, as she often used to, about how Black people were at the origins of humanity, because *Homo sapiens* first evolved in Africa. She needed my reassurance that Women of the Year had been worthwhile and wanted to know it would continue. We held hands, we ate together, and I stroked her hair and sang to her when she went to bed. Our bond was unbroken.

She passed away a few days later, after my return to London, and Keith and I hurried back to Scotland for a quiet funeral attended by relatives and close friends. The night before, I went to see her in the family crypt, surrounded by yellow daffodils. Tony had been very religious, a Catholic so committed that she was made a Dame of the Papal Order of St Gregory the Great in 2002. This, and her OBE, were honours she valued far above the many aristocratic titles she also possessed, because both of them were for her own achievements, in ecumenical work and charitable fundraising. In June 2007, her family bestowed on me the enormous honour of giving the final address at Tony's memorial thanksgiving service in Westminster Cathedral. There I would sing 'Bye Bye Blackbird' for her for the last time.

As I write this, it makes me happy to say that her legacy lives on through her granddaughters. Lady Louise Fitzroy is now the chair of the Women of the Year Lunch and Lady Emily is on the organizing committee.

Mourning the loss of my dearest friend and second mother, my angel of angels, I returned to London, where it soon became clear that Dardie was unlikely to be leaving hospital. His departure from life was protracted and distressing, and our only consolation for what he went through was the fact that because it took so long, my brothers and sisters and I were able to gather and spend plenty of time with him and Marmie in his last weeks and days.

An explorer and adventurer, he'd had a good life, enjoying rich experiences in music and politics all over the world. Of course, as we sat with him, we talked a lot about his younger days as a jazz musician, at Ronnie Scott's and elsewhere. But I knew he was dying not entirely fulfilled. Had circumstances allowed, he might have been a politician, or a more successful musician in his own right, instead of supporting others. Still, at least he knew that every one of his children had made something of their lives, and that was an achievement in itself. He knew he was in our blood and our spirit and had made us who we were. Long, long ago his White boss, Veasey, had told him how foolish it was for a man to try to make it in London with six children. My father knew he'd proved him wrong.

Although Dardie had never been a churchgoer, and didn't seem to us to be a religious man, he'd been brought up to know his Bible and had never lost the ability to quote from it at length. We were taken aback when he asked for it on his deathbed.

I was disturbed by how hard it was to get good care at that time. I didn't feel he'd been well looked after in hospital. I sometimes had to change the sheets myself, and wash the floor when I came to visit him, because I'd turn up and find them soiled. Old people were left to fade away as if they were irritants, or worthless. Nobody seemed to have time for them. But when I complained about the state of the ward, Dardie said anxiously:

'Don't say anything! They'll come and get me!'

So, I've always worried that they did treat him badly when we weren't there to watch out for him. But I'll never know, and of course, since opioids can affect your sense of reality, and make you paranoid, it could have been the painkillers talking.

In the end he died alone, but peacefully. Marmie had just left him in the hospital, and a nurse phoned to let her know when she got home.

'Show respect to your father,' Marmie always used to say when he was alive. I wanted to see him, and to pay my respects again now, so I went alone to the hospital morgue the following day. I've never been afraid of death, not since seeing a dead old man when I was a child in Trinidad. All his wrinkles had disappeared, and his skin was completely smooth. My dad looked as if he were asleep too, quite beautiful. I broke down in tears, and hugged him.

'Thank you, Dardie. Thank you,' I said. He was a great man, a hero, and he had done so much for me, and now he was gone, the first in our family to die. At his funeral I sang 'The Lady is a Tramp' and Sandra read the famous Martin Luther King speech in his honour. Dardie represented something so huge in my life. We even look so alike that I catch something of him when I look in the mirror.

In his lifetime, he had never expressed his enormous pride in all his children's achievements. His expectations of us were always so high, he seemed to take our successes for granted. We never got away with anything less than the best we were capable of. Yet after he died, I discovered he had kept every single newspaper cutting about me, every theatre programme, every record of every television credit; he'd treasured and collected mementoes of all our lives and triumphs. I was amazed and touched to the bottom of my heart. We'd all proved Veasey wrong.

Chapter Thirty-six

My mum had been a typical 1950s housewife, devoting her entire life to her husband, and even more to her six children, if such a thing is possible. Years ago, at a publicity event for *Black Joy* at the Café Royal, a reporter had said to her:

'You must be very proud of Floella, Mrs Benjamin.'

Fiery and forthright, she always had a fast comeback:

'Listen to me! I've got six children and I'm proud of every damn one of them.'

Her chest puffed out with pride.

For years, at eight o'clock each morning, my sister Cynthia, now a businesswoman and financial adviser, would call Marmie, and they'd chat for at least an hour. At five o'clock in the afternoon, it would be my sister Sandra's turn. She was now chair of an NHS trust in Cornwall, a school inspector and a charity volunteer for Mind. At ten or eleven o'clock at night, after I'd finished work and before I went to bed, it would be me on the phone, telling her every trivial event that had happened that day. My brother Lester went to see her every Friday. Ellington and his wife Pauline took her out regularly. He was a quantity surveyor and property developer. Junior, who lived in San Francisco, would call for two or three hours every Sunday. A computer analyst, he helped create the supermarket self-checkout system. Marmie used to tease him about this, saying, 'I bring a child into this world to put people out of work?' Whenever the phone rang, my dad would know who it was before she answered. If we didn't call, he'd ask what happened.

Something changed after Dardie's death, and she became more reflective. We were staying at the Waldorf together one night, getting dressed for a charity event, and suddenly she began to talk about the miscarriages she'd had.

'I could have had eight children, but two of them I lost.'

She'd never spoken about this to me or my sisters before, not even when I was having my own miscarriages. I wonder now if it was the first time she'd told anybody. I was glad she finally felt able to talk about it.

In her last years, all six of us thought hopefully that she would be truly free to enjoy her life. If we took her out for the day, she wouldn't worry about rushing home, saying:

'I've got to get back and cook for your Dardie.'

She wouldn't worry about leaving him alone. We could all take turns to whisk her away for treats at the Ritz, on holidays and outings, giving her wonderful experiences and showing her exotic places, and for once in her life, she could just think about herself. We planned to go all out with these treats. What a life she could lead! A life she'd earned through her unstinting hard work and resilience.

In January 2008 Sandra treated Marmie to a Caribbean cruise, just the two of them. They took Dardie's ashes with them, and buried them in Trinidad in the grave of my Uncle Milton, Auntie Olive's husband, who used to meet my parents under a particular tree in Port of Spain each year for Carnival.

Marmie loved that cruise, but she hardly had a chance to spread her wings, because when they came back to England, she began to feel quite ill.

She had been diagnosed with bowel cancer a few years earlier, and quite quickly given the all-clear.

'Veronica, you won't die of cancer,' the surgeon had assured her then. But all of a sudden, less than a year after Dardie had died, the cancer did come back, with a vengeance. Even then the doctors didn't tell us her prognosis, or how far it had spread. We had no idea that it was already in her liver and her spine and goodness knows where else. Trying to solve her terrible back pain, I took her for acupuncture and bought her back braces, to no avail.

She was offered an experimental new treatment at St Thomas's, but when I mentioned this to the health campaigner and broadcaster Lynn Faulds Wood, who'd had bowel cancer herself, she cautioned against it.

'Tell your mum not to do it. There comes a point in time when it's better to die of the cancer than of the treatment. Your mum's too old to go through that.'

But the doctors had persuaded her it would help other people if she did it, so Marmie was adamant she had to try it.

She had been reintroduced to God by two of my dearest and devout friends Marsha Rae Ratcliff OBE, a generous soul, and Mini, who had appeared like a guardian angel to help us while filming in Cuba, and ever since has been part of my life, giving me guidance and affirmation. Now Marmie read the Bible every day, but as her pain grew worse, and she steadily weakened, I would overhear her heartbreaking prayers:

'Lord, why are you making me suffer so much? Why don't you take me?'

Although I had most of the responsibility for looking after Marmie in those months, as Cynthia lived in Cyprus by then, and Sandra in Cornwall, I wasn't a very good carer. If we hadn't already spent the evening with her, eating supper, watching a bit of television, Alvina snuggling next to her, Keith would often drop me off to spend the night with her so Marmie wasn't alone, but I'd always fall asleep before she did. And it was hard to look after her because she treasured her independence and wanted to keep her dignity, so she never let me help her wash, for example. But Marie Curie nurses used to come and do her hair and paint her nails.

One night I couldn't stay with her, so I made sure she came downstairs to lock the door behind me.

'If you don't use it, you lose it,' she used to say, determined not to become bedridden, and she made her way down, step by step.

At the last minute, I turned back and peered through the letter box, to reassure myself she was all right. I saw her crawling back up the stairs on her hands and knees, no faster than a snail. She didn't want me to know she'd lost so much strength, and managed to keep her last reserves of energy until she thought I was safely gone. That was when I realized we were really losing her.

Soon after that the doctors said she had about six weeks to live.

That chemo was really, really aggressive. I always wonder if we should have tried to stop her doing it. Even when the cancer first came back, she looked fantastic. Then all of a sudden, the world seemed to close in on her. Her face was drawn to nothing. Her body crumbled. From a healthy-looking and buxom woman, she shrank to almost skin and bone. Towards the end I couldn't bear to see her lying there, still hiding how terrible her pain was.

Almost a year earlier, I'd been invited to do a talk on a cruise through the Norwegian fjords. I was very excited about it, and Marmie was thrilled for me. It was late July 2008 when she asked me:

'When are you doing that cruise again, Flo?'

'End of August, Marmie.'

She asked me again the next day, and again the next. Two weeks later, they told us not to expect her to live for more than twenty-four hours. But she kept on going, and still she kept asking me:

'When are you going on that cruise?'

'In a week's time, Marmie.'

'You're going on that cruise,' she said firmly.

I was due to leave on Saturday. She died on Thursday night. She was determined to get me on that ship.

We all helped wash and dress her and then she lay like an empress. But she was gone. Part of my soul went with her. She was our everything. Even now, when things aren't going the way I want them to, or I'm feeling in despair about the world, I speak to her:

'Marmie, Marmie, where are you? I need you. I need you now.'

We were all so used to Marmie sorting out our problems and sharing our lives, so dependent on her emotional, spiritual and physical power. She was a visionary who could see every side of a situation and always came up with a solution. 'This is what you tell them . . . this is what you do . . .' She sorted everything out. I think she should have been a president, a world leader.

And now she was gone. This was just before the August bank holiday. We had everything already prepared, but we learned the funeral would have to wait until the following week.

'Go,' my family told me. 'That's what she wanted.'

When we'd embarked, and begun to sail across the North Sea, I locked myself in my cabin with Keith and couldn't bear to come out. That time at sea was another time out of time in my life, which gave me a chance to mourn with no distractions. I hadn't told anyone on board what had happened, and after a few days, the company began putting notes under my door, trying to find out what was wrong.

When the day arrived that I was due to speak, I had to emerge, and stand up, completely vulnerable, in front of a thousand people.

For the third time in my life, from out of nowhere, a tremendous force swept right through me. It was like having my mother right by my side. I could feel her power and spirit inside me, coursing through my veins. As usual, I hadn't planned in advance what I was going to say, but I found myself telling the audience all about what had happened, and about Marmie, her great influence on me, and her wisdom and strength.

I wept, and the whole room wept with me. The strength of shared emotion was palpable. Over the next few days, one person after another came and hugged me, and thanked me, crying, for sharing the gift of my mother. They also told me their own stories of bereavement. So many of the people there had experienced a similar loss to me, and my speech had really hit a chord with them.

Coming back to England, I felt as though an earthquake had shaken my foundations. These three important people, to whom both Keith and I had so long looked for guidance, advice, support, love and leadership, were all gone. They had given us such confidence as a family. Life without them was going to be tough.

I sang at Marmie's funeral: 'Amazing Grace', unaccompanied, without a microphone. Each one of her six children talked in turn about how much she meant to us, so often taking care of us alone while our father was gallivanting around the world pursuing his musical ambitions. Everyone present felt privileged to be there to say farewell, and could feel the power and strength of this remarkable woman. Against all the odds, through all the traumas and challenges she'd faced, she had triumphed, guiding us all like the captain of a ship steering through tempests and sunshine.

Though she died in 2008, whenever I'm with any of my brothers and sisters, we talk about Marmie, without fail. What would Marmie do? How would Marmie feel? To all of us, she is a continuing daily presence. In her memory I became a patron of Beating Bowel Cancer.

When Tony and Dardie died, I felt acceptance. Death is not something I fear. But when Marmie died, I had bad dreams. For six months I tormented myself, worrying that we could and should have done more for her as she was dying. Normally, my sleep is deep and dreamless, but every night was filled with anxiety. I felt angry with the doctors for not being more explicit about what they knew so we weren't better prepared. But I also now had nobody to talk to about the lighter things in life, or discuss trivial things with like who was wearing what where, and who said this, that and the other, or who I'd met that day. All the thoughts I used to share with her became trapped inside my head, disturbing my nights.

Sorting out the old family home after all those decades brought some surprises. Discovering little things I'd never known about Marmie often brought humour, and even comedy, to the whole process of grieving. She was a secret hoarder: dozens and dozens of plastic bags fell out when we moved her big wardrobe. She must have been stuffing them behind it for years. In every drawer we opened, we found another packet of out-of-date batteries. I knew she liked to be prepared, but who needs that many batteries? That made me laugh. What a god-send laughter can be in the middle of trauma!

One day, I was hoovering our own front room and under the coffee table in front of the sofa I found a white feather on the carpet. Strange, I thought.

'Keith, what's this feather doing in here?' I called.

'I've no idea!' he replied.

A few days later, I found another white feather on the doorstep. I didn't think much of it at first, but it just kept happening. Coming back from an award ceremony one evening, as we were talking about how much we missed Marmie, who often came with us to such events, a white feather fluttered down onto our windscreen. For our sixtieth birthdays, Keith and I spent the weekend at the Ritz with Aston and Alvina. Marmie had loved the Ritz. She used to walk in with a sense of ownership and pride. So, we raised a glass to her as we ate our dinner, and went upstairs to our room. The corridor had a long red carpet, which was always spotless, of course. Yet outside our bedroom door, we found a white feather. The next time we were in Barbados, Keith and I were swimming in the blue Caribbean sea with Alvina, regretting never having taken Marmie to the island, and once again, a white feather appeared from nowhere, floating on the sea.

Something strange was going on. It made me feel that my mum was still with me, still watching over me. And with this understanding, I let go of everything that was making me feel so terrible. Blessed once again, I felt I could float back into life at last.

PART 4

WHO WOULD
HAVE THOUGHT?

Chapter Thirty-seven

Growing up in Britain as a Caribbean or Black person in the 1960s, you constantly heard from your parents that you'd got to be ten times as good as the next person. You're continually forging forward, persistently trying to impress, all the time making sure that people understand you and where you're coming from.

But working with Steve Smith and Dave Allen at Exeter taught me the value of easing off, and not trying to force or prove anything. Dave gave me a piece of life-changing advice: 'Just be,' he said. It was only then that I discovered a certain inner calm and stillness. I learned how to develop further my spiritual connection with people. It was great preparation for stepping into a bigger arena.

There had been a few attempts to get me into the House of Lords over the years by various parties. Baroness Jay was behind one of these, and Joan Ruddock another, and I'm so grateful to everyone for their efforts. But it wasn't the right time for me. It would have been like force-ripening a mango. You don't want to pick a fruit too early, or it will be hard and bitter, instead of sun-warmed and sweet.

I've always believed in supporting any politician who does good for society but I had never wanted to nail my colours to any party mast until the Iraq War. I was convinced invasion was a grievous mistake, and at the time of the huge demonstrations of February 2003, I wrote to Tony Blair to tell him so. For the first time ever, he didn't reply. For me, as for many voters, this was the beginning of my disenchantment with New Labour.

And so, I joined the Liberal Democrats, publicly declaring my out-and-out support for the party and actively campaigning for their policies. I was welcomed as a good voice for the party at a national level, not just because I'm a woman of colour, but because of the impact I had on local audiences. When Nick Clegg became party leader in 2007, he made it his mission to claim a radical centre ground in British politics.

I can't help feeling that Black people have a lot of affinity with the Lib Dems. We know we have much to offer but we're rarely given the opportunity. You're never taken seriously. You're not thought of as important. People use you when it suits them. So, if you're a Black athlete of Jamaican heritage, like Linford Christie, and you win, then you're described as British! If you lose, you're Jamaican-born. If England's football team had won the European Cup, Marcus Rashford and his Black teammates would have been British heroes. Instead, they were subjected to racist abuse.

Since 2004, Navnit Dholakia, Baron Dholakia, has been the deputy leader of the Liberal Democrats in the House of Lords. He grew up in Tanzania and India, and devoted most of his life to race relations, criminal justice and racial justice, working for the Commission for Racial Equality and the Commission on the Future of Multi-Ethnic Britain, among other roles. He had also sat on the selection panel for crossbench peers. After watching me make a speech, he said to me:

'You've got to be in the House of Lords. You are loved by my children as well as the nation's children.'

When Nick Clegg heard me speak, he asked me this:

'If you were to enter the Lords, what would be your priority?'

'Children!' I said.

'Exactly,' he replied, and a few months later, after the party conference in September 2009, he rang me up.

'I want you to represent us on the red benches.'

I'm not often speechless but on this occasion I was lost for words. I just blurted out:

'Yes. Yes, I will.'

My entry to the House of Lords as a Liberal Democrat peer was confirmed soon after the momentous May election in 2010 which eventually ousted Labour after thirteen years in power. Finally, my nomination had been approved by the new prime minister David Cameron. There had been a long nine month wait because when Gordon Brown became prime minister he signed off very few peerages. Then in June 2010, everything began to happen very quickly, with lots of meetings all in one week. First, I had to go to see the Garter Principal King of Arms at his wood-panelled office in the seventeenth-century red-brick building opposite St Paul's Cathedral called the College of Arms.

'So, what are you going to call yourself?' Sir Thomas Woodcock asked me. 'If there's nobody in the House of Lords who's ever shared your surname, you don't need to have a place name in your title.'

Perhaps because it was traditionally a Jewish surname, and the first Jewish peer wasn't titled until 1885, I am actually the very first Benjamin to sit in the House of Lords.

'I do want a place name,' I said quickly. 'I would like to be called Baroness Benjamin of Beckenham in the County of Kent.'

Keith and I had discussed this at great length, considering all possibilities and also what names had already been taken. Brixton? Tulse Hill? Herne Hill? Chiswick? And then it dawned on me. Beckenham. It was all because of Marmie. When she decided we'd upgrade our house and move there, she wanted to go somewhere she could be sure of getting the best healthcare, the best education and the best jumble sales and charity shops. Beckenham was a very White and conservative part of London, and it ticked all those boxes. Yet when we moved there, we were told to 'go back home'. Marmie dug in her heels, and lived in that house for more than forty years. So, in calling myself Baroness Benjamin of Beckenham, I wanted to remember my mother, her fortitude in the face of our hostile neighbours and the life she built for herself in Beckenham, Kent, and also my father. My new title was a way of recognizing how much Britain had moved on, too. And after I'd got confirmation that my peerage was definitely going through, I'd gone straight to Beckenham Cemetery, where her ashes lay, and I knelt beside the memorial plaques for her and my dad.

'Marmie! Dardie! I'm going to claim Beckenham for you,' I told them proudly. If only they could have known.

And what should I see at the cemetery but a white feather?

The date was set for me to be introduced to the Lords. This very formal ceremony marks the solemn recognition of both a peer's past achievements and also their new duties and responsibilities. The second chamber of the UK parliament, the House of Lords is independent from the more powerful House of Commons, and shares the important task of making and shaping laws as well as scrutinizing and, if necessary, challenging the work of the government, through committee work, questions and debates. Since the radical reforms of 1999 which abolished hereditary peerages, the membership of the Lords has changed a great deal and also expanded enormously. We're appointed because of the work we've done in all kinds of fields, and the expertise and experience we can bring to parliament, not because of the families we were born into. As well as these 'Lords Temporal', as life peers and hereditary peers are called, there are up to twenty-six 'Lords Spiritual', all currently Church of England bishops and archbishops, and, like cross-bench peers, not politically aligned.

For the official 'introduction' to the Lords, you have to choose two 'supporters'; mine were Ros Scott, Baroness Scott of Needham Market, then president of the Lib Dems, and Lord Navnit Dholakia. Both were so kind to me. Three years later, I would be Doreen Lawrence's proud supporter, when she was introduced to the House of Lords as a Labour peer in 2013.

I also had a meeting with the Lib Dem leader and the Chief Whips Lord David Shutt and Lord Tom McNally, who needed to know if I would be attending and participating regularly. I promised I would truly be a working life peer, devoting myself to working in the House for most of the week. As a peer, you only get paid a fixed daily allowance for the days you attend. The House of Lords often sits until ten or eleven at night. At times, for example during the coalition and Brexit crises, I've sat till four in the morning.

We were due at Westminster for the Ceremony of Introduction at eleven a.m. on Monday 28 June 2010. We almost got stuck in France the night before because of flight cancellations, but one of my *Play School* babies who was working at Nice airport that evening came to the rescue and got us home on the only departure. Keith, Aston and Alvina came with me to the Lords, but of my siblings, only Sandra and Lester were in the UK at that time and able to join us. Besides our official 'supporters', Ros and Navnit, our other guests were my surrogate daughter Ros, and Tim Snowball, a representative from Nick Clegg's office and a great ally of mine.

Our first stop after an early lunch was one of the most beautiful rooms in the Palace of Westminster: the Robing Room. This is where Her Majesty the Queen is arrayed in her ceremonial garments for the State Openings of Parliament. The Imperial State Crown is placed on her head while she sits on the canopied Chair of State. Sumptuously decorated with gilded oak panelling, it's more like a hall than a room, and was big enough to contain all the peers during the Second World War, although there are too many now to fit into any room or chamber in Westminster. The Robing Room is very grand, very gold, and very Victorian. Everywhere the Queen walks, there's a blue carpet, even in the Chamber, and the emblems of the portcullis, rose, lily and lion are repeated everywhere. Heraldic badges are stencilled on the coffered ceiling, and on either side of a magnificent mosaic marble fireplace there are brass statuettes of St George slaying the dragon and St Michael overcoming the devil. Allegorical wall paintings show scenes from the legend of King Arthur representing the chivalric virtues: hospitality, generosity, mercy, religion and courtesy. They never got round to finishing the paintings for fidelity and courage.

Nobody had given me any advice about clothing, so I decided to wear a cream-coloured Jackie-O-style silk suit underneath the robes, with matching shoes and a string of pearls over my heart necklace. I'd bought the suit years earlier with my mum, and I always stuck to Tony's excellent advice: when you're doing something special, you should never wear new clothes, but instead choose an outfit you know you're comfortable in. I'd put my hair in my usual topknot style. I stood in this extraordinary room, being dressed in my long red ermine-trimmed robes by somebody from Ede & Ravenscroft, who supply robes to parliament, enjoying all the splendour very much, and running through the lines of the Oath of Allegiance in my head:

I, Baroness Benjamin, swear by Almighty God that I will be faithful and bear true allegiance to Her Majesty Queen Elizabeth, her heirs and successors, according to law. So help me God.

I had never felt so special.

We walked in procession to the Moses Room, a replica of the Chamber, which is used for extra debating and for meetings of grand committees. This is where everyone congregates before the ceremony. From there, we were led in complete and utter silence into the Peers' Lobby, and there we faced the open doors of the Chamber: a most magnificent sight. Glittering in the June sunshine, the gleaming golden throne and cherubs took my breath away. First in the procession was the Gentleman Usher of the Black Rod, who maintains order in the Lords, then the Garter King of Arms, followed by Ros, then me and finally Navnit. Although there are marks on the floor to help everyone walk spaced at the right distance from each other, there was still a lot to think about and my stage experience was certainly useful.

I handed my letters patent to the Reading Clerk, who speaks the sovereign's words; with this reading the House hears the terms on which a new peerage has been created.

I can't believe today. I can't believe this.

These words kept running through my head as I glanced up to the gallery, smiling at Keith, Aston and Alvina. Just as I swore my oath, Sandra and Lester were suddenly lit up by a strong ray of sun like a spotlight, and for an instant they seemed to become Marmie and Dardie, watching me proudly. With the biggest smile in the world on my face, I silently addressed them: *Marmie! Dardie! Your little girl is here!*

319

Four hundred years ago, in the House of Lords, peers, many of them plantation owners, decided the fate of my ancestors in Africa and the Caribbean. Now here I am, and I can help make change. I can help formulate process and policy. Oh Marmie! Dardie! Why couldn't you be here to see me now?

Then we processed out, still in silence, until I reached the Lord Speaker, then Baroness Helene Hayman. She was the first person elected to take on that newly created role in 2006. As I shook her hand, the House erupted into noise: rah, rah, rah, rah. (Clapping is forbidden.)

And when I returned to the Robing Room for photographs, and to disrobe, guess what I found? A white feather, lying on the carpet. As if to say, *We're here! We're here!* I was the happiest girl in the world.

After that, guided by my supporters, I went to sit in the Chamber for the first time. The extraordinary thing is that when I was first asked to become a peer, I always assumed it would mean sitting on the opposition benches. The Lib Dems had never been in power in my lifetime. But the previous month, the 6 May general election had left no party with an absolute majority. It was the first hung parliament since 1974. I'd stayed up all night at home with Keith, watching the election results, unable to believe my eyes.

After five tense days of negotiations between my party and the Conservatives, they struck a deal, and in the early hours of 12 May, Nick Clegg emerged as Deputy to David Cameron as Prime Minister. That meant that I was unexpectedly now heading left for the government benches in the House of Lords, instead of right. And in coalition with the Conservative Party. We were no longer a voice in the wilderness. I was in a position I'd never dreamed of reaching.

The evening after my introduction ceremony and elevation, we came home with the red box containing my official documents and seal, and Keith and I sat in our kitchen drinking a cup of tea and watching *Newsnight*, as we always do. Suddenly my ears pricked up.

'Something rather wonderful happened today,' said the presenter. 'Somebody we all know and love went in through one door, and came out of another.'

And then I heard the theme music for *Play School*, and that familiar image of the square house logo appeared on the screen. And the image cut to me walking through the door of the House of Lords, while the presenter joked about the neo-gothic window. Now that really made me smile.

The 2010 election had brought more Black MPs into parliament than ever before: Labour's Chi Onwurah was the first African woman to win a seat, and Helen Grant became one of the first women of colour to represent the Tories. They followed in the footsteps of Bernie Grant, Diane Abbott, Paul Boateng and David Lammy, among others. I was the only Black woman on the coalition government benches in the Lords.

There was naturally a great sense of euphoria among Lib Dems, whose new peers also included Baroness Meral Hussein-Ece, the first woman peer of Turkish Cypriot heritage. We all felt we finally had a chance to make a real difference, even if we were unlikely to be able to achieve all our goals as a party in the first term. As coalition partners, we had to make many compromises to win the first stages of battles, and I often found myself in a dilemma. There were numerous things the government was doing with which I couldn't agree, particularly relating to austerity and the NHS. Had I consistently voted with the government, I would have been letting down the very people I'd been working to help for so long through my charitable work. So, in these cases I usually abstained from voting.

Other Lib Dem peers, such as Baroness Shirley Williams, similarly couldn't stomach the attacks on the NHS, and being more experienced, she could be more vocal about her opposition to government policy, despite being part of the coalition. Unlike MPs, peers don't have to follow the party whip.

I had a lot to learn. I was given a substantial rule book – the *Companion to the Standing Orders and Guide to the Proceedings of the House of Lords* – which explains exactly how a bill is put together, privileges, how select committees work, negative and affirmative and hybrid instruments, royal assent, and all the terminology of government and Westminster itself. So, for two months I simply sat and watched, absorbing the mood of the House, listening to people's maiden speeches, learning procedure, technicalities, language and etiquette, how to find my way around, how different designs of the robes signify a peer's rank. I stood up once to speak in a sleeveless dress and was reprimanded by the formidable Baroness Trumpington. 'No sleeves! No sleeves!' she shouted, even though there are no written rules about this dress code in the *Companion*.

But all the same, I love the rules and costume and pomp and ceremony of the Lords. It's there for a purpose. Until the world changes substantially, and there is true equality for people of colour in all walks of society, I believe we need to keep all these markers of hierarchy so that people can measure how much progress they've made by the height that they reach. Some people may take all the trappings of the establishment for granted, and think them unnecessary, but for others it's all relatively new. They're an important and visible part of a message about change to the general public, and particularly important for children to see. As my father knew so well, everyone needs role models. You have to see yourself to know you belong.

The first Black peer only entered the House of Lords in 1969. He was the great Learie Constantine and he was born near San Fernando, in Trinidad and Tobago, as I was, and first came to England and made a name for himself as a cricketer. In a landmark 1943 legal case which eventually led to the first Race Relations Act, he was the first to sue a hotel for refusing to accommodate his family after racist complaints from White US servicemen. He later became a barrister, and served on the Race Relations Board and as a governor of the BBC. I'm proud to follow in his footsteps as the first woman Trinidadian peer. From Lord Constantine's appointment until 1990, only three more life peerages were awarded to people of colour. In 1997 Valerie Amos became the first Black woman to be awarded a peerage. Later, in 2003, she went on to become Leader of the House, and the first Black woman to sit in Cabinet. In 2022 she was the first Black person ever to be appointed into the Order of the Garter.

In November 2021, there were 52 peers of colour, out of a total of 784. And although the House of Lords is incredibly diverse in so many ways – in terms of religion, disability, gender, sexual orientation and social background – when I look across the Chamber I feel there still seems some way to go to achieve complete diversity nirvana.

Chapter Thirty-eight

You're not permitted to speak in a Lords debate until you've made your maiden speech, so you have to wait until a debate is scheduled that is close to your interests and expertise. On Tuesday 5 October 2010, the very day that the House resumed sitting after the summer recess and the party conference season, the Conservative life peer Lord Taylor of Holbeach proposed the motion that 'this House takes note of the role of the charitable sector in strengthening civil society'. David Cameron had launched the Tories' 'big society' plan in July, and the Charities Act 2006 was coming under review. That would be my ideal moment to speak for the first time. I would soon discover that six other noble Lords were also going to make their maiden speeches in this debate: 'a galaxy of new talent', as one peer put it, and a record number. I planned my speech very carefully, not wanting to miss anything out, and knowing that I only had eight minutes to get everything in.

My Auntie Olive came specially from Trinidad and sat in the public gallery with Sandra. Keith sat 'Below Bar', where visitors must not cross into the Chamber and where MPs stand to listen to the Queen's speech during the State Opening. At 3.37 p.m., the discussion began. The breadth and depth of experience and understanding gathered together in the Chamber that day was truly impressive. Different peers declared their own interests in a huge range of different charities and voluntary sector organizations, from Breakthrough Breast Cancer to the Refugee Council. At 5.50 p.m. I rose to speak, without notes. I began by thanking all those who made me feel welcome, especially the Attendants for their diligence.

'I love being part of this establishment,' I declared, 'and as I wander round the maze of corridors, soaking up the rich symbolism, I think to myself, *Surely I have reached the summit of life's mountain, the zenith of a career stretching over four decades.* Like the coat worn by the Garter King of Arms, my life has been a rich tapestry of experiences which have led me to a lifelong mission of ensuring that children's well-being is at the heart of society's thinking.'

I explained why I had chosen Beckenham as my title as a legacy for my parents, and in recognition of just how much Britain has moved on, and told the story of how our neighbours had called the police to arrest us when we went to view our future home. As a 'Hall of Fame' NSPCC supporter, a trustee of the paediatric medical charity Sparks, and as Barnardo's vice-president, I declared my interest in these charities, and talked of how I had seen at first hand the tremendous contribution the charitable sector makes to civil society.

Afterwards I had many admiring comments about the fact that I had spoken entirely without prompts, so clearly from the heart, and several peers apologized to me for not having stood up against the injustices I had highlighted. But although everyone was so positive about my speech, I resolved to hold visible notes in future, in case the lack of them might give the impression I was still 'just' an actress, rather than a committed, working peer. I didn't want to give anyone any reason not to listen to me, or to dismiss me because of my acting career. But I do believe that when you speak from the heart, you can win hearts and minds. After my maiden speech, everyone began to see me differently: not simply the bubbly, smiley *Play School* presenter from the telly, but a serious individual, with a mission I had pursued for decades. Now they knew what I was doing there.

However, a few people continued to question my presence in the House, making it clear they didn't think I had earned my peerage, and much of this was politically motivated. Some Labour peers were hostile, angry about the Lib Dems being in the coalition government. But overall I was greeted warmly by all sides of the House. Although there was one Labour peer who would single me out, criticize me and publicly comment on my presence in the Chamber. This made me very angry. It felt like he was taking unfair advantage of the fact that as the first-ever actress in the Lords, I was already in the public eye. It made working very hurtful and, about six months after my elevation, it got to the point where I could take it no more. Heading for a vote one evening, I just happened to find myself beside Baroness Royall of Blaisdon, then the leader of the opposition in the House of Lords, with whom I got on very well.

'I'd really appreciate it if you could ask one of your members not to speak negatively about me publicly,' I said to her. 'I think it's unfair to comment about my presence in the Chamber.'

'I'm terribly sorry, Floella. Who is it?'

Just at that moment, the man himself approached us, so I just said, 'It's him.'

Then I turned to him myself. Quietly and firmly, I made my position perfectly clear to him.

'Listen you, back off. Don't you dare comment about or criticize me publicly ever again. Just back off.'

I had to put my stake in the ground and say this had gone far enough. It might have been that he wasn't happy with the

Lib Dem's being in coalition. But he wasn't expecting a response like that and he certainly never did it again, and he's been respectful ever since.

Not long after, I was offered another significant political opportunity. Nick Clegg called me to his office in Whitehall, where he and Simon Hughes MP asked me to run as the Lib Dem candidate for the Mayor of London against Ken Livingstone and Boris Johnson. I had only just been made a peer and decided it was too soon to consider such a role.

However, the press got hold of the rumour and it appeared in the media with the headline Flo-Bo in Low Blow for Bo-Jo. To my surprise several wealthy donors offered to support my campaign as they thought I offered a credible alternative and a good chance I might win with all the second preference votes.

Nick was none too pleased when I declined, but I think he understood that I wanted to focus my energy on the Lords.

Every time I enter the Palace of Westminster I pinch myself. Never more so than the day I sat in Westminster Hall, listening to President Barack Obama addressing both Houses in 2011. It's the oldest part of the building, over one thousand years old and steeped in history. I sang an impromptu rendition of 'Smile' there once when I hosted an event to celebrate the two hundredth anniversary of the abolition of slavery. It was where the trial of Charles I took place, and is one of the only settings where MPs and peers can sit together. This historic hall has only hosted a handful of speakers, including Pope Benedict XVI, Nelson Mandela and Aung San Suu Kyi.

Now it was the turn of President Obama. He spoke with

passion about his connection to Britain, through his father who had served as a chef in the British army, and how we need to ensure children are given opportunities to go out into the world to make a difference. As I sat there I could hear the voices of Dardie and Marmie, who had died before Obama became president but had prayed for it to happen. He received rapturous applause from the hundreds of people present and as he made his way through the crowds everyone rushed to shake his hand, including the cleaners and canteen staff, who were also invited.

I sat at the end of a row at the back of the Hall near the North Door with the huge stained-glass window, which allowed the sunlight to flood in. When he reached my row I spontaneously hugged him and said:

'Thank you, Mister President, for everything you do to give hope to children, for giving them the feeling they can achieve anything. Promise me you will continue to do just that.'

By now his security people were getting rather nervous as I held on to him, but I knew he wouldn't mind because his wife Michelle is a hugger too. He looked me in the eye with a smile.

'I will, ma'am,' he told me. 'I'll try my best, ma'am'.

The event was televised live and immediately I received many messages from people thanking me for hugging him, saying the hug was on their behalf too. Mind you, I was told by a fellow peer that it wasn't protocol to hug a president. I said, if you were Black, you would understand the significance.

In the five years of the coalition government, there were major disappointments for the Lib Dems, such as the Alternative Vote referendum, which did nothing to change the electoral system or forward the cause of proportional representation, for which I'd campaigned, the downgrading of the cabinet level Minister for Children to the most junior ministerial status, and the huge cuts in early years service funding. Hundreds of Sure Start children's centres had to close, and their services became much harder to access, with terrible consequences for the most disadvantaged children.

Everyone in the House of Lords is an expert on something, and we tend to stick to our areas of expertise. I knew about children, about the media, and about diversity. One of my early campaigns was to change the regulation of child performances, which was unchanged since 1968, as licensing decisions varied from borough to borough, even for children attending the same school, and it was against the law for children to perform in front of a live camera after seven p.m. This was causing particular problems for productions in London such as at the Royal Opera House or National Theatre or Royal Albert Hall that wanted to livestream performances into cinemas in the provinces, which had recently become technically possible. It even affected television shows like *Britain's Got Talent*.

I raised this problem with Lord Nash, who had become a life peer and Schools Minister in 2013, and we worked together on the issue, organizing repeated meetings at the Department for Education. After several years apparently making little progress, despite the support of my noble friend Lord Mike Storey, I was just leaving the offices in Great Smith Street when I bumped into an old friend who was trying to start an academy. As we were chatting in the lobby, who should appear but Michael Gove, then still serving as Education Secretary?

'Oh Michael . . . Do you know Baroness Benjamin?' asked my friend.

'No, but I've always wanted to meet her,' Michael Gove replied, making me a low bow. 'I grew up watching her.'

'I'm so pleased to know that you're one of my *Play School* babies!' I said. 'Now, this is what I want you to do.'

I explained the problem and how I thought it could be solved.

'Done!' he said, and shook my hand. That was it. Suddenly I got a completely different reception at the Department for Education. Just before Christmas, Lord Nash called me for a meeting.

'I don't want bad news,' I warned him. 'Not at this time of year.'

'Well, you'll be pleased to hear that we're going to repeal all the various laws currently in place.' He explained all the changes they had in mind to remove outdated rules and red tape surrounding child performance.

I literally cried. Thanks to my determination and persistence, the law was going to change.

A personal approach also helped in ensuring key Black heroes secured a place on the national curriculum. The department tried to argue that this should only be *if* there was a need for it – for example, in inner-city areas with lots of Black people.

'No, no, no, no! Black children are more likely to know already. I want the children of middle England to know about Britain's Black history,' I argued. 'They should be learning about the pioneering nurse Mary Seacole, and the composer Samuel Coleridge-Taylor and about the *Windrush* history in schools in Gloucestershire and Northumberland and Somerset, where the Black presence is very small, and nobody's ever heard of such things.'

I would not give up. More than thirty-five thousand people signed a petition organized by Operation Black Vote in 2013, led by Simon Woolley, now Lord Woolley, and David Laws MP, then the Minister for Schools, was also at the forefront of this battle. Eventually Michael Gove had a change of heart and neither Mary Seacole nor Olaudah Equiano were ultimately dropped from the curriculum as planned. All people of all races need to know those parts of history which had always been left out of school books. As I write this in 2022, schoolchildren across the country are reading my book *Coming to England*, which as Colin Webb predicted is becoming a classic, and learning about *Windrush*. It took the *Windrush* scandal and the death of George Floyd for many people in England to have their eyes opened to Black history, but perhaps we shall now see real change in education.

All-Party Parliamentary Groups, informal cross-party alliances of members of both Houses with a common interest in particular issues, are a very good way to push forward matters dear to your heart. I helped to create and then co-chaired two APPGs – one on A Fit and Healthy Childhood and the other on Children's Media and the Arts – and have participated in many others. One of my major battles was getting tax relief for making children's television, to encourage producers not to be deterred by the relative lack of income from advertising. I was getting terribly concerned because only 1 per cent of children's programmes broadcast in the UK were actually being made here. Ofcom couldn't help, because that body can only regulate, not change the law.

Fortunately, I can usually get a meeting when I want to, because so many ministers now are my *Play School* babies. Karen Bradley was one of these, and as Secretary of State for Digital, Culture, Media and Sport (DCMS), she was keen to help me realize my ambition of persuading all the major UK broadcasters to make a financial commitment to creating television programmes for children every year through an amendment to the Digital Economy Bill, extending Ofcom's powers to support children's television in other ways if necessary. She wrote to me on 14 February 2017:

Dear Floella, I'm really sorry to tell you this, but I don't think we'll be able to do it after all.

I was bitterly disappointed. All those months and years of meeting and lobbying and persuading, and just when I thought it would happen, she was saying no? This amendment wouldn't go ahead? I was beside myself. Shortly afterwards I found myself walking beside Lord Ashton of Hyde, the DCMS Parliamentary Under Secretary of State, the minister in the Lords dealing with that bill.

'How can you do this? You know how important it is for the children of this country to have programmes that reflect their lives. British children can't see the diversity of their own land. Why have you done this?'

'I'm really sorry,' he replied. 'It's out of my hands. But why don't you contact the bill manager?'

Bills are proposals for new laws. To become actual legislation, they need to pass every stage of scrutiny in the two Houses of Parliament and then receive royal assent so they can become acts of parliament. Bill managers are civil servants working in the Ministry of Justice who project manage each stage of a bill. Often when a bill comes into the House of Lords, it's quite short and basic, but when it leaves, our scrutiny means it can be three times the length because so many peers have put forward amendments. We add the meat to a bill, and make it workable.

At Lord Ashton's words, I had a glimmer of hope, so I ran upstairs to my office on the second floor, which looks out onto the back of Westminster Abbey – I'm always running up and down as fast as I can, always wanting to keep fit – and got on the phone to arrange a meeting right away. The bill manager came with his people and we sat around the circular table we have in the alcove of our shared office, and we chatted about the protest outside, and the view, making small talk as we got to know each other. Being a forty-something dad, and a fan, he obviously wanted to talk about *Play School*. Then I told him the plan behind my amendment.

'It's a chance for so many creators – actors, musicians, producers – and for British children too, to ensure they all see their lives reflected. In the past, the world looked to Britain for top-quality children's programmes. Now children's production companies are going out of business and only the BBC ever sells children's programmes at MIPCOM, the global entertainment market. Children will grow up to become creators if we set the right example. They must not be left behind. We can change that and make the ailing children's television production industry great again.'

He had been sitting back in his chair, nodding as I spoke. Now he suddenly leaned forward.

'Lady Benjamin, you were there for me, when I was a little boy of four, watching you. Now I have a four-year-old daughter, and I want someone who will inspire her. Let's do this.'

He looked at the calendar on his watch.

'We've only got two weeks to change the law, but we're going to do it. I'll speak to Ofcom this afternoon.'

Everything went swimmingly until the five p.m. deadline for me to put down an amendment which the government would not oppose, when I realized that nothing had come through from government. Everyone seemed overwhelmed with impending Brexit legislation. What a cliffhanger! All that hard work could be wasted, disappearing like water into sand. I'd been campaigning for this for a decade: with John McVay OBE of the screen sector trade body Pact, I'd launched a petition to save homegrown children's TV programmes in 2007. Was I now being double-crossed somehow? I called the bill manager to ask this question and he reassured me it would happen the next day. Brexit was taking priority but government would take time to clear this amendment.

The ups and downs and ins and outs of what happened next are too complex to go into, but at the last minute the Benjamin amendment was saved. Normally, an accepted amendment goes forward in the government name, but because of my tenacity it was put forward in my name. I lay flat on the floor of my office, feeling utterly drained, as if I'd run three marathons on the trot.

The following day, Wednesday 22 March, I was in parliament, waiting excitedly for the amendment to be read, when I realized that the Chamber wasn't filling up as usual. Then the doorkeeper told me to go back to my room immediately. I didn't know why, and thinking I'd soon be back, I even left my handbag on my seat. At the office I found Keith, who'd been told the same thing. He'd gone to try to meet six media students from Glasgow who were coming to watch the ceremonial opening and the debate, and he'd advised them to come early. No sign of them. We had no idea what was going on. Suddenly, all hell broke loose. All you could hear was one police siren after another.

'Stay in your room,' we were told. 'There's been an incident.'

So of course, we turned the television on. We were horrified at the news of a terrorist attack on parliament. We were confined to the office for six hours, while they cleared the palace, and then they marched us out.

There are two types of police officer at the Lords: the heavy-duty kind with big guns and the unarmed chatty sort. PC Keith Palmer, who was tragically stabbed to death by Khalid Masood on the palace forecourt that day, one of five people killed in the Westminster atrocity, was the second type, and we always had a friendly exchange. Later, we left flowers where he fell. That was one of the most shocking days of my life.

We managed to get the Benjamin amendment through the following week, just before recess. Then the bill went back to the House of Commons, but at that point someone tried to put forward a further amendment to it, delaying and possibly jeopardizing the next stage. Terrified that time would run out and the bill would fail, we watched on television as the minutes ticked by. Introduced in the House of Commons on 5 July 2016, the Digital Economy Act finally became law on 27 April 2017, and I was hailed as the saviour of children's television by Pact and children's practitioners, who now have many more programme-making opportunities.

The Lib Dems were demolished in the 2015 election, which gave David Cameron his first outright majority. Up and down the country on the campaign trail I heard the same thing: 'I'm never voting Lib Dem again. You didn't keep your promises on tuition fees.'

Many people felt betrayed that the Lib Dem policy (set by the party members, not the MPs) to keep tuition fees at the same level (and eventually phase them out) had not been kept by the coalition government. I understood why people were angry but had learned that government is a compromise between what you would like to achieve and what is actually possible. Steve Smith, vice-chancellor of Exeter and president of Universities UK, had told me that direct funding was going to be cut again. He explained that the Labour government had already cut university funding by about £900 million in 2010, the economy was in a downturn and the money simply wasn't there to fund tuition fees. The alternative was to reduce student intake and support a smaller number at the same level as before. The students who would be prevented from going to university would be those with lower grades and they tend to be those from lower socio-economic groups.

Some hated Nick Clegg simply for agreeing to be Cameron's deputy. I tried to persuade voters that without us, we would never have made advances such as the Same Sex Couples Marriage Bill championed by Lynne Featherstone MP, and pupil premium which provided additional funding for pupils who needed it most, a passion of Nick Clegg's. Most of the achievements of that term were things which the Lib Dems had pushed for, including environmental policies, advocated by Ed Davey MP. I argued that true visionaries use the opportunities they have to make change. But we were the punchbag for everything that went wrong, and never given credit for anything good. I believe that if we had been given a second opportunity in coalition, things would have been very different today.

Losing so many seats was devastating. People like Paddy Ashdown and Charles Kennedy had worked hard for so many years to lift the Lib Dems from obscurity. But suddenly we had only eight MPs left. Though we'd lost our status as the third biggest party in the Commons, and rarely had a voice at Prime Minister's Questions, thankfully at least we had a Lib Dem voice in the Lords. Since the 1999 reforms abolishing hereditary peerages, the Conservative Party had ceased to dominate the Chamber. I became one of nearly a hundred Lib Dem peers who continued to hold the government to account, putting down amendments and speaking out wherever possible. At least no longer being in coalition made it easier to speak out against the government.

At a time of such high stakes, I felt that the country needed us in the Lords more than ever, as a voice of compromise, fairness and justice. I continued to spend many late nights in the Lords, battling to get cherished amendments through on bills that were dear to my heart, such as the Education Bill and the Adoption Bill. We even kept a camp bed in the office, as the division bell could ring to summon peers to vote at any time. So, my duty was unchanged.

Chapter Thirty-nine

When I was a little girl at school in Trinidad, singing 'God Save the Queen', I wondered if one day I might meet the sovereign who lived in a palace far away across the ocean in London yet graced our stamps. On one of our regular outings with Marmie, visiting famous sights like Big Ben, Trafalgar Square, Hyde Park and Oxford Street, I stood outside the gates of Buckingham Palace with my brothers and sisters and wondered what it was really like inside.

It would be more than thirty years before I finally did meet the Queen, in 1995, when she came to BAFTA to mark the foundation of the Elizabeth R Broadcasting Fund, of which I was president. I met her again several times, including when she gave me my OBE in 2001 for services to broadcasting. I also met quite a number of other royals, either through my charity work or through Tony, and got to know some of them quite well, including Prince Philip, to whom I gave as good as I got. When we first met at a charity lunch in 1998, I was asked to sit next to him. He spoke to the person on his right for twenty-five minutes before turning to me and asking:

'Who are you and what do you do?'

With a twinkle in my eye I replied, 'You tell me who you are and what you do and I'll tell you all about myself.'

He threw his head back with laughter and after that we got on like a house on fire. He loved and empathized with my book *Coming to England*, and told me that he too came to Britain as a child with very little. He knew what it was like to be an outsider. We often wrote notes to each other right up until he died.

Princess Diana and I supported many of the same children's organizations, so I would encounter her regularly. The first time I spoke to her properly was at a charity lunch in 1986 at the Silver Jubilee celebration of the Pre-School Playgroups Association, now called the Early Years Alliance. Diana was their patron. We were all very excited. Wearing a little grey suit with rolled-up sleeves and white shoes, looking very mid-eighties and *Miami Vice*, four-year-old Aston presented her with a drawing he'd done for her. The princess was terribly sweet, and bent down to talk to him at his level, as she always did, and didn't once touch his hair, which he always hated.

After speeches and presentations there was a finger-food buffet lunch, but she didn't want to eat. Instead, she rushed over to me as soon as she possibly could.

'I've always wanted to meet you!' the princess exclaimed, as thrilled as a little girl. 'I wanted to work with young children because of watching you on *Play School*. Do tell me all about *Play School*.'

We talked and talked, sharing our experiences of motherhood, and children's charity work, and although her royal minders tried to move her on, she just wouldn't leave my side. They brought a plate of food over to her, and her fork fell on the floor. Rather than letting someone else pick it up for her, she immediately bent to retrieve it herself.

Soon afterwards, she was the guest of honour at the Women of the Year Lunch, and this time Tony had invited Marmie too. Princess Diana and Marmie chatted together when they were introduced and, being an earth mother, Marmie sensed Diana's deep unhappiness and talked to her quite intimately and directly, giving her just the kind of advice any mother would offer her daughter. Diana held a bouquet in one hand, and with the other hand she started rubbing my mum's arm gently and persistently, like a child with a comforter. Once you touched my mum's skin, you found it was so soft and beautiful, you couldn't stop. She leaned her head on one side and said:

'Oh Mrs Benjamin, I do wish you were my mum.'

After that, whenever we met, even if she was on the other side of the room, she'd always call over:

'Floella! Floella! How's your mum? Send her my love!'

Princess Margaret was equally enamoured with Marmie, whom she met at a National Children's Home event at the Guildhall.

'Bother!' she said when her aide called her away from their conversation. 'I love being with you. It reminds me of when I'm in the Caribbean.'

At one of the earliest Women of the Year Lunches, Tony had thrown me in the deep end without warning, giving me the job of going to meet and greet Princess Michael of Kent at The Savoy. In 1991, I was a guest speaker at the luncheon with the Duchess of York, speaking on the theme of 'Harmony'. So, over the years, my work and friendship with Tony had given me a good training in royal protocol, and dealing with introductions and titles.

When I learned that the Queen was visiting Exeter University on her Diamond Jubilee tour in 2012, and it would be my responsibility as chancellor to look after her, I was full of excitement rather than trepidation. However, I was warned that any speech I made had to be approved in advance by the palace, and on no account could I deviate from the text once it had been approved. Of course, on occasions like this I never usually speak with notes, and so this time I planned my words very carefully, and learned my lines thoroughly, as I had always done as an actor.

The Queen and Prince Philip were coming for the official opening of the stunning new Forum building, an incredible £48 million campus development. It houses a new student services centre, library, theatre, shops, learning spaces and it's set in a beautifully landscaped piazza, with views across the city towards Dartmoor. The ruler of Sharjah, an alumnus and major supporter of the university, would be another honoured guest. I had the joy of visiting his magnificent palace in Sharjah with its glorious English-style rose garden, amazingly set in the desert.

The year 2012 was a great one for Exeter. We had joined the prestigious Russell Group in March, and within months Exeter would rise to the top 200 in the international league table of universities. On 2 May, thousands of students turned out to see the Queen. When I stepped out of the car, a wall of sound greeted me, like a physical force, cheers and applause amplified by the structure of the vast new buildings. I'd never encountered anything quite like it. The roar of delight when the Queen herself arrived was even more overwhelming.

After initial introductions, we enjoyed some entertainment: singing and dancing and poetry reading, which we watched from the side of the four-hundred-seat auditorium, which is now familiar to many as the courtroom in *Broadchurch*.

I never get nervous, and I always do my breathing exercises before any public speaking . . . breathe in for four . . . hold for five . . . out for six . . . in for four, hold for five, out for six. Smiling as I breathe out, I repeat my mantra: *Peace. Be Still. Peace. Be Still. Peace. Be Still.*

So, I sat beside the Queen, perfectly calm and collected in my trusty Alexander McQueen outfit. The Queen was dressed in a lilac wool coat, with piped vertical stripes, a high-brimmed matching hat and an amethyst and diamond bouquet brooch. I felt completely relaxed and confident as I rose to welcome the special guests and the audience, and embark on my brief and well-rehearsed speech.

This is going rather well, I thought to myself, as I neared the end. A big mistake!

Suddenly my mind went blank. I had lost focus disastrously. Imagine that terrible moment when the computer screen turns black and everything disappears without warning. Everything I was supposed to say and do had completely vanished from my brain. Usually on stage, if the exact words escape you, it's easy to make something else up, and nobody need ever know. And it's not as if I'm someone who's ever stuck for words. But this was different. I knew I absolutely couldn't deviate from the ninety seconds of text the palace had already approved. I had no choice but to stick precisely to my script. So, what on earth was I supposed to say next?

Outside I looked perfectly serene. Inside, my heart was beating furiously, as if about to leap out of my body. I smiled.

Then I looked around at the audience, smiling still, acknowledging their presence, playing desperately for time. Still outwardly as cool as a cucumber, I turned back to face the Queen. And at that moment, just beyond her chair, I saw the painting for the sovereign mounted on a stand. That was it! That was my next job, to present that painting. All the right words came flowing smoothly out of me, as if nothing had happened.

Applause. Relief. Keep smiling.

'Your speech was marvellous,' someone said afterwards. 'And that pause was perfect! It allowed us to take everything in.'

Little did they know. It was my secret – mine and Keith's, of course, since he knows me far too well not to have noticed that unrehearsed pause.

341

So, the moral of that story is never panic. Keep smiling, and keep *looking* in control, and everyone will be reassured, including yourself. Before you know it, you *will* be back in control.

As I accompanied the Queen into the Great Hall for lunch, and began to show her around, it was like watching a people-skills masterclass. She was like a walking encyclopedia. I learned quickly to understand when she wanted to move on, or was keen to talk to someone at more length, especially if they were from the Commonwealth: a small movement of the hand-bag signalled so much. We sat down at a table for eight and ate our lunch together, me on one side, the ruler of Sharjah on the other. At that point I felt we really gelled, as we talked about family and food and whether she might write a private record of the Jubilee tour, so that her children, grandchildren and great-grandchildren might one day know about all the different people she'd met and her personal thoughts.

'Do you do much cooking, ma'am?' I asked.

'I don't have much time, but I do like having a barbecue in the summer for the family,' the Queen replied.

I had been told this by Bill Tinsley, my university driver, who used to be a royal protection officer. He had fond memories of the Queen and her husband cooking for their guests, and had enjoyed several occasions of this kind.

She was very witty and seemed to be enjoying having a very natural, relaxed conversation, woman to woman, exchanging thoughts and ideas about all kinds of subjects, including the Commonwealth, which I could tell she loved. She asked me about my views on the House of Lords, and what I was working on, and she made me feel I could be perfectly honest with her, so I took the opportunity to say:

'One of the highlights of my family's life was when I received my OBE and I got a telegram of congratulations from your husband, Prince Philip. It really meant a lot to us all, because when I was a little girl in Trinidad, I used to stand in the playground and sing "God Save the Queen" every day. I was told the Queen loved me and that I was part of the Motherland. But when I came to England, it wasn't like that at all. How badly I was treated. I had to face so much adversity, so much racism, and break down so many barriers. But my parents always told me I was a winner, and I worked hard and kept my focus. And although lots of people did wicked things to me, I don't hate them, and I have no resentment in my heart.'

The Queen leaned back in her chair, and she looked at me with her deep blue eyes. Her head on one side, she said something rather wonderful to me:

'Listening to you like this reminds me of my conversations with Nelson Mandela. He had the same forgiving philosophy, and bore no hatred.'

I thought she had real empathy and generosity of spirit. We all know of her dedication to duty, but that day I also witnessed close up a side of her not many people get to see.

When she drove away, I couldn't help thinking of Marmie. If only she had been able to see her little girl hosting the Queen and taking charge of such a special day, and proving herself more than equal to the task. Returning to Reed Hall, where the chancellor's apartments are, I opened the huge front door and there on the red carpet lay a white feather. Loud and clear, I could hear Marmie's voice in my head: 'Girl, I'm not going to miss this day.'

'Marmie! Marmie! Marmie!' I said. 'Isn't it wonderful?'

By the time I left Exeter in 2016 I'd greeted over 35,000 graduands in 172 ceremonies over the course of more than ten years, and also presided over ceremonies in Sharjah, in the United Arab Emirates, celebrating the strong academic connections between Exeter University and the Gulf States. But the success of the university and the ever-growing numbers of students wanting to attend graduation ceremonies meant it would be impossible for me to be there to hug every single one, as I'd promised, and I felt it was time to go. It would have been unfair to pick and choose and I didn't want anyone to be disappointed. In February 2017, I returned with my family to unveil a bronze portrait bust of me on the university's Streatham Campus, made by a renowned sculptor called Luke Shepherd. Every so often, I hear, a student in need of solace will come and give my statue a hug.

Chapter Forty

People write to me with their problems all the time, and whenever I can, I take action.

Soon after I became a peer, I began to receive a great many letters and emails from parents saying their child had been sexually abused by another child at school, and the abuser must have watched sexual images. One distraught mother I got to know at a charity function told me her four-year-old daughter had been abused by a ten-year-old boy, who told her, 'I'm going to rape you and you're going to like it.' The daughter was given counselling, but every time the TV news reported that a woman had been raped, the daughter asked, 'Did she like it, Mummy?'

Realizing the damage being done to children who were targeted by predators or accidentally accessed horrific and harmful sexual content while playing games online, or even just carrying out research for their homework, I began to campaign in parliament through the All Party Parliamentary Group on Children's Media and the Arts, which I co-chair. I became determined that age verification was the best barrier – not to stop grown-ups watching pornography if they wanted to, but to prevent children from growing up with unwanted and often violent sexual images in their heads. These are images that can damage people for life. They effectively programme children to believe certain sexual behaviours are 'normal' and acceptable.

My concerns were reinforced by the many prison visits I have done, and the countless prisoners I've spoken with. After visiting HMP Rye Hill in Rugby, which houses over six hundred sex offenders, I came away with the overwhelming message that their problems had started in childhood.

'Please, please, Floella,' one young man said to me there. 'Please ensure that no ten-year-old ends up in prison like me because of what I saw.'

At the 2013 Lib Dem party conference in Glasgow I put forward a motion to stop children from easily accessing online pornography.

At every previous conference at which I'd spoken, I had been applauded vigorously. This time I was greeted by dead silence. For once, virtually nobody in the auditorium was on my side. Anyone who might have supported me had vanished, and it seemed that a completely different crowd had marched in to vote me down. Although someone from the organizing office had tried to warn me, I was shocked nonetheless by this response from my party. I wasn't demanding that we ban pornography, but that we protect children from its terrible effects. Yet the principles of free speech and the spectre of censorship proved more important to the majority of the party membership than the protection of children. Or, misunderstanding how it would operate, perhaps these members imagined that age verification would mean they'd have to release their personal details. Lib Dem policy is decided democratically. Without the membership behind me, there was nothing I could do.

The cameras caught me open-mouthed with disbelief. Two significant people wrote to me after the conference to express their support: Shirley Williams who had been watching from her hotel room and told me not to give up the fight; David

Cameron also said he was with me all the way. The former Bishop of Liverpool, the Rt Revd James Jones, a friend and kindred spirit, encouraged me to face this adversity with a smile and keep going.

In July 2015 the Prime Minister's Office put out a press release about introducing age verification mechanisms to restrict access for under-eighteens to pornographic websites. That year, they reported, a Childline poll found nearly one in ten twelve- to thirteen-year-olds were worried they were addicted to adult content. Baroness Joanna Shields, the Minister for Internet Safety and Security at the Department of Culture, Media and Sport, began to work with industry and government, and she did everything in her power to change the legislation on this matter. She was utterly committed but it took an incredibly long time to make progress. Every year, for nine years in total, we met new stumbling blocks, and, with the exception of stalwarts Baroness Elspeth Howe, Lord Mike Storey and a few crossbenchers, we had little support even from my own party, so we were often the only peers speaking in favour of reforms. That was hard to take.

'I feel this is a seat belt moment,' Baroness Jane Bonham Carter eventually said to me. 'When my father was in parliament, Liberals were against seat belts, because they were seen as an infringement of liberty. But eventually we saw that they made sense, and look how effective that's been. I'm on your side, Floella.'

One by one, people came across to my point of view – that the internet was leading children on an unstoppable march into a moral wasteland. That by not regulating it, we were generating terrible problems for the future because the ease with which children can simply access violent pornography was creating a conveyor belt of sexual predators. Yes, education can play its part, but if the violent sexual content is still available, then it's like trying to wean a cocaine addict off the drug while making it readily available at the same time. When Theresa May became PM, she also supported the policy. At last the government announced that under the Digital Economy Act, age verification for online pornography would come into force on 15 July 2019. But unfortunately, the DCMS had failed to notify the EU Commission – an administrative oversight which Lord Ashton promised the noble Lords would be investigated. So, there was a six-month delay in implementation. And in that time, there was an election, a new government came into power, and despite all the work with stakeholders and all the tax-payers' money spent to ensure a workable technical system was in place, Boris Johnson instantly scrapped the policy. I was devastated. I wept for days and still do when I think of the damage done to children's innocent minds.

In 2021, I wrote to him with the support of children's charities, headteachers, women's organizations and other parliamentarians pleading for him to reverse the decision. At last, the government have now promised to include age verification in the upcoming Online Safety Bill, but it will take years to implement and, in the meantime, because of the delay, many young lives will be blighted.

By the time I entered the Lords, Aston and Alvina were independent adults making their way in the world. Aston had qualified as a solicitor, and in 2013 he moved abroad to work as a successful international hospitality lawyer. Alvina graduated from the University of Brighton with a Geography degree in 2010. On a walk together in the Lake District, as we had sat in a field surrounded by sheep on Loughrigg Fell, admiring the magnificent view over Ambleside, and she explained to me the geological foundations of the beauty all around us, she'd had a kind of revelation. She realized at that moment that her vocation was to become a teacher, and she's now a much-loved inspirational Head of Geography and housemistress at the secondary school where she herself was educated. Every night she phones me and her voice sounds just like Marmie's. My own two children were all grown up, and thriving, and so were their rose bushes.

Yet I never forgot those early miscarriages and the pain I had experienced before Alvina's birth. How hard it was when nobody wanted to acknowledge your loss, and you just had to shut up and get on with life, however miserable and frightened you felt. Decades had passed, but there still seemed to be so much silence around pregnancy loss, in society and law alike. The Births and Deaths Registration Act 1953 only allows death certificates to be issued for babies who have died after twenty-four weeks' gestation, but many women go through the trauma of labour and have to give birth to a dead baby much earlier than that. Some babies born at twenty-two weeks can now survive because of recent advances in foetal medicine. So, the law on this no longer made any sense.

One day, I saw an impressive woman on TV called Zoe Clark-Coates MBE who had set up an organization called the Mariposa Trust to offer support to anyone who has lost a baby in pregnancy, at birth or in infancy, whether recently or in the past. I contacted her right away. I'd had an idea.

As well as putting forward amendments to government bills, individual peers and MPs can also introduce private members' bills – PMBs or backbench bills – which in the Lords are usually prioritized by 'first reading' by a ballot held at the start of each new parliamentary session. Very few ever get as far as receiving royal assent and becoming law, so it's always a long shot, and if the parliamentary session ends before the bill's gone through, you have to start all over again from scratch. But

PMBs are very useful for drawing attention to an issue: they can influence future public bills and amendments, and that way they can often change legislation indirectly.

Could grieving parents be helped by a bill that allowed them to obtain a certificate of pregnancy loss in cases of miscarriage and stillbirth before the twenty-four-week cut-off? Not everyone wants or needs one, but for many it could make a huge difference, both emotionally and in order to get time off from employers. With the help of the Bills Office, Zoe and I worked together on the best wording for a private member's bill which, after three unsuccessful ballots, I finally introduced to the Lords on 7 July 2017. There were no amendments put forward at the second reading, and many people, including Lord Robert Winston, gave harrowing evidence at this debate. But unfortunately, there wasn't enough time before the next State Opening to get it to committee stage. I've been trying to get this bill through for five years now, and it may take another five, but I won't give up. It can sometimes feel like a game of snakes and ladders, but one thing I've learned is that 90 per cent of politics is patience.

Chapter Forty-one

Although I am a workaholic, which I cope with by meditating, I do manage to find time to get away from it all every now and then. In our old age Keith and I have decided to try harder to take more frequent breaks from our hectic life. I love the beautiful scenery and the food in the south of France, especially at one of my favourite restaurants, La Colombe d'Or in Saint-Paul de Vence. On weekends we often go dancing and even though Keith doesn't enjoy dancing, he bravely makes the effort as he knows how much I love it. But one thing we both adore is walking in the Lake District, my spiritual home. Playing and watching all sports, and understanding both the physical and the psychological side of it, gives me a buzz. I would love to be a football manager and motivate a team but what excites me most is Formula One and seeing Sir Lewis Hamilton drive. He is truly one of the all-time sporting greats who from an early age was motivated by our dear friend, his determined father, Anthony Hamilton, to keep on rising. Keith and I were lucky enough to be invited on board a superyacht in Monaco to watch him race in the Grand Prix. It was a sensational weekend and, to make it even more special, one of the other guests was Dame Shirley Bassey, who I have long admired. I said to her, 'I've always wanted to meet you!' She replied, 'I've always wanted to meet you!' Years ago people would regularly ask me if I was Shirley Bassey, which was very flattering. We gave each other a big kiss and a hug of mutual respect.

In February 2013, I was asked to give a speech on a Saga cruise on board the MV *Quest for Adventure*, starting in Accra, Ghana. I leapt at the chance to go all the way along the west coast of Africa, visiting Sierra Leone, Senegal and Gambia, to see for myself where my people came from. I was the only Black person on that cruise. It was my first time in Africa, and I was very excited. The first excursion in Ghana was to go to one of the slave forts. Elmina Castle, built in 1482 and one of the oldest European buildings outside Europe, marks the site of the earliest encounters between Europeans and sub-Saharan Africans. From that date on, forts were built on the edge of land and sea all along what was known then as the Gold Coast. The trafficking of human beings became a lucrative business and African people quickly became just another com- modity for Europeans to trade and exploit.

Men, women and children were dragged from their villages, shackled together and marched to the forts.

I can't tell you how powerfully the vibrations and spiritual presence of those millions of people who passed through Elmina Castle coursed through me when I stepped inside. We learned the full horrors of what happened to people in these hell holes – men hanged, women raped, babies murdered. The tour party stood in the dungeons in silence with bowed heads, as shocked as I was.

The horrific experiences and emotions of those African souls seeped through the walls and into me. Down there was a tiny cell reserved for the men and women who rebelled. Their pun- ishment was to be locked into the windowless room, no higher than five feet, no wider than a few yards, with the thickest doors I've ever seen. Thirty people were locked in the cell, and the double doors barred. They never came out alive. One by one they suffocated and only when they had all died were another thirty enslaved souls forced to clear out the bodies, before being locked in there themselves. Can you imagine the screams of those people, thrown on top of each other? How can people be so cruel to other human beings?

Upstairs were huge rooms filled with beautiful furniture where the White slave traders lived in luxury. In darkness below lived human cargo, their freedom denied. They could be there for months, waiting for the ships that would take them four thousand miles across the Atlantic. Imagine a doorway, huge and arched. Thick, wooden doors. This was called the 'Door of No Return'. When those doors opened, you saw the sea. And then you knew you would never see your homeland again. You knew that life would never be the same.

The traumatized captives were packed on board ships like sardines. If they got ill or fought back they would be thrown overboard alive. When they reached the Caribbean they were auctioned like animals. People often say that it was other Africans who co-operated with the Europeans and captured and sold their fellow countrymen. Yes, the culture in Africa was to have servants and slaves, but Europeans, especially the British, *industrialized* slavery. They didn't think these people were human beings. They had no feelings for them at all.

When I was in that dungeon I could hear my ancestors' screams. I could feel their horror and fear. I remember standing there with tears rolling down my face, shaking, wondering what goes on in people's minds that allows them to behave like that. I'd come to Africa with a happy, full heart, but nobody had prepared me for this. What I saw was not a clinical account of slavery. It was evil. It was cruel. It was vindictive. My ancestors

353

were torn apart as families. They were scattered across the Caribbean.

And I thought about how Caribbean people were treated by some people now, denied the justice and opportunities in life that they deserve, having gone through so many atrocities for hundreds of years. The *Windrush* generation had worked hard to rebuild Britain, sometimes at the expense of their own children's well-being, the 'left-behind' children; some who never saw their parents again were testament to this. The sad breakdown of family bonding, love and attachment and being separated took a terrible toll and that trauma still plays out today.

When you think of the *Windrush* scandal it's clear the powers-that-be don't give Caribbean people the dignity and respect that they deserve. They are still judged by the colour of their skin and rejected as unworthy, inferior, by some.

But George Floyd didn't die in vain. The nine minutes twenty-nine seconds which became a symbol of police brutality after Chauvin knelt on Floyd's neck and killed him changed perceptions and opened millions of people's minds to empathize with people of colour. Sometimes terrible things have to happen to bring about good.

As a young child in Trinidad, thanks to Dardie's teachings, I didn't believe the Hollywood stereotype version of Africa as the land of savage cannibals I saw in movies, or in Britain the television images of Africa portrayed as one big country, full of starving children and conflict. So, remembering my father's positive stories, I embarked on my African adventure, happy and joyful at the prospect of learning more about my own origins and heritage. But on that first day I was totally crushed by what I saw. For three days I wept.

All those families separated, never to see each other again. Never to speak their own languages. Never to practise their own culture or religion. Branded across the chest with the mark of their owners – as enslaved people, they were not even allowed to keep their own names. If you weren't strong, you were dead, you were gone. If you protested, you were hanged, you were drawn, you were quartered.

I wept and wept and wept. Until one night I woke up and asked myself this:

Why are you crying, Floella? Tears aren't going to change anything. You are now in the House of Lords. You are now in the place where people once made decisions about your ancestors. Stop crying. Keep on paving the way for the future. Press that reset button and change things.

A few days later, I got a standing ovation for my speech. My companions on that journey really understood what I was talking about, and the indignities I had faced after my own four-thousand-mile journey across the ocean. I realized I am a proud Caribbean survivor and it is my duty to build on the sacrifice and suffering of my ancestors.

Later that year the Foreign and Commonwealth Office asked me to go on an official visit to Trinidad and Barbados. I had been back to the Caribbean several times but never in this capacity: this was a high-level occasion with police outriders clearing the road ahead. The Trinidadian Prime Minister, Kamla Persad-Bissessar, the country's first woman in that role, asked me to address her cabinet, something I never imagined as a little girl. I spoke about the need for the Caribbean to work together with Britain and to proudly take their place in the world for the sake of their ancestors. The British High Commissioner Arthur Snell held a reception in my honour and I invited Auntie Olive, who represented Marmie. Afterwards, when we stood on the manicured lawn for the official photographs, I looked down, and there was a white feather.

The next stop was Barbados, and Keith and I got on a small six-seater plane for the twenty-minute journey which nearly ended in disaster. Just as we took off, a powerful tropical storm erupted. The sky turned black and the plane was tossed around violently.

'I can't find Barbados,' the pilot said to us. 'We are going to have to fly to the next island, St Lucia.'

Keith turned to me and said:

'This doesn't look good. I think this is it!'

Now Keith is my hero and he is usually right about technical things. But I'm a great believer that when your number is up, that's it. I didn't feel my time had come. I looked out of the window and saw far in the distance beyond the darkness a chink of light and declared in my usual optimistic way:

'Everything will be all right.'

After what seemed a lifetime, the plane landed heavily with a thud on the tarmac at St Lucia airport as the heavens opened and the storm caught up with us. We were safe but all hell had broken loose as Paul Brummell, the British High Commissioner in Barbados, thought he had lost a baroness. The next day we flew to Barbados and continued our visit as if nothing had happened.

In 2016, aware that the seventieth anniversary of the arrival of HMT *Empire Windrush* at Tilbury Dock on 22 June 1948 was fast approaching, Keith and I began to discuss different ways it could be publicly commemorated. I was already an ambassador for the Royal Horticultural Society, and working with schools to encourage children from all cultural backgrounds to get involved with gardening, and took great pleasure in visiting the Chelsea Flower Show for decades. So, I thought a

Windrush-themed garden at Chelsea would be the perfect way to draw attention to this historic event.

But when it came to getting sponsorship, there was bafflement. People had never heard the name *Windrush*, let alone knew what it represented for thousands of people of Caribbean origin in the UK. The arrival of the first ship from the Caribbean, marking the dawn of multicultural Britain, had been all but written out of history. So many high-profile companies said no to us. Banks, businesses, big stores: nobody understood what we were trying to do. They all said they were interested in diversity and supported corporate social responsibility, but they couldn't see how this idea fitted into their business goals.

The recent Brexit vote and scapegoating of migrants had brought increasing animosity to those people in Britain who in some quarters were not perceived as truly British, or not British enough. I was queueing in a supermarket when a man deliberately pushed his trolley into the back of my legs and asked, 'What are you still doing here?'

'Changing the world,' I snapped back.

Rather than engage in arguments about immigration, I wanted to offer a counterbalance, putting forward a constructive and positive contribution to the role of people of Caribbean origin in our country. At a high-profile event like the Chelsea Flower Show, which is watched by millions across the globe, I could make a strong point about who belongs in Britain in a celebratory way. Our *Windrush* garden would win hearts with the beauty of the unexpected, and so increase its impact. It could also help counteract the widespread ignorance about why there are Caribbean people living in Britain in the first place, highlighting the fact that we were invited to come, and the contribution we've made to the nation, not just since *Windrush* but from the time the Atlantic slave trade began over four hundred years ago. But nobody wanted to listen.

Normally you have to have your finalized proposal in to the RHS for Chelsea by September. Fortunately, the RHS had great faith in us and very much wanted the garden to go ahead, so they held open the space while we continued to hunt for funding. Then in November 2017, just as we were losing hope, the RHS put us in touch with Birmingham City Council. Birmingham usually had a garden in the pavilion, and were gold medal winners, renowned for their incredible displays, but had put nothing forward for 2018. So, I emailed Darren Share MBE, Head of Parks, and explained I was looking for someone to partner with. I outlined my concept for the garden, with the *Windrush* ship as its centrepiece, symbolizing a bridge between communities.

The week before Christmas it was all settled – the best Christmas present I could have had. Darren's ideas and drawings were fantastic. Recreating the imagery and history of Caribbean–British relations in exotic flowers, he'd included flying fish, and a chattel house, one of those small movable dwellings for enslaved people used on plantations, and given it a round window, a square window and an arched window. Keith came up with the idea of small 3-D printed figures who looked out and waved from the deck of a model of the *Windrush* ship. On the other side of that, in the British section, Darren had created floral images to represent the NHS and manufacturing, and a big red London bus. There would also be an educational element created by Louise Bessant and a looped film from a programme Keith and I produced called *When I Came to Britain* with people aged from sixty to a hundred talking about their adventures, my father included. I knew the finished garden would be incredible.

Meanwhile, however, the story of the scandalous and catastrophic treatment by the Home Office of so many members of the *Windrush* generation was beginning to break in the mainstream media, not least thanks to the efforts of Arten Llazari at the Refugee and Migrant Centre in Wolverhampton, *The Voice* newspaper and the award-winning *Guardian* journalist Amelia Gentleman. The problem had arisen as a direct result of the hostile environment policy which came into force in October 2012 in order to make it as difficult as possible for people without 'leave to remain' to survive in the UK. Theresa May, then Home Secretary, didn't want illegal immigrants to have any chance of getting work, receiving NHS medical treatment or claiming benefits. It also became harder to rent property, receive education or report crimes. This implicitly encouraged racial discrimination and suspicion, and undermined trust within communities, because doctors, landlords, teachers, university staff and other public sector workers became responsible for immigration checks.

The government quickly began to detain, deport and threaten to deport large numbers of people suddenly reclassified as illegal immigrants. Many were people who had arrived from the Caribbean as young British children, just as I had, or who were even born in Britain, but who didn't have documentation or passports to prove their right to live here. This was either because they had never needed them or because the Home Office itself had destroyed crucial records, such as landing cards. It was devastating to discover this had been allowed to happen, over a number of years. People were pressurized to provide absurd proofs of long-term residence, such as school reports dating back half a century. Some were even being sent to islands where they had never lived, where they had no living family or friends.

More and more people began to write to me about this issue, from High Commissioners to those directly affected and organizations trying to help them and their families. Caribbean governments had been warning the Foreign Secretary for some time that many *Windrush*-generation residents were being treated as illegal immigrants, and older Caribbean-born people were being targeted by the Home Office, yet deeply distressing cases of unfair treatment kept on emerging. But every time my colleagues in parliament or I tried to raise this, or even call for an official national Windrush Day on 22 June to get recognition for the history of Caribbean presence in Britain – something for which the social commentator and cultural historian Patrick Vernon OBE had been campaigning since 2010 – or if we asked the government how they planned to commemorate the seventieth anniversary, we were fobbed off with wishy-washy answers. By December 2017, over sixty MPs, academics and campaign groups sent an open letter to the Home Secretary, Amber Rudd, objecting to the 'inhumane' hostile environment strategy, saying it had no place in a compassionate society.

Everything began to snowball in February, when senior Caribbean diplomats urged the Home Office to act. It came to a head in April 2018 when the Barbados High Commissioner, Guy Hewitt, revealed that Downing Street had initially rejected a formal diplomatic request to discuss the immigration and deportation problems at a forthcoming London Commonwealth Heads of Government meeting, hosted by the Queen. Finally, Theresa May, now prime minister, realized how embarrassing this was and agreed to meet all the High Commissioners. Unfortunately, I couldn't attend this meeting myself. On 30 April, the day I was honoured with the Freedom of the City of London for making a difference to society, Home Secretary Amber Rudd resigned, saying she had 'inadvertently misled' MPs over targets for removing illegal immigrants. The scandal was intensifying.

Suddenly, with all this adverse publicity, everything changed. I got a phone call from Nero Ughwujabo, special adviser on social justice to Theresa May, a man I'd had a number of meetings with already, and who knew all about my *Windrush* garden plans. He told me that the Prime Minister now wanted to create not only an annual Windrush Day, but also a permanent national memorial to the *Windrush* generation.

'Lady Benjamin, she wants you to chair the Windrush Commemoration Committee to oversee this. Are you happy to do so?'

Fantastic. An opportunity at last to consolidate everything I'd been fighting for.

In March I'd been to see Darren Share in Birmingham, and he'd taken me round the city council nursery where all the plants for our garden were being grown. Thanks to so much new interest in *Windrush*, a BBC film crew came to film our meeting. It had been a terrible winter and the plants were coming along worryingly slowly. But on one of the leaves, I spotted a white feather.

'It's OK,' I said. 'My mum is here and she'll make sure these plants grow.'

And, come May, when Darren constructed the garden in Chelsea, sure enough, it looked perfect.

Out of the blue, I got another call from Number 10. The Prime Minister herself wanted to open the garden.

At this point I had to be extremely diplomatic. I didn't want *Windrush* to be entirely defined by the scandal and people's anger about it. My ambition for the garden was to draw attention to the pride and resilience and dignity of Caribbean people.

'This is a celebration,' I explained carefully. 'This garden is about thanking the people who came to give their contribution to British society, people who have been forgotten, whose history has never been properly recognized. I'm so sorry, but if the Prime Minister comes, all that will be lost and the focus will change to the current political crisis. I can't let that happen.'

So, I opened the garden myself. But Theresa May did turn

up very early in the morning, the first PM ever to come to the Chelsea Flower Show, and she asked to see the *Windrush* garden before the public were allowed in.

I don't care what mistakes people make, so long as they learn from them. It's thanks to Theresa May that we now not only have a Stephen Lawrence Day on 22 April, first observed in 2019, but also a Windrush Day with a guaranteed budget of half a million pounds to support celebrations up and down the country for people whose voices have been silenced. She also allocated a million pounds to create a permanent and prominent national monument in central London, and gave me responsibility, as chair of the Commemoration Committee, for organizing this. We've chosen a site already full of heritage, and therefore protected, which is also synonymous with the arrival of Caribbean people to London – Waterloo station, where I arrived as a ten-year-old. Little did I imagine then what would transpire sixty years later. I'm so grateful to my ever-supportive colleague Lord Bill Bradshaw, who shares my office, for putting me in touch with another of my *Play School* babies, Andrew Haines, the chief executive of Network Rail, and his colleague Tracee Grenardo, and smoothing the way for this.

Sadly, it's been like turning round a tanker ever since the scandal broke. We're still asking questions in parliament about why *Windrush* compensation claims are not being settled. I told the Lords in November 2021, more than three years later, that an independent overseeing body is urgently needed to deal with these claims. There's still an overwhelming feeling of distrust and a fear that some victims of the *Windrush* scandal won't be paid before they die. The hostile environment policy was renamed but not ended. You have to keep on speaking out and demanding answers.

'You have to vote,' I tell Black people, at every opportunity. 'You have to stand for council elections, you have to apply for the civil service, you have to get into politics and aim high, because if you don't take part and you don't have a seat around that table, you can't change people's minds and perceptions. As Operation Black Vote promotes, you have to take part in the social and political system.'

For real change to happen, we need more people who know what they're talking about and who have true compassion in positions of power. The key qualities for working in government or organizations at any level should be morality, integrity and honesty. Trust is essential.

Dear Baroness, My mummy said I could write to you because you want to know what people think about the Windrush Monument in Waterloo station. I like the one with the suitcases, because that's like the stories my nanny tells me. The little girl standing on the suitcases is my nanny. But I think you should also have a little boy who looks like me, because I'm part of Windrush too.

This letter from a little boy called Nathaniel was one of hundreds responding to the open consultation we held which confirmed to me that with our monument we're creating a legacy for the past, the present and the future. We've had Zoom calls, organized by my Deputy Chair Paulette Simpson CBE, with people joining us from right across the country telling us what they think of four possible statue designs – people of all ages from Birmingham, Newcastle, Peterborough, Manchester, Bristol and elsewhere. In July 2021, we revealed a shortlist of concepts by four artists of Caribbean heritage, Basil Watson, Jeannette Ehlers, Thomas J. Price and Valda Jackson. Basil Watson's family looking out from a pile of 'grips' (suitcases) seems to have resonated most with the public, and was ultimately chosen. Many have told me they were so moved by the image of the winning statue that they cried. For some, it opened conversations about the past, and unburied the hidden trauma of childhood separation.

'What a beautiful image of myself,' one young man said when he saw the final choice. 'I feel so proud.'

Eventually, I'd like to see monuments in all the places where Caribbean people went once they had arrived in Britain, including Brixton; monuments which inspire hope, not anger. In years to come, when I'm dead, people will walk by that statue of me in Exeter and wonder who I am, and ask about my three Cs. There's even a time capsule waiting to be dug up one day, with messages from the thousands of students I hugged as they graduated. I feel so happy to leave that legacy behind.

I know change is coming. When Marcus Rashford MBE, whom I greatly admire, missed that penalty at the European Cup in 2021 and the mural of him in Manchester was defaced, it was White people who went to clean off the disgusting comments. On their knees, with scrubbing brushes, White people said, 'Black Lives Matter. Leave Marcus Rashford alone.' That's how you know that change is coming. You have to face up to what's happened in the past, and then decide how the future should be.

All young people need to live with hope and opportunities. We all need to dig in, and get our positive messages out there in order to achieve lasting change.

Feel it. Know it. Be it. Prove to the world who you are and what you can do.

Chapter Forty-two

Often what's happening in my life seems unreal, beyond my wildest imagination. For example, in 2019, Tony's son-in-law, Richard Dalkeith, now the Duke of Buccleuch, who had been on the Moscow trip with me and sat with me on the Millennium Commission, was appointed as Lord High Commissioner to the General Assembly of the Church of Scotland. To celebrate, he invited me and Keith to be house guests at the magnificent Palace of Holyroodhouse, the Queen's official residence in Edinburgh, to watch the ancient Ceremony of the Keys, which he was receiving on behalf of the monarch that year.

It was a simply splendid occasion, mingling with the good and the great in the palatial seventeenth-century surroundings where so much history has been made. What was really unforgettable was staying overnight at the royal palace, being greeted by a Downton Abbey-like receiving line of staff, and being looked after by a lady-in-waiting and a maid, as I'd been instructed to bring five changes of outfit, one for each part of the itinerary . . . who would have thought?

Then, later that year, one morning in November, a brown envelope landed on our doormat, marked 'Her Majesty's Service'. Keith brought it up to me in the bedroom, where I was still in my pyjamas. Even when I read the letter, the words didn't sink in.

The Prime Minister is recommending that HM the Queen may be graciously pleased to approve that the honour of Dame Commander of the Order of the British Empire be conferred upon you . . .

I read it again. And then again.

'What is it? What is it?' Keith kept asking me.

'They want to make me a dame!'

Alvina was visiting that day, and arrived shortly after the letter. We danced round the bedroom together singing. 'A dame! There ain't nothing like a dame!'

I eventually discovered that I had Lord Bill Bradshaw to thank for this extraordinary surprise. Bill and I had shared an office for almost ten years, so for a very long time he'd watched me at work with lots of different charities, overheard countless conversations, and seen me rushing from one meeting to another. He knew, for example, all about two charities that became particularly close to my heart during this time: The World Heartbeat Music Academy, founded by Sahana Gero MBE, and Transplant Links, created by Dr Jennie Jewitt-Harris and her daughter Aimee, which saves lives by carrying out kidney transplant operations. These are usually in the Caribbean, and often parent-to-child. Watching this intricate and miraculous procedure in the operating theatre was a great privilege and one of the most moving experiences of my life. Bill had secretly contacted a huge number of different people whose work I'd supported and they added their backing to his suggestion that I should receive an honour for my outstanding contribution to charities, stretching back over fifty years.

When you're Black, when you're a woman, when you work with children, it sometimes seems that the higher you go, the harder it becomes. Whatever you achieve, someone out there will doubt that you are worthy. When it was announced, the media went wild. Still I had a naysayer on Twitter who wanted to know what I was doing there – a single MP who assumed I'd done nothing in life but jump up and down on *Play School* in a pair of dungarees. But my thousands of followers soon put her right.

Eleven days before the UK's first official lockdown, I went to Buckingham Palace with Keith, Alvina and my sister Sandra who has taken on the role of family matriarch and keeps us all in touch with each other just as Marmie used to do. Poor Aston was stuck in Dubai because of the emerging Covid crisis. Sandra and I both decided to take something with us that had belonged to Marmie, so she would also have a presence at this special day – Sandra wore her scarf and I carried her handbag. The beautiful gold embroidered coat I chose to wear was like the many interwoven threads of my life, so I felt I was at the palace representing the past and the future at once.

Being the only woman receiving a damehood that day, and at the top of the alphabet, I was the first to be presented to Prince Charles, who greeted me so warmly. He was one of the first royals to publicly condemn the horrors of the slave trade. He pinned on my medal, and we talked for so long about climate change and working together with Caribbean countries and the Commonwealth that I began to worry he would never get through all the other people waiting behind me. Unable to shake hands, we each put our palms together in the traditional *Namaste* greeting and he sent greetings from his wife.

I left walking on air, feeling elated, and then headed for the Ritz for a celebratory lunch with the family – including Ros, who took Aston's place. Interviewed by the press as I was leaving the palace, I told reporters that I was dedicating my honour to my parents, who made me who I am:

'I've given my heart and my soul to children to make sure that they understand that they're loved too and that there is so much they can do if they feel confident about themselves, because that's what my mum and dad did for me, just like the song "The Greatest Love". My whole life is about giving, unconditionally. I don't expect anything for it but when something like this happens, you do feel bowled over.'

I'm an optimist. I believe in the power of positivity and long-term thinking, and I feel extremely happy with my lot here in Britain. It certainly turned out to be the land of opportunity for me and I continue to strive to make it the same for others. I'm convinced that the more you give, the more you will receive, and I receive so much love and affection every day, especially from those I call my *Play School* babies. Marmie's idea of complete success was to sit in the Royal Box at Wimbledon and be a guest on *Desert Island Discs*. I've fulfilled those dreams for her and found a white feather on both occasions. How could she have imagined that I would also be summoned by Lord Dick Newby, the Lib Dem leader in the House of Lords, and asked to consider standing for election as the Lord Speaker, the presiding officer and highest authority of the House of Lords. I thought about this long and hard, and received support from all sides of the House, led by Lord John Lee, who pointed out it would have made political history and demonstrate just how much Britain has changed. It would be a symbol of hope. I was incredibly proud to have been considered, but I realized it would mean giving up too much of my life with Keith, and our continuing work together: Keith is still the creative director in everything we do, including all the exciting projects we have on the go. Our work and lives are inextricably linked. So I regretfully declined to stand for Lord Speaker. However, it has been decided that a portrait of me by June Mendoza OBE (if the canvas was ever X-rayed it would reveal a previous painting of

Princess Diana underneath) should be hung in the Cholmonde-
ley Room in the House of Lords. What a shame Marmie and
Dardie are not here to see it.

Life has come full circle for me and Keith. We started off
together in theatre and now we are producing a stage musical
of my childhood story *Coming to England* for children and
families with a world premiere at The Birmingham Rep as part
of their fiftieth anniversary. I've also adapted it into a picture
book for four to seven-year-olds, with illustrations by a brilliant artist called Diane Ewen. On 1st October 2021, I proudly
watched this book being read on television as a CBeebies Bedtime Story by none other than the outstanding historian and
broadcaster David Olusoga OBE, who said he was reading it
for his own four-year-old daughter.

Thanks to *Coming to England*, I hear four and five-year-
olds speaking with empathy and understanding about difference
and belonging. I meet many of their teachers, and often discover they were my *Play School* babies. On one Zoom call in
2021 in the midst of the pandemic, I spoke to thirty thousand
children across the UK, from over a thousand different schools.
It was the day of the State Opening of Parliament, 11 May
2021, so I wore my peer's robes, as I would have done if I had
been able to attend in person, as I always do.

At this Zoom event, each child could feel I was speaking to
them personally, that I was there in the room with them, just
like when I was presenting *Play School*. *Wow!* they thought
when they saw me dressed up so grandly.

'I'm meant to be sitting on the red benches in parliament
right now,' I told them. 'That's why I'm wearing these robes.
But instead of being with the Queen, I'm with you today.'

And then I took my robes off, and started telling them my
story.

Of course, I told them about Marmie, and how she taught

369

me to understand that although you might not be able to make sense of what's happening to you in the moment, as time goes by, it will all make sense. So I use everything as a positive, believing that out of bad, good will prevail. Many people have begged forgiveness for what they did to me. I smile and say there's nothing to forgive – you made me strong, you made me who I am – complete with no bitterness in my heart. Just the power to face challenges without breaking. I know that whatever is happening is ultimately going to get me where I want to be, to show me what I'm doing here on earth.

The older you get, the harder it can be to hang on to that knowledge. When you're younger you can feel that you're climbing, but you do get to a certain point when you know the finishing line is coming. I know my days are numbered. And I would like to be sure, when I do reach the finishing line, that I can say, 'Yes! I made a difference! Change happened!'

But I also know that, no matter what, there'll be someone coming up behind me who shares my total commitment, so I'll just pass the baton on. Others paved the way for me. Now I'm paving the way for future generations. So I hope I've been a role model and that I leave a lasting legacy.

What gives me hope is that more and more people are beginning to agree with me about the need once again for a cabinet-level Minister for Children. Because everything we do effects the lives of children. These are people I never dreamed would one day share my belief in the importance of a child's early years and the impact they have throughout a person's life. I'll say it one more time: '*Childhood Lasts a Lifetime*.'

The world is waking up at last to something I realized long ago, thanks to the power of *Play School*: the importance of seeing the world through the eyes of a child. Awakening that vision in others has been my life's mission.

That's what I'm doing here!

Acknowledgements

From the moment I entered this world I have been surrounded with love. First, by my beloved Marmie and Dardie, Veronica and Roy, two of the most wonderful parents any child could wish for. They were the perfect combination – Dardie opened my eyes to the world and showed me what was possible; Marmie gave me the confidence to go out and capture it. Together they gave me and my five sisters and brothers – Sandra, Lester, Ellington, Roy Jr and Cynthia – everything that was needed to succeed: love and a sense of belonging. So I want to thank my siblings for allowing me to share our story in the hope that it inspires others. I am incredibly proud of them and everything they have achieved throughout their lives.

I am also grateful for the love of all my guardian angels who have guided me along the way and shone a light on the path as I forged forward. There are some I have not been able to acknowledge fully in this book as there have been so many occasions when individuals have come fleetingly into my life to help me navigate hurdles and obstacles. So I want to take time to acknowledge their unselfish love and show my appreciation to them for watching over me as they have been a source of inspiration and hope.

I want to thank my wonderful editor Ingrid Connell at

Macmillan, who always made me feel anything is possible. Her calmness kept me on an even keel throughout, so I'm grateful for her support and guidance as I took each step along the way to creating this book. Thanks also to Charlotte Wright, Bethan Miller, Lydia Syson and Paul R. Jackson for their diligence and professionalism.

At the age of seventy-two, I have had a full, extraordinary and exciting existence and not all my amazing stories are in this book. Many people, apart from my guardian angels, have touched my life in one way or another. They know who they are. So I also want to acknowledge them – I will be forever grateful for their love and support over the years.

The love of my children must also be acknowledged because they have always been supportive from their earliest years. Aston, who was masterful when we appeared together in the theatre, and reminded me of my lines before I went on stage. He's now a brilliant international lawyer. And Alvina with her teaching background helps me with my House of Lords speeches, especially when they are about schools and education.

Finally, the greatest love of all is shown to me by my handsome, clever, witty and devoted husband Keith who has been by my side for the last fifty-two years. I always wear the silver heart necklace he gave me when we first met – it's a symbol of our love. He proclaimed it was written in the stars that we were meant to be together, and that it was preordained we should meet even though we were born thousands of miles apart. Destiny is a wonderful thing and has served us well.

I am known for my hugs and smiles and want to thank all those who have returned them back with unconditional love.

Now you know why I always sign off with the words 'keep smiling'. It's my mantra. It's because I feel like a winner having received so much love and I want to pass it on.

Picture Acknowledgements

All photographs are from the author's personal collection apart from:

Page 5   top, page 6 bottom right, page 8 top, page 9, page 10 top right, page 11, page 12 bottom right, page 13 bottom, page 15 bottom, page 16 top © Keith Taylor

Page 6   top © Christina Burton/ArenaPAL

Page 7   top © BBC

Page 7   bottom left © Bill Kennedy/Daily Mirror/Mirrorpix/ Getty Images

Page 7   bottom right © Walter Brown/ANL/Shutterstock:

Page 8   bottom © Yves Coatsaliou

Page 10   top left © H. Tempest Ltd

Page 15   top left © Alvina Benjamin-Taylor

Page 16   bottom © Mark Thomas/Rex Shutterstock